LONDON

Rebuilding the City after the Great Fire

To Bos
with lots of love
from Sheila

Christmas 2009

LON

Rebuilding the Cit

DON

fter the Great Fire

written and with illustrations by
T. M. M. Baker

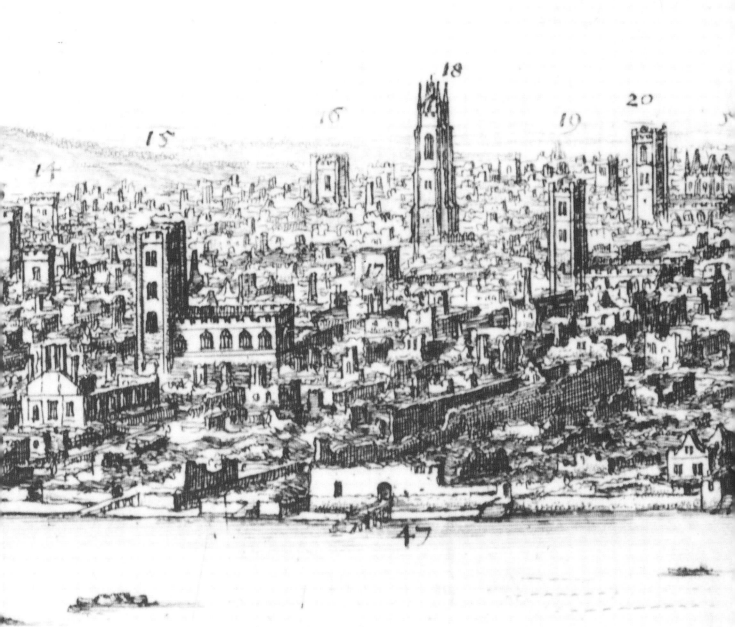

 Phillimore

2000

Published by
PHILLIMORE & CO. LTD.
Shopwyke Manor Barn, Chichester, West Sussex

ISBN 1 86077 113 0

Printed and bound in Great Britain by
BUTLER & TANNER LTD.
London and Frome

CONTENTS

LIST OF PLATES

PREAMBLE

LONDON'S HISTORIC CORE, the City, is one of the most-rebuilt square miles on earth. The razed sites and construction projects which the rapid pace of office building technology and the competitive demands of astronomical land values entail have long been a familiar feature of the London scene. Things were much the same in the late 19th century, when the demands of managing the world's greatest trading empire swamped the new City which Londoners had provided for themselves in the less ambitious rebuilding of the late 17th century.

Twice since the Middle Ages, half of London has been a vast building site. The last such occasion was during the post-war reconstruction of the 1950s and 1960s; even that great rebuilding becomes today ever more threadbare as the mighty juggernaut of the commercial property market sweeps backwards and forwards through it.

The post-war planners explicitly drew inspiration (albeit with less happy results visually) from London's response to its greatest building site of all, the 437 acres left behind by the Great Fire of 1666. Then the heart of the City was rebuilt according to a consistent scheme which emphasised good standards of construction, solidity, and permanence, and which was a wonder of its age. Today, little more than 300 years later, precious little of that new London still stands.

This work attempts the impossible – an illustrated representation of the process, which extended for half a century, by which the ashes of 1666 were superseded by a modern City – the City which witnessed much of London's rise to global commercial pre-eminence. The attempt is impossible because black and white drawings on a scale of 1:255 do scant justice to the lost magnificence of what they represent; because the evidence for what many of the buildings looked like is so limited (particularly beyond the churches and major public buildings) and so much is therefore educated guesswork; because elevations and sections cannot convey the crowded, tangled urban fabric within which the buildings were set; and because any effort to people them with the teeming multitude of Londoners who were their *raison d'être* (except by means of descriptive text) would be pastiche.

Yet it is worth the attempt, not least because it has not been done in any systematic or comprehensive way before (not, at any rate, since Clayton drew the City churches in the middle of the 19th century). Here, in however inadequate a form, are restored to Londoners the buildings with which a confident and vital age once embellished their City, and which formed a familiar backdrop to the daily lives of their predecessors, until London's very success made so many of them redundant, or until sudden violent destruction swept them away. Many of the views are probably the first attempt at accurate representation (including features which were obscured or replaced by the passage of time) since the originals were built.

At one level this work is an illustrated guide to the City of London as it was in the late 17th and early 18th centuries. At another it is an analysis of the physical fabric of that City, and how and why it came to be like that. At yet another it seeks to place the City in the context of its people – how they lived, how they governed themselves, how they worshipped, and how they traded – tracing not only change and decay, but also what continuity is evident in the City today, in both its fabric and its commercial and administrative organisation.

All levels demand a large measure of imagination, but the magnificent survivors of the renewed London continue as a vibrant reminder of the reality which these drawings represent and, for all the shortcomings of what follows, the effort is worth it.

'… The flames march along both sides of the way with such a roaring noise as never was heard in the City of London: no stately building so great as to resist their fury …'

Thomas Vincent, 3 September 1666

1 The burning City: anonymous contemporary painting, *c.*1666. (Museum of London)

'In my way do observe the great streets in the City are marked out with piles driven into the ground and if ever it be built in that form with so fair streets, it will be a noble sight.'

Samuel Pepys, 29 March 1667

INTRODUCTION

THE DREADFUL FIRE

When Thomas Farynor, a King's baker (of ship's biscuit), and his family woke at 2 o'clock in the morning of Sunday 2 September 1666 to find their house burning around them, they little knew as they escaped (all except for an unfortunate maid whose fear of heights sealed her fate) over the neighbouring rooftops of Pudding Lane what their misfortune was starting. The catastrophic destruction of 437 acres of the heart of one of the richest cities in the world, a loss estimated by John Strype in 1720 at £10,788,500 (in 1666 values, the equivalent of some £2 billion today) necessitated the rebuilding over the next decades of a completely new City, visually entirely different from the one which had gone up in smoke, and including some of the masterpieces of world architecture. The magnitude of the devastation and of the building programme which ensued gave birth to an enduring Great Fire myth, a blend of tragedy, nostalgia, pyromania, anti-Popery, triumph in adversity, and the genius of Sir Christopher Wren, which has been one of the mainstays of London's popular culture, tourism, and publishing ever since. From the moment when Farynor's house fire got out of control, London would never be the same again.

1666 is one of the most famous dates in English history. It inspired a bevy of 'urban myths', ranging from the misinformed to the malicious, including the following:

'The Fire was started by Roman Catholic agents' – a particularly tenacious myth, which persisted for 200 years, perpetuated by inscriptions on both the Monument and the site of Farynor's house in Pudding Lane. A Frenchman called Hubert (who was however a Protestant) suicidally confessed to setting fire to London deliberately, and was duly hanged, but he almost certainly had nothing to do with it.

'Only a few people were killed' – unlikely in such an inferno in a crowded city, with people desperately trying to save their goods and property from the rapidly advancing flames.

'London was rebuilt within three years' – this was inscribed on the Monument too (it is still there); in fact serious reconstruction did not start until 1668, the housing stock was not fully replenished until the early 1670s, and many of the public buildings, especially the churches, took much longer.

'Christopher Wren was denied the opportunity to build a magnificent modern city, with broad, straight thoroughfares, by short-sighted vested interests' – Wren's and others' idealistic plans, produced in the immediate aftermath of the Fire, were simply impractical in the circumstances, and could never have been realised.

'The Great Fire eradicated the Great Plague of 1665 by sweeping away the rat-infested houses in which it had festered' – the Plague raged at its worst in the slums which fringed the City, and which were largely untouched by the Fire. It had already exhausted itself by September 1666, although plague continued in endemic form until 1670. Gradual improvements in health and housing, and a large measure of good fortune, were the main reasons for the non-recurrence of the epidemic.

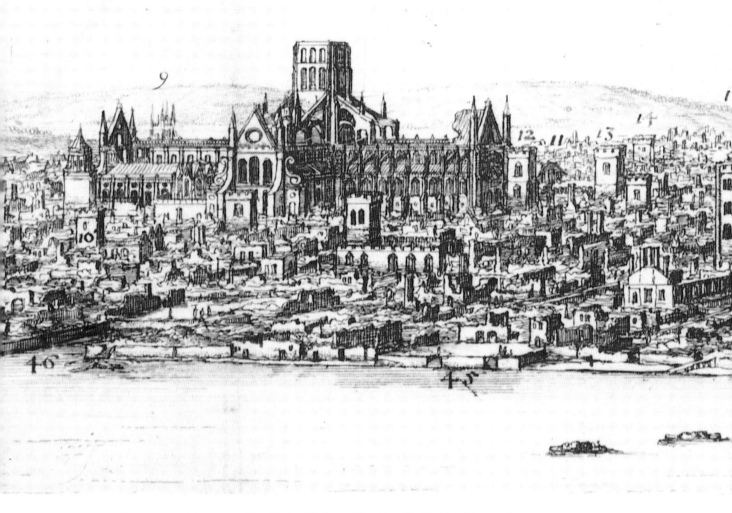

2 Panorama of the burnt City, Vaclav Hollar, 1666 (detail). (British Museum)

'All of the City churches and major public buildings were rebuilt to Wren's designs' – it is true that the office of works was under Wren's control, and he played the crucial leading role in getting the huge task done; he also contributed some magnificent designs; however modern scholarship is increasingly recognising the major contributions made by Robert Hooke and Nicholas Hawksmoor to the design of the churches, while many secular public buildings were the work of local architects, most notably Edward Jerman.

Fires were common enough amongst the crowded timber-framed tenements of the City of London but, perhaps surprisingly, there had not been a universal conflagration since the great fire of 1133 (which probably started in the house of Thomas Becket's father, a wealthy Cheapside mercer). Samuel Pepys, woken at 3 o'clock by his maids to observe the fire from his roof in Seething Lane, went back to bed again, comfortable that it was 'far enough off'. The Lord Mayor, Sir Thomas Bludworth, summoned, also at 3 o'clock, from his bed in Gracechurch Street to supervise the fire-fighting effort, allegedly offered an opinion which turned out to be one of the most spectacular hostages to fortune in all history: 'Pish! A woman might piss it out!' None of them bargained for the hot, dry, easterly wind at the end of a long, dry summer, nor for the nearby Thames Street warehouses and wharves, crammed with tallow, pitch, tar, hemp, timber and coal.

For four days and nights the great old rich crowded combustible wooden City burned. Eye-witness accounts testify to the terror and noise of the flames and of the struggles of a populace fleeing with what goods they could salvage, but also to the strange beauty of it all.

Vincent, in his *God's Terrible Voice in the City*, described the burning Guildhall, with the fire gnawing away at its huge Gothic timber roof, one of the many benefactions to his City of Sir Richard Whittington: 'a fearful spectacle, which stood the whole body of it together in view, for several hours together, after the fire had taken it, without flames (I suppose because the timber was such solid oak) in a bright shining coal, as if it had been a palace of gold, or a great building of burnished brass'. The Dreadful Fire, or the Lamentable and Dismal Fire, as contemporaries called it, swallowed up some 13,200 houses together with 86 churches, St Paul's Cathedral, 44 Company Halls, two Exchanges, all the important markets except Leadenhall, the Custom House, the Guildhall, the prisons, and numbers of other public buildings. Charred fragments of London, driven along by the breeze, rained down as far away as Henley-on-Thames, and Kensington was coated in soot. In the Museum of London hangs an anonymous painting of the Fire at its height which shows, between the confused mass of refugees in the foreground and the great arc of flame in the distance, the hillside of the City, the gaunt ruins of its churches stranded eerily amidst a huge sea of charred debris.

By Thursday morning, 6 September 1666, the heart of London was reduced to rubble and smouldering ash, still so hot that John Evelyn, wandering through the devastated City, burnt the soles of his shoes. One Alexander Fleming wrote that 'You may stand where Cheapside was and see the Thames', and compared the landscape to his native Westmorland: 'The houses are laid so flat to the ground that the city looks just like our fells, for there is nothing to be seen but heaps of stones'.

THE GREAT REBUILDING

The task which faced weary and homeless Londoners, many of them camped out on Moorfields, on that Thursday morning was daunting and immense – little less than rebuilding an entire City. Speed was of the utmost importance so that:

- London could retain its pre-eminent entrepôt status,
- trade and rental payments (both of which, in the absence of developed systems of insurance or government assistance, would have to provide the bulk of the funds for rebuilding) could be resumed, and
- the dispossessed populace could be rehoused and the pattern of their business life resumed before they settled permanently in other parts of the metropolis, or in the provinces.

Central government in Westminster also had an interest, since its finances depended critically on the prosperity and continuity of London's trade, already severely disrupted by the previous year's Great Plague. The Bohemian topographical engraver Vaclav Hollar was commissioned to produce his plan of the devastated City on 10 September. The clearing of rubbish and surveying of streets continued throughout the autumn and winter, and at least one householder was rebuilding within a week of the Fire itself.

But the authorities were determined that the rebuilt City should be commodious, efficient, magnificent, and above all fireproof. The opportunity which a *tabula rasa* offered to create a better London than had been there before was too good to be missed. The London which burned down was crowded, irregular, and dangerously combustible. The Elizabethan and Stuart population explosion had laced it with huge warrens of tangled alleys and courtyards, lined by houses whose crowded rooms were often intermingled with each other in defiance of party walls, and whose structure was little more than lath and plaster ('paper work', Defoe called it; his opinion of old London was that 'the buildings looked as if they had been formed to make one general bonfire'). 'Such a congestion of misshapen and extravagant houses', John Evelyn called London in *Fumifugium* in 1661. The maze that was London explains why the baroque *sistemazione* at Rome, with broad straight avenues radiating from piazzas towards grand public buildings sited for deliberate visual effect, had such a profound impact on English cognoscenti such as John Evelyn (who had been to Rome and admired it) and Christopher Wren (who in early 1666 had been in Paris, where Louis XIV and Jean Baptiste Colbert were planning similar developments). They wished to build a rational City which would be in keeping with the spirit of its age and sweep away all traces of its barbaric medieval past. Within days of the Great Fire Wren, Evelyn, Robert Hooke and others were submitting plans for just such a City whose layout would have borne no resemblance whatever to old London. The King caught the mood, and on 13 September a royal proclamation banned all rebuilding pending decisions on the form that the new 'much more beautiful city than that consumed' was to take.

The stern dictates of economic necessity clouded these Utopian visions. London needed to be restored as quickly as possible (starting with the 1667 building season) so that its trade did not drift to the West End or the provinces. Everybody wanted a City that would be modern and that would work, with broad streets, and regular and magnificent buildings. But nobody wanted his own property rights to be infringed, and funds for widespread compulsory purchase of sites did not exist. This was England, so the solution was compromise. The idealistic schemes for a completely new layout were rejected in favour of selective widening of existing streets in order to eliminate the worst bottlenecks, to allow the passage of carts down the narrowest lanes, and to enhance the potential of the streets as firebreaks. Existing property boundaries were retained, thereby encouraging owners and occupiers to rebuild quickly (the resources and legal mechanisms for large-scale reallocation of land did not in any case exist). A few new streets were introduced. The Fleet River was canalised and provided with broad flanking quays modelled on the Parisian *quais*. (A similar broad quay along the Thames, designed partly to provide easy access to warehouses, partly to furnish a firebreak between inflammable shipping and the City, and partly for magnificence, was also projected, but never received the impetus to be realised.) The houses, although rebuilt on their old sites, and often on their original foundations, were subject to strict regulations as to the manner of their construction. As a work of practical administration in a crisis, it would probably have been difficult to better the mechanism which was put in place, and the result was town-planning of a scale and consistency which was unprecedented, and which set a model for the extensive late Stuart and Georgian developments of London's suburbs.

The Commission for Rebuilding was appointed in October 1666. Its three Commissioners (Christopher Wren, Roger Pratt, and Hugh May) were appointed by the Privy Council; they were joined by the three City Surveyors (Robert Hooke, Peter Mills, and Edward Jerman). Wren was appointed 'Principal Architect' for rebuilding the City. John Oliver filled the vacancy created by Jerman's death in 1668. The Commission's job was to manage the survey of streets and sites, and to consider the form of the new streets and buildings. It came up with the following general principles (many of which had already been prefigured in the royal proclamation of 13 September), which formed the basis of the Rebuilding Bill submitted to Parliament in late 1666:

- Buildings were be faced with brick or stone.
- The principal streets were to be broad enough to act as firebreaks.
- The narrowest lanes and alleys were to be widened (to 14 feet) or eliminated.
- 'Noisome' trades – such as tanning, dyeing, soap-boiling, brewing – were to be removed from the City (they had been concentrated along the River, to take advantage of the water supply, but ended up polluting both it and the City air; it turned out to be impractical to do more than banish them from the main streets – a similar watered-down prohibition was applied to trades which presented a fire risk).
- Minimum use was to be made of timber structures on the outsides of buildings, and shop-fronts were to be built of fire-resistant oak.
- Four standard categories of house were to be allowed, depending on what type of street or lane they stood on.

On 27 February 1667 the Fire Court was established by Act of Parliament, consisting of Judges of the Court of King's Bench and the Court of Common Pleas, and Barons of the Exchequer. Its job was to deal with property disputes. When delivering its decrees, from its headquarters in Clifford's Inn just off Fleet Street, it cut where necessary through strict legality (leases usually required tenants to rebuild a house if it was destroyed by fire) in favour of ensuring that those who were able and willing to rebuild (whether landlord or tenant) were given the legal wherewithal and the financial incentive (by means of adjustments of rental obligations or lease terms) to do so.

The Rebuilding Act, passed in 1667, incorporated the proposals of the Commission, as well as the following:

- The regulation of building workers, and of the cost of materials, in order to avoid opportunistic exploitation and sharp practice (Stephen Primatt published *City and Country Purchaser and Builder* in 1667 as a guide to landlords and tenants on the going rates for the costs of rebuilding).

- The liberalisation of restrictive practices in the building trade for a period of seven years.
- A tax on coal entering the port of London, at 1 shilling per ton until Michaelmas 1677, to finance public works and the compulsory purchase of property.
- Provision for the rebuilding of not more than 39 of the 87 parishes churches which had been destroyed.
- Provision for the City authorities to appoint Commissioners for Sewers and Paving.
- Provision for the new Thames quay, Fleet canal, and better street access to the riverside.
- Provision for the building of a Monument to the Fire, and for 2nd September to be observed as a 'day of public fasting and humiliation' in perpetuity.

The framework for rebuilding thus encompassed not just the replacement of structures, but also the pioneering establishment of a modern (by 17th-century standards) urban infrastructure.

In the spring of 1667 work on reconstruction began. Hooke and Mills worked on laying out the streets (in which enterprise they had to contend with householders who at dead of night moved the marker stakes out into the street in a surreptitious expansion of their plots); the markets which had encumbered them were removed to special off-street sites, usually those of churches which were not to be rebuilt. The building of houses got off to a slow start, apparently because of the initial shortage of necessary materials; many were still built with timber frames (even timber was not easy to come by immediately), but they had to be faced with bricks.

By 1668 the pace quickened, and Pepys refers several times to the 'fine' and 'brave' streets and houses which were going up all over the City. By the end of 1668, 1,600 houses had been built, by 1669 3,950, by 1670 6,000, and by 1672 7,700 (out of a final total rebuilt stock of 9,000). The stopping of the Exchequer in 1672 and the Second Dutch War of the early 1670s affected confidence, but by then the major part of the rebuilding job was done (even though almost half of the houses were still unlet in 1673). The Fire Court's jurisdiction was concluded at Michaelmas 1672.

The inscription on the pedestal of the Monument to the Great Fire, which was built on the site of the church of St Margaret Fish Street Hill, close to the head of London Bridge, claims that the City was entirely rebuilt in three years. This is something of an exaggeration. The rebuilding even of houses took six years and more, and the replacement of public buildings and churches was a much longer and more piecemeal process. The slowness with which the City revived is demonstrated by the fact that the City Corporation had to introduce various legislative measures in the early 1670s to encourage or compel the citizens (and even provincial traders and craftsmen) to repopulate it. However, considering the size of the task and the absence of any fire insurance or public provision for rebuilding private premises, the speed with which London got back on its feet was remarkable, and testimony to its vigour as a commercial organism. No doubt the process was helped by London's embryonic speculative commercial property market, as manifested by the accumulation of landholdings for rebuilding by such men as Nicholas Barbon, who developed much property around Fleet Street, and Alderman Edward Backwell, the great goldsmith and financier of government, who developed a large estate in Lombard Street and Cornhill.

By 1670 the need for further legislation, particularly in respect of church building, had become evident, and the second Rebuilding Act was passed in 1671. Its main provisions were:

- The Coal Tax was to be extended to Michaelmas 1687, and to be increased to 2 shillings per ton; three quarters of the fund was to be spent on churches, and one quarter on public buildings. In 1677 it went up to 3 shillings per ton.

- 51 churches were to be rebuilt, but the old parish structure was to be retained, with some parishes sharing church buildings.

The authorities had still underestimated how much it would cost to finance the programme of church building. The Coal Tax had to be extended again, at the reduced rate of 1s. 6d. per ton, until Michaelmas 1700, then yet again, until Michaelmas 1716. Even then, when the Coal Fund finally ran out, there still remained unsatisfied demands by a few of the parishes to furnish their churches with elaborate steeples similar to those of their neighbours. The replacement of the structurally unsound post-Great Fire rebuilding of St Mary Woolnoth and the new steeple of St Michael Cornhill were financed under the 1711 New Churches Act, a piece of legislation which was directed primarily at the suburbs of London, and effectively marked the end of the half century and more of restoration work on the fire-ravaged City.

Year	House plots surveyed	Houses finished	Public buildings finished	Company Halls finished	Churches started	Churches finished
1667	843	150			1	
1668	2375	1450		3	1	
1669	2349	2350	1	5		
1670	1316	2050	3	10	12	1
1671	760	1100	3	9	6	2
1672	283	600	5	3	1	1
1673	41	200		3		1
(1,000 plots unbuilt, 3,500 houses unoccupied)						
1674		100		1	2	
(309 plots surveyed 1674-1696)						
1675						1
(St Paul's Cathedral started)						
1676			1	1	4	
1677			2	1	6	4
1678					2	2
1679					1	6
1680			1		1	1
1681				1	4	2
1682				1	1	2
1683			1		3	1
1684					2	4
1685					2	
1686					2	4
1687						10
1688			1			
1689						1
1690						
1691						
1692						1
1693						
1694						
1695						
1696						
1697						1
1698-1727 17 church steeples completed; 3 churches rebuilt again;						
St Paul's Cathedral completed 1710						

THE NEW LONDON

By the 1720s the new City of London stood pristine (although steadily disappearing under a layer of the very coal-soot which had financed so much of it), a modern heart to what was rapidly becoming the greatest commercial city in the world. Strype in his update of John Stow's *Survey of London*, published in 1720, expressed the pride of Londoners in their new City: 'Divers churches, the stately Guildhall, many Halls of Companies, and other Publick Edifices; all infinitely more Uniform, more Solid, and more Magnificent than before: So that no City in Europe (nay, scarcely in the World) can stand comparison with it'.

The City was rebuilt according to new standards of construction and design. Never before had there been such wide-ranging control of building activity. The standardisation of house-building, with precise specification of ceiling heights, wall thicknesses, and materials, although it was a codification of accepted practice, was another aspect of the City's pioneering of new town planning techniques. It resulted in a City which was orderly and regular, but which was visually varied and never monotonous. Purged by the Fire of the remaining vestiges of the once numerous medieval town mansions of the aristocracy and gentry, the new London was also and above all a commercial City. The houses of its merchants and craftsmen were not just houses but shops and warehouses and workshops as well. The City's purpose-built trading facilities were of an unprecedented scale and standard. Its inns, taverns, and coffee houses served commercial functions as well as hospitable ones, and in many cases the entertainment became merely a convenient adjunct to business. Even the churches and charitable institutions, while extensively financed from public funds, were substantially embellished and endowed by the proceeds of trade. Those public funds in their turn derived from a tax on London's fuel, so that a large proportion of it represented a charge against the profits of Londoners' trade.

Nor were the visible improvements the only ones. For the first time London had a permanently established highways and sanitary authority, the beginning of a long process of amelioration of London's long history of disease and mortality. Improved fire-fighting technology supplemented the new building standards to reduce yet further the risk of catastrophic destruction. Scientific fire insurance furnished for the first time an alternative to bags of gold under the bed as a means of funding rebuilding. New and improving methods of credit provision and storage of wealth did even more to reduce merchants' exposure to risk, thereby boosting yet further in a virtuous circle the explosion of London's prosperity.

The Gresham Lecturer in Physics, John Woodward, nicely expressed the general enthusiasm for New London in a letter to Sir Christopher Wren:

> So many thousand Houses, of even private Citizens, built in such a manner as to render them not only more convenient ... but even superior in Design and Architecture to the Palaces of Princes elsewhere ... Then, which I and everybody must observe with great satisfaction, by means of the Inlargement of the Streets, of the great Plenty of good Water convey'd to all Parts, of the common Sewers, and other like Contrivances, such Provision in made for a free Access and Passage of air, for Sweetness, for Cleanness, and for Salubrity, that it is not only the finest, but the most healthy City in the World.

In the 18th century London was the place to be, and for all the landed wealth which was invested in its West End, the newly built City at its core, Wordsworth's 'mighty heart', was the engine which kept it going.

BUILDINGS FOR GOVERNMENT, ADMINISTRATION AND JUSTICE

The Great Fire gutted the Guildhall, the centre of the Corporation of London's administration of the City, as well as all of its prisons. In the immediate aftermath of the Fire it was to the reconstruction of these that the authorities gave priority, in the interests of smooth administration. The prisons were among the earliest structures to be financed from the Coal Tax, and all of them were complete by the early 1670s. Many of the civic buildings had been sturdily built of stone, and much of their fabric was sound enough to be reused. Thus the City gates, including the prisons at Newgate and Ludgate, retained in their repaired state much of their original appearance, as did Guildhall and Bridewell (a blend of prison and hospital).

The Monument, a purely ornamental structure, and the expansion of the Guildhall Offices were the only substantial post-Fire additions to London's stock of public buildings. The lawyers' residences and courts at Doctors Commons were rebuilt after the Fire on a new and ampler site, as were those of the Temple. The Navy Office, untouched by the Great Fire, was rebuilt after a fire of its own in 1673.

BUILDINGS FOR TRADE AND COMMERCE

Trade is the *raison d'etre* of cities, and has always been the essence of the City of London, ever since the Romans first spotted the potential of a site which offered the combination of a good natural harbour, the lowest feasible bridging point over the Thames, and easy access to the Continent. London succeeded almost from the moment of its foundation, and prosperity brought power. At various times in its early history the local political authority resided in Colchester or St Albans or Winchester, but the magnetism of London's wealth and influence drew kings and governments to settle there, albeit ultimately beyond the immediate influence of the City, safely two miles upstream at Westminster.

The proximity of the two great powers in the land set the scene for centuries of struggle for mastery and influence, a process which persists to this day. Westminster provided the stable political environment which was essential for the City to prosper, but the City provided the finance on which the government depended. Each pushed the other as far as it could, the City ratcheted up its rights, and eventually the merchants and tradesmen of London acquired a degree of civic independence from central government that was unparalleled in England.

The close interdependence of the political and commercial powers was demonstrated by their cooperation in the calamity of 1666, both to fight the Fire itself, and to rebuild the stricken City. Government provided the legal mechanism for the rebuilding, and the Coal Tax which financed so much of it, but government had an interest in ensuring that the City continued its business with as little interruption as possible so that loans raised there and custom duties collected there could continue to fund the extravagant Stuart court and the wars against the Dutch.

The Great Fire of 1666 destroyed not just the physical fabric of the City, but also the delicate web of business relationships that was built upon its topography. Until quite recently London was a place where business, even if international in its scope, was done with the neighbours. The Fire laid waste the heart of the City, and scattered its traders to the outskirts. The civic authorities were justifiably alarmed at the disruption which physical dislocation might cause to trade. They responded by designating Gresham College, the old mansion of Sir Thomas Gresham in Old Broad Street (on the site now occupied by the National Westminster Tower), as a temporary Royal Exchange; the great financiers leased nearby houses, and for a few years unburnt Bishopsgate became the financial centre of London. The

Royal Exchange and the cloth exchange at Blackwell Hall, vital as central facilities for merchants to meet and trade, were palatially rebuilt as soon as possible.

The 17th century was a time of transition in London's commerce. Already in the late Middle Ages, and increasingly during the Tudor and Stuart periods, the expansion of the scale of trade was reflected in the strain which was placed on the wealthy individual merchants and goldsmiths who dominated the London economy, their vulnerability to financial shocks, and the subsequent development of associations of merchants in chartered trading companies (notably the Merchant Adventurers, who controlled the woollen cloth trade, London's most valuable, and the East India Company which monopolised the lucrative trade in Far Eastern luxuries) to provide a larger pool of capital for the riskier ventures. Much of London's commerce, as well as its administration, was still governed by the powerful livery companies, guilds whose organisation reflected medieval trading practices. But the oligopolistic control of many of the livery companies over their trades had already weakened substantially since the Middle Ages; the 'custom of London' in any case meant that a member of a company was not constrained to follow the trade which it nominally controlled, and by the 17th century the greater companies in particular were already well on the way to becoming the social and charitable associations of wealthy general merchants which they are today. The relaxations of legal restrictions on 'foreigners' (i.e. non-Londoners) trading in London, necessary to help get the City running again after the hiatus of the Great Fire, eroded the remaining control of the livery companies over London's business even further.

3 The River Thames with St Paul's Cathedral on Lord Mayor's Day, *c*.1747-8 (oil on canvas) by Canaletto (Giovanni Antonio Canal) (1697-1768). (Lobkowicz Collections, Nelahozeves Castle, Czech Republic/Bridgeman Art Library)

The livery companies were, however, more interested in grand buildings than were the trading companies. They regarded reconstruction of their Halls as a priority, since the Hall functioned as both administrative headquarters and embodiment of the prestige of the guild. The Great Fire left many of the companies in severe financial difficulties. Forty-four of their Halls were destroyed (only those of the Ironmongers, Carpenters, Leathersellers, Bricklayers, Armourers and Brasiers, Loriners, Cooks, and Glovers survived). Their resources had already been depleted by the 'donation' of much of their gold and silver plate to finance the Parliamentary cause in the Civil War. Much of their income derived from rents of property in the City. The destruction of a large part of this estate reduced many companies to virtual penury. In order to meet the financial crisis the companies admitted new members on a large scale, and by the mid-1670s most of the Halls had been rebuilt. Some, belonging to the major companies, were large and elegant palaces. Most were domestic in scale, with little more than an elaborate doorway with the company's coat of arms to announce their presence to the street. Almost all, however, were furnished with carved wooden fittings of the highest quality, and some also boasted elaborate plasterwork. Only a handful (the Poulters', Bowyers', Upholders', and Woodmongers') were not rebuilt at all.

HOUSES

The 1667 Rebuilding Act provided for four categories of house. On the six 'principal streets' houses were to be of four storeys with attics; because of their location these houses were often highly ornamented in the robust and not always classically literate City baroque style. Houses fronting the 'other streets and lanes of note' were to be of three storeys; on the back lanes of two storeys. Finally, 'mansion houses' were to be of four storeys, but were subject to less restriction as to their dimensions.

External timber framing was not allowed. Although the Act allowed stone or brick walls, brick was by far the predominant facing material; stone was sometimes used for dressing and decorating frontages. The Act also specified thicknesses of external and party walls, with a view to reducing the risk of fires spreading between properties.

Generally speaking the new houses followed the provisions of the Act. With the exception of the largest medieval mansions, the houses of the City were rebuilt virtually on their old sites, so that the new London replicated the ground plan of its predecessor, consisting of three elements:

- the narrow-fronted houses, usually with a shop, which lined the streets;
- the mansion houses which were usually set back from the street behind a courtyard opening off it, and often had a substantial garden behind;
- the meaner houses which lined the maze of courts and alleyways that filled in the gaps between everything else.

Nicholas Barbon claimed to be able to tell to what trade the builder of each house belonged from its appearance:

> some being set out with fine brick-work rubbed and gaged, were the Issue of a master bricklayer. If stone coyned, jamb'd, and fascia'd, of a stone mason. If full of windoe, with much glass in compass, and reliev, a Glazier's, if full of Balcone, and balustrading, a Carpenter, and so others … one may in ye face of most houses, discerne ye calling of some builder or other most conspicuously.

Particular features of the new City houses were the narrowness of the frontages (which led one foreign visitor to liken them to birdcages, with the inhabitants jumping from floor to floor via the stairs at the back), the widespread use of rubbed brick for decorations, particularly of window and door surrounds, the plat bands of projecting bricks which marked the storeys, the cornices which topped each house-front, the railed balconies at first floor level on the principal streets, and the far-projecting signs, hanging from richly ornamented iron brackets, which in the days before house numbers were introduced in the later 18th century were the only means of identifying houses, and the principal means by which shopkeepers advertised. The competition to have the most prominent specimens eventually led to signs which were so large and projected so far over the street that they were liable to collapse, sometimes even bringing the house-front with them, and legislation of 1762 required all signs to be flush with the front of the house.

BUILDINGS FOR ENTERTAINMENT

Eating and drinking have long been an integral component of doing business in London – the City lunch is a venerable tradition, and the taverns and coffee houses were vital oilers of the wheels of commerce from the time of the Great Fire until the 19th century. As early as 1668 Samuel Rolle noted that most of the few new houses that had by then been rebuilt were let out as alehouses and food shops to provide for the army of builders.

Until the railway stations took over their role in the mid-19th century the inns of the City and Southwark were the main servicers of transport between London and provincial destinations, as well as providing accommodation, warehousing, sustenance, and a convenient place to meet for visitors to London and traders in its markets. They were thickly studded along several of the main streets, particularly those leading out of the City, usually with several gallery-fronted ranges surrounding an off-street yard. Survivals of this type of inn are exceptionally rare in England as a whole, quite apart from London, where the sole remnant is one range of the George in the Borough (itself rebuilt after Southwark's great fire of 1677). The inns serviced and acted as termini for coaches, and carriers plying trade to a range of towns and cities, each inn specialising in traffic to particular parts of the country, many with extensive stabling and accommodation. The detailed appearance of only a handful, including some of the most famous, was recorded, often immediately before or actually during demolition.

The appearance of the taverns and coffee houses with which the City also teemed, especially thickly in the vicinity of the markets and exchanges, is even more sparsely recorded, although their general appearance was effectively identical to the houses.

Apart from these premises, which were designed to service trade, the facilities for public entertainment were sparse indeed. The City had a traditional hostility to theatres, partly the result of Puritan sentiment, and all of the great Elizabethan playhouses were built just outside its jurisdiction (even Shakespeare's Blackfriars Playhouse, though within the City boundary, was located in a quasi-autonomous district which had a dubious reputation, as was the Whitefriars Playhouse). Nevertheless plays were sometimes performed in inn yards, whose galleries provided practical accommodation for audiences, and influenced the arrangements of tiered seating in the playhouses themselves. The Duke's Theatre in Dorset Gardens was the only purpose-built theatre in the 17th-century City, and even it followed fashionable society to the West End before the century was out.

SCHOOLS, HOSPITALS AND COLLEGES

Charitable provision in London was extensive by the time of the Great Fire, largely as a result of munificence by the Crown, the City, the livery companies, or individual merchants. With a few exceptions, space for schools, almshouses and colleges was extremely limited, because of the high value and cramped scale of City property generally. Those built on a more palatial scale, such as Christ's Hospital, Bridewell (a prison, although it had some of the features of a hospital), and the Colleges of Physicians and Arms, occupied the buildings or sites of dissolved monasteries or disused aristocratic mansions. Bethlehem Hospital, rebuilt on a new site in Moorfields in 1670s (although its old cramped buildings were not damaged by the Great Fire) was the vastest and most magnificent of all.

Many of the almshouses were built on sites towards the fringe of the City which were less in demand for commercial purposes; there was a particular concentration around Cripplegate, represented here by Nicholas's Almshouses. Because they were not in the central area most almshouses survived the Great Fire, although they were eventually removed elsewhere during the 19th-century boom in demand for and prices of City property. The same fate befell all of the schools and most other charitable institutions of the late 17th-century City. Nowadays only the College of Arms and Trinity House remain within the City boundaries, and only the former retains anything substantial of its original buildings.

CHURCHES AND CHAPELS

The reconstruction of churches did not officially start until 1670 (although some parishes whose churches were less badly damaged jumped the gun before then, often making use of surviving walls where latent fire damage necessitated extensive subsequent rebuilding), and for many years Londoners had to worship in 'tabernacles' – 27 of these temporary churches were built from 1669 onwards.

The Rebuilding Act of 1667 did not specify which of the 87 parishes whose churches had been destroyed in the Great Fire were among the 39 where rebuilding and reconstitution was proposed. The result was inter-parochial squabbling, each parish jealous of its privileges and most keen to have their own church rebuilt. The Rebuilding Act of 1671 finally settled the number of churches to be rebuilt at 51, although the parish structure was left intact, with some of the church buildings belonging to more than one parish. It also appointed a Commission for rebuilding the churches, consisting of the Bishop of London, the Lord Mayor, and the Archbishop of Canterbury, by virtue of his proprietorial rights in 13 of the City parishes which were his 'peculiars', and not subject to the London diocese's jurisdiction. Provision was made for the King to approve the designs of churches. The Commissioners appointed Christopher Wren as their principal architect and contractor, with responsibility also for the finance and administration of the enterprise. Wren authorised disbursements from the Chamber of London, which accumulated the receipts of the Coal Tax. The Coal Tax continued until 1716, and £326,000 of it was eventually disbursed against work on the churches, £747,000 on St Paul's Cathedral.

Wren appointed two other surveyors to work under him on the repair of the churches: Robert Hooke and Edward Woodroffe. Woodroffe was replaced on his death in 1675 by John Oliver (himself replaced by William Dickinson in 1695), while Hooke retired in 1693 and was replaced by Wren's protégé Nicholas Hawksmoor. Both Hooke and Hawksmoor appear to have been closely involved with Wren in the design work; Woodroffe and his successors worked rather as surveyors, liaising with the builders and measuring work done.

There was keen competition between parishes to obtain priority in the building programme, intensified by the fact that in the early years funds from the coal tax were limited and sparingly allocated. To start with a distinction emerged between churches which were built 'on the ordinary', financed immediately from the

4 The City from Somerset House, Samuel Scott, mid-18th century. (National Monuments Record)

Coal Fund, and those built 'on the extraordinary', where an eager parish deposited funds out of its own resources (to be repaid subsequently when the Coal Fund had accumulated) in order to get construction under way. In the late 1670s it became clear that, given the funding constraints, the building of steeples alongside the churches was impeding new starts, and from then on steeple building was given a much lower priority until the bulk of church building was completed. Through the 1680s funding became easier; the last churches were begun in 1686, and the church campaign was effectively completed by 1695. The raising of steeples continued well into the 18th century. The new St Paul's was not started until 1675, and not completed until 1710.

The churches have long been noted for the originality both of their planning and of the design of their steeples. Several patterns and features can be identified with a fair degree of consistency throughout the building programme:

- Wren aimed to provide 'auditory' churches on centralised plans, reflecting the Protestant mode of worship and its focus on the pulpit.
- In the interests of economy the old foundations and even surviving sound medieval masonry were incorporated; structural considerations often dictated lightweight structures, without heavy roofs, in order not to put too much strain on them.

- Awkward or cramped sites were exploited for dramatic baroque effects in the interiors of many churches.
- Exteriors tended to be relatively unadorned, except where there was a street frontage to be made the most of, and the most elaborate decoration was reserved for the plasterwork and furnishings of interiors, and for the steeples.
- The steeples became increasingly elaborate and baroque as the years progressed (although St Mary le Bow set a high standard from the outset). Many of the later steeples were probably strongly influenced by the emerging talent of Nicholas Hawksmoor.

The steeples gave the new City a characteristic baroque skyline, especially when viewed from across the Thames, as recorded most memorably in the Buck brothers' 1749 panorama (part of which featured on the old £50 note) and the paintings of Canaletto and Samuel Scott – a procession of elaborate spires stretching from St Bride's in the west to St Dunstan in the east and washing around the dominating dome of St Paul's. The white stone towers, black lead spires, and gilded weathervanes stood out not only against the sky, but also against the red bricks and tiles of the buildings around them. Each was different from the rest, but the way in which they picked up themes from one another imposed a stylistic harmony on the whole, which was arguably the supreme artistic achievement of the entire rebuilding programme.

The established church with its government funding dominated church building in the new City. There were, however, substantial elements of non-conformity in the City population. In the climate of hostility towards Roman Catholics which had been reinforced by the supposed Papist plot to fire the City, no Catholic chapels were put up in the immediate aftermath of the Fire (it was not until James II's reign, in 1686, that a Catholic chapel was opened in Lime Street; there was a riot). Churches were however built by the French Protestant and German Lutheran communities, and there were also several meeting houses for various non-conformist sects; of the appearance of the last nothing seems to have been recorded except for the late 17th-century rebuilding of the Presbyterian Kings Weighhouse Chapel in Eastcheap.

DECAY AND DESTRUCTION

By the 18th century the new City was already becoming out of date. The rebuilding occurred at a turning point in London's history. The old City had been an essentially medieval one, and its replacement, in spite of the up-to-date smart brick houses and public buildings, retained many medieval echoes. The 18th century saw substantial extension of British colonies overseas, the beginning of large-scale industrialised production (particularly in textiles), and a boom in British international entrepôt trade. London, as the source and user of much of the capital that fuelled this extraordinary expansion, and as far and away the largest English port, was at the centre of this boom, and in the mid-18th century the city overtook Constantinople to become the largest in Europe.

Such a city could not stand still. In addition to the normal deleterious forces of decay, accident, economic progress, and changing fashions, the late 17th-century City of London has suffered the almost complete departure of its resident population, repeated redevelopment of its warehouse and office space to meet the demands of its booming and ever-changing economy, and the hugely destructive German aerial bombardment of the Second World War, whose effects, especially in the textile warehouse district of the western part of the City, were not very dissimilar from those of the Great Fire itself. Considering these pressures it is remarkable not how much has disappeared, but that so much has survived.

Inevitably, in a context where rapid reconstruction was of the essence, there must have been some jerry-building. Many City houses were rebuilt in Georgian times, and it was not unknown for houses to collapse (a particular problem was the heavy, far-projecting wrought-iron signs by which shopkeepers advertised their presence – they had a tendency to pull the house-front down). Certainly many developed picturesque irregularities over the years. In spite of the emphasis on fire-resistant buildings, fires continued to afflict quite substantial areas, notably the Temple fire of 1677, the Lower Thames Street blaze of 1715 (which did for Wren's Custom House), the Cornhill fire of 1748 (which consumed many of the great commercial coffee houses), and the Royal Exchange fire of 1838.

During the 18th century, as wealth increased, the great London merchants joined the aristocracy in the new suburbs of the West End, City living gradually ceased to be fashionable, and an exodus began which was not to stop until the number of City dwellers dwindled in the 20th century to a handful of thousands, displaced by an army of a quarter of a million businessmen and clerks who went home every evening to London's burgeoning suburbs.

Much of the post-Fire rebuilding of London did however survive into the 19th century, and it was really only with the large-scale provision of purpose-built warehouses and offices to accommodate the substantial firms which were emerging in a number of City trades, particularly banking, textiles, and commodities, that demolitions occurred widely throughout the length and breadth of the City.

As the 18th century progressed the needs of London's trade steadily outgrew the buildings which the late 17th century had provided for them. It was a gradual process at first, with the houses around the Royal Exchange being taken over by a multitude of coffee houses which provided specialist commercial and information services as overflows from the overcrowded courtyard of the Exchange itself. Eventually the coffee houses themselves burst out of their modest premises, and developed into exchanges in their own right – the Stock Exchange, Lloyd's, the Baltic Exchange, the Metal Exchange, and other commodity exchanges, most of which built and rebuilt larger and grander premises for themselves as the 18th, 19th, and 20th centuries unfolded. In a similar way the Ship Tavern was the origin of the Corn Exchange.

Meanwhile the goldsmith bankers responded to the increasing demand for capital by developing into partnerships, and eventually were overtaken by upstart joint stock clearing banks. Several of the merchant houses developed into merchant banks, whose global reach and sound credit, combined with the relative political stability of England, led to London's becoming the world centre of international trade and finance in the 19th century. Wave after wave of banks responded to the booming appetite for finance and credit, each able to respond to demand more flexibly than their predecessors, leading eventually to the global international investment houses which dominate the City today. Hand in hand with these changes, the physical fabric of the City was modified to accommodate them. From the middle of the 19th century onwards the old housing stock became increasingly unsuitable. The second half of that century witnessed a building boom in which some four-fifths of the City was replaced by substantial and ostentatious Victorian warehouses and office blocks, forming the fabric of another new City of London which endured for half a century until it was devastated by German bombs. Commerce took over and workers increasingly commuted daily from the suburbs, until the late 17th-century City had been almost entirely replaced by mercantile palaces which were, and continue to be, rebuilt on larger and grander scales with seemingly ever-increasing frequency.

Meanwhile the influence of the institutions which dominated London's trade at the time of the Great Fire, and for which the City was rebuilt – the Royal Exchange, Blackwell Hall, the private bankers, the merchants, the chartered trading companies, the livery companies – waned. They either faded away, or changed their nature to occupy specialist niches in the economy of London, or transformed themselves into social or charitable institutions, prominent elements in City life, but not its mainstream. Fires, wars, changes in fashion, and commercial pressures have taken an overwhelming toll of their premises, so that except for half a dozen or so livery company halls hardly a brick of the 17th-century commercial City still stands upon another.

From the early 19th century onwards ambitious street improvements – the London Bridge approaches, the Cannon Street extension, Gresham Street, Moorgate, Queen Victoria Street, the Victoria Embankment, cut swathes through the tightly-packed fabric of the City. Later in the 19th century the railways (both those on the surface and the cut-and-cover underground) had a similar effect.

By the beginning of the 20th century hardly any of the 17th-century houses were left, and by its end the survivors barely number above single figures. Only in some of the older enclaves of Westminster, such as Queen Anne's Gate, or in the surviving fragments of the old Temple, can one gain a slight impression nowadays of what the 17th-century City of London looked like.

The churches and the parochial spirit which sustained them thrived until the pressures of booming commerce and declining resident populations began to take their toll in the 19th century. The parishes remained fiercely loyal to their churches to the last, but the diocese of London was eager to realise the commercial value of the sites and building materials in order to assist in the provision of new churches in the exploding suburbs of

London. The Union of City Benefices Act was passed in 1860. Before it only four of Wren's churches had disappeared, three of them in the interests of street improvement, but for half a century afterwards there ensued a steady stream of demolitions. Plans in the 1920s for a further extensive cull were abandoned.

In 1940 most of the major churches survived, but many of the smaller ones had already gone. St Paul's Cathedral was then and still remains the single greatest manifestation of the energetic late 17th-century resurrection of the City. Otherwise, a handful of company halls and houses had escaped the Georgian and Victorian appetite for larger and grander buildings. Even though fire-resistant by 17th-century standards, these fragile structures were easy prey to German high explosives and fire-bombs. In among the sturdily-built banks and exchanges in the eastern part of the City their survival rate was relatively high, but further to the west the textile warehouses, just like their predecessors of 1666, provided ample fuel for an inferno that obliterated virtually everything in its path. Now only half of the new churches are still structurally complete, and most of these are 20th-century rebuilds whose interiors particularly often have little similarity to their pristine appearance.

The disappearance of many of the steeples has been compounded, particularly over the past 40 years, by the mushrooming of London's skyscrapers, so that the late Stuart skyline is now, in spite of height restrictions around St Paul's, a shadow of its former self. Occasional glimpses of it remain, however, as for instance in the view across the River from the Globe Theatre on Bankside.

THE SURVIVORS

None of the late 17th-century buildings of London survives completely unaltered. Several are so close to their original state, however, or have been so sensitively restored after wartime damage, that they still have something of a genuine 17th-century 'feel'. Some of these are not illustrated in this book, since no drawing can hope to do justice to the real thing; where they are illustrated it is because of some significant change to their appearance. They are:

- St Paul's Cathedral – Later furnishings and monuments intrude, especially the mosaics in the choir vaults; but on the whole Wren's masterpiece, the culmination and focus of the post-Fire rebuilding, remains unchanged, one of the finest works of baroque architecture and decoration anywhere in the world; it retains most of its superb fittings, including magnificent woodcarving by Gibbons and wrought iron by Tijou. (Only the old choir screen and organ case, now dismembered, are illustrated here.)
- The Monument – A commemorative column close to Thomas Farynor's house where it all began. (It is illustrated here, to show its scale in relation to the houses of Fish Street Hill.)
- St Martin Ludgate – A fine small church, which survived the Blitz and its furnishings are more or less intact. (It is illustrated here to show its relation to the adjacent Ludgate.)
- St Benet Paul's Wharf – An attractive small church; it has one of the best-preserved of City church interiors, with most of the original fittings. (The illustration here is a composite of an unrealised design for the south front and the existing steeple.)
- St Mary Abchurch – An exquisite domed church magnificently restored after extensive bomb damage in the Second World War, with most of its original fittings; one of the finest churches in the City. (The illustration here is a composite of an unrealised design for the east front and the existing steeple.)
- St James Garlickhithe – A fairly large church, where judicious restoration of war damage and fittings brought in from demolished churches have successfully recreated

a 17th-century atmosphere. (Illustrated here to show how it looked before minor structural changes.)

- St Margaret Lothbury – A relatively simple but largely undamaged church which relies for its effect mostly on its rich collection of furnishings, many of them imported from demolished churches. (Illustrated here to show the original arrangement of the doors, and the shops which fronted it.)
- St Margaret Pattens – A largely undamaged church which retains many original furnishings. (Illustrated here to show the original decoration of its spire.)
- St Magnus the Martyr – A church which suffered a number of structural vicissitudes during the 18th century, but preserves most of its 17th-century furnishings intact. (Illustrated here to show its substantially different structural appearance.)
- St Peter Cornhill – Another church which retains much of its original fittings, although marred by inappropriate stained glass and the removal of its pews. (The interior is illustrated here to show the original pewing.)
- St Stephen Walbrook – The finest of the Wren parish churches, not seriously damaged either by restorations or German bombs, and retaining many of its original furnishings, but aesthetically substantially changed by modern fittings. (Illustrated here to show how it appeared from Stocks Market, and the original pewing of the interior.)
- St Edmund King and Martyr – A relatively plain church with a well-preserved interior. (Illustrated here to show how it appeared before structural changes.)
- St Clement Eastcheap – Another plain church, with many of its original fittings. (Illustrated here to show the original gallery.)
- St Mary Aldermary – A structurally intact important example of a 'modern Gothick' church, but embellished and refurbished in the 19th century. (Illustrated here to show its unrestored state.)
- St Mary Woolnoth – Hawksmoor's major accredited contribution to the City churches, intact apart from the removal of its galleries and box pews (which the illustration here shows as they were originally).
- Skinners' Hall – A relatively well-preserved and all-too-rare survival of the post-Fire rebuildings of the livery companies' halls.
- Tallow Chandlers' Hall – A uniquely well-preserved hall of one of the minor companies.
- Vintners' Hall – The interior is largely intact, with fine decoration, although the exterior is completely new. (The original exterior is illustrated here.)
- Stationers' Hall – Another well-preserved interior with high-quality decoration; here also the exterior has been altered. (The original exterior is illustrated here.)
- Apothecaries' Hall – A well-preserved company hall (the original form of the exterior is illustrated here).
- Innholders' Hall – Parts of the interior, and a new copy of the original elaborately decorated entrance survive.
- Deanery of St Paul's – A rare survivor of the larger brick houses which were once common in the City.
- Chapter House of St Paul's – The exterior survives of the chapter house which was gutted by Second World War bombs.
- King's Bench Walk (Inner Temple) – Several of the fine brick houses survive.
- Whittington's College – Former almshouses in College Hill, with two spectacularly decorated gateways.
- College of Arms – substantially altered in association with the driving of Queen Victoria Street past it, but still with its finely decorated court room intact. (The original appearance of the exteriors is illustrated here.)

- St Leonard's Parish School – The only surviving 17th-century school building in the City.
- Master's House (Inner and Middle Temples) – The exterior is an accurate reconstruction of the original, destroyed by German bombs.
- Nos.1 and 2 Laurence Pountney Hill – A pair of fine early 18th-century houses.
- Nos.5 and 6 Crane Court – Two of Nicholas Barbon's houses, with well preserved exteriors, and interiors restored after fire damage.
- Dr. Johnson's House, Gough Square – A well-preserved late 17th-century brick house.
- Ye Olde Cheshire Cheese, Wine Office Court – A much-altered 17th-century tavern, refronted in the 18th century.
- Nos.79 and 81 Carter Lane – Two examples of the smallest class of houses.
- Nos.1, 2, and 3 Amen Court – A row of late 17th-century brick canons' houses.
- Nos.3, 4, and 5 Wardrobe Court – Three houses built in about 1710.
- The Old Bell, Fleet Street – A plain house overlooking St Bride's churchyard.
- Ye Olde Watling, Watling Street – A much-restored and plain house of the intermediate category.
- Shades, Martin Lane – Another much-restored house of the intermediate category.

Apart from these, all that is left is 12 churches (St Andrew Holborn, St Andrew by the Wardrobe, St Anne and St Agnes, St Bride, St Lawrence Jewry, St Mary at Hill, St Mary le Bow, St Michael Cornhill, St Michael Paternoster Royal, St Nicholas, St Sepulchre, St Vedast) whose exteriors are largely original, but which internally are more or less Victorian restorations or mid-20th-century rebuilds, often in a loose interpretation of the Wren style, sometimes deliberately modern; six dismembered steeples (Christ Church, St Alban, St Augustine, St Dunstan, St Mary Somerset, St Olave Jewry); and a handful of interiors of secular buildings.

A few other structures survive, usually as a fragment, as a result of being moved to new locations, often outside the City, saved from the onslaught of progress. Notable examples are:

- Aldermen's Court Room (ceiling painting in the Guildhall Art Gallery).
- All Hallows the Great (furnishings at Halstead, Essex, and St Margaret Lothbury, City of London).
- All Hallows Lombard Street (tower and furnishings incorporated in All Hallows Twickenham, Middlesex).
- Bethlehem Royal Hospital (statues at new hospital, Beckenham, Kent).
- Boar's Head Tavern (stone sign in Museum of London).
- Christ's Hospital (part of façade and statuary at new school, Horsham, Sussex).
- Doctors' Commons (wood carving at Fulham Palace).
- German Church(reredos at Hamburg Lutheran church, Hackney).
- Ludgate (statues at St Dunstan in the West, City of London).
- Mark Lane (Richly carved wooden street entrance in Victoria and Albert Museum).
- Mercers' Hall (façade incorporated in Swanage town hall, Dorset).
- Old Mansion House (fragments at St Margaret's Bay, Kent).
- Pewterers' Hall (parlour at Geffrye Museum, Shoreditch).
- Royal College of Physicians (Censors' Room at new College building, Regents Park, wood carving at Mayfield, Sussex).
- Royal Exchange (statuary at various locations in the City and at Goudhurst, Kent).
- St Alban Wood Street (west window of nave incorporated in Wrotham church, Kent).

- St Antholin Watling Street (top of spire a garden ornament, Forest Hill, Kent; reredos at Nunhead, Kent; pulpit at Blandford Forum, Dorset).
- St Mary Aldermanbury (rebuilt, incorporating much of the original fabric, Fulton, Missouri, USA).
- St Matthew Friday Street (reredos at Polesden Lacey, Surrey).
- St Michael Queenhithe (furnishings at St James Garlickhythe).
- Stocks Market statue (park ornament, Newby Park, Yorkshire).
- Temple Bar (park ornament, Theobalds, Hertfordshire).
- Waldo's House (room in Cheapside, City of London).
- Wren's House (room at Sir John Cass's School, Aldgate, City of London)

Many furnishings from City churches are scattered in churches in the City and suburbs of London. Otherwise, there remain only photographs, prints, paintings, drawings, memories, and (all too often) obscurity.

LONDON RENEWED

This book is an attempt to recapture an echo of the London which was rebuilt in the decades following 1666, the chimera which resulted when the first modern city in England was grafted onto a layout and mode of organisation which retained much of its medieval past. This is done by means of sketches of elevations and sections of as many as possible of the 'show' buildings of the new City, together with what is necessarily a selection from its domestic architecture. Sketches, not drawings, because the level of detail of many of the sources for these buildings' appearance is often not sufficient to guarantee absolute accuracy; in all cases, however, the aim has been the most accurate representation possible.

The sources for the appearance of the new buildings of late 17th-century London are various, although not as numerous as one might have hoped – widespread accurate topographical representations of London's streets and buildings did not get under way until well into the 18th century, and acquired substantial momentum only in the 19th, by which time much of the fabric of the City, particularly its domestic buildings, had already been modernised or rebuilt in the Georgian period. The main sources used in this work to reconstruct post-Fire London are:

- Elevational and sectional drawings, particularly those of the original architects, and of Clayton and Crace;
- 17th-, 18th-, and 19th-century prints, drawings, and paintings, particularly those of Cole, Bowles, the Shepherds, Scharf, and Schnebbelie;
- 17th- and 18th-century verbal accounts of the appearance of London's buildings (particularly Edward Hatton's 1708 descriptions of the churches);
- 17th-, 18th-, and 19th-century maps, notably Morgan's 1682 map (whose schematic views of certain buildings are the only record of their appearance; some have formed the basis here of speculative reconstructions);
- Photographs;
- Surviving structures.

The idea in *London: Rebuilding the City after the Great Fire* has been to show the City's principal buildings as nearly as possible according to their original appearance. With wear and tear, changing fashions, and new technology, many changes occurred over the years, so that later pictures are often rather different from what was originally there. Such changes sometimes occurred fairly soon after construction – for instance the introduction of sash windows around the turn of the 18th century. Thus, because London took half a century to rebuild completely, this book should not be taken as a representation of what the City 'looked like' in, say, 1720; it is rather a somewhat idealistic conception of what its builders originally intended.

Because of the imperfection or late date of many of the sources, a number of conventions have been adopted to attempt to convey the 'original appearance' of these buildings:

- Windows: sash windows, although known in 1666, were not widely introduced in England until the last years of the 17th century. Until then 'Italian' windows, with crossed mullion and transom, were widely used; all of the earliest representations of the City streets show Italian windows to have been the norm, and they have therefore been generally depicted even when the earliest known pictures of buildings show sashes, except when a late construction date makes sashes more likely.
- Shops were generally open to the street, with shutters which folded down to form a counter for the display of wares. The shop windows in the Royal Exchange, however, with their removable shutters, presaged a new fashion which became general. 'Penthouses' at first-floor level provided protection from the weather for the shop-fronts; they, too, often disappeared to make way for the more capacious Georgian shop-front technology. Even more than the windows, the shop-fronts shown in these drawings are schematic.
- Roofs generally descended to projecting cornices, although some were fronted by parapets (sometimes balustraded); parapets were widely introduced at a later date; these reconstructions reinstate corniced roofs where it appears reasonable to do so.
- Downpipes are not shown, nor, generally, are the elaborate projecting shop signs which festooned London's streets.

In order to assist comparisons the scale of all the sketches is the same, at approximately 1:255, or 21¼ feet to the inch. On this scale a six-foot man would stand about three-tenths of an inch high.

THE CITY WHICH MIGHT HAVE BEEN

As described above, the schemes for rebuilding London according to a modernistic layout were never realistic enough to develop beyond simple ground-plans. Within the pattern of rebuilding that was adopted there were, however, a number of projects which, while they got as far as detailed exposition on paper (or even as models), never had the funds or backing to be realised. The convoluted history of the development of the design of St Paul's Cathedral (culminating in the magnificent Great Model which shows how Wren would have built St Paul's if it hadn't been for the tiresomeness of his clients) has been told and illustrated so amply elsewhere that no repetition is attempted here. This book does, however, include:

- Some of the early designs for the churches and their steeples.
- Wren's scheme for the north frontage of St Stephen Walbrook, intended to give the Stocks Market the grand aspect of a Roman forum.
- Wren's/Hawksmoor's scheme for a grand loggia in Cheapside, to adjoin St Mary le Bow.
- Hawksmoor's early 18th-century scheme for improving and elaborating St Paul's Churchyard, including his proposed 'baptistry' opposite the west end of the cathedral.
- The most spectacular of the rejected designs for the Monument – the gilded flames springing from its shaft would have been an apt memorial to the conflagration that changed London forever.

THE BUILDINGS

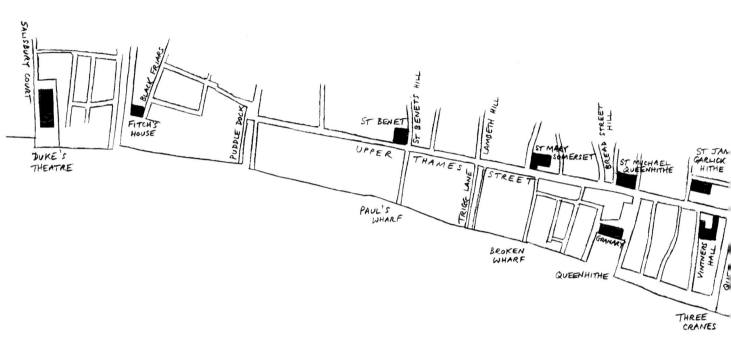

5 Panorama of London, Nathaniel and Samuel Buck, 1749
(detail), showing St Paul's Cathedral, the City steeples and the
waterfront. (Guildhall Library)

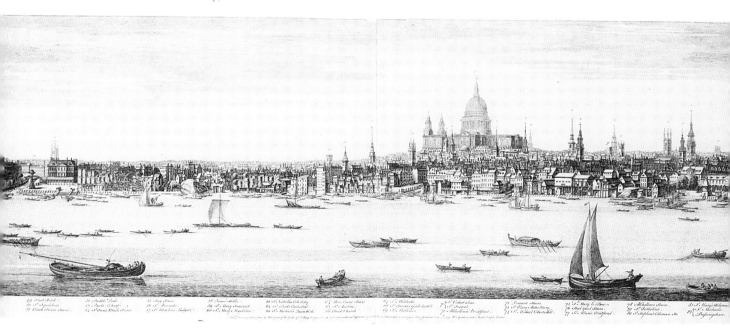

THE RIVERFRONT

THE CITY OF LONDON'S façade to the world, through which so much of its trade passed. London lived on the River to a vastly greater extent than today – sea-going ships loading and unloading below London Bridge (with the Custom House strategically placed to extract finance for the state), the upriver trade above the bridge, passenger traffic in all directions. As befitted a great commercial City, the new London was almost 'designed' to be viewed from the River, and all the great panoramas of the City showed the view from the Southwark shore, the greatest of them all the Buck brothers' 1749 panorama of the new City in all its bustle, prosperity, pride and beauty. Today London's waterfront is hardly recognisable as a port, and the skyline has all but disappeared.

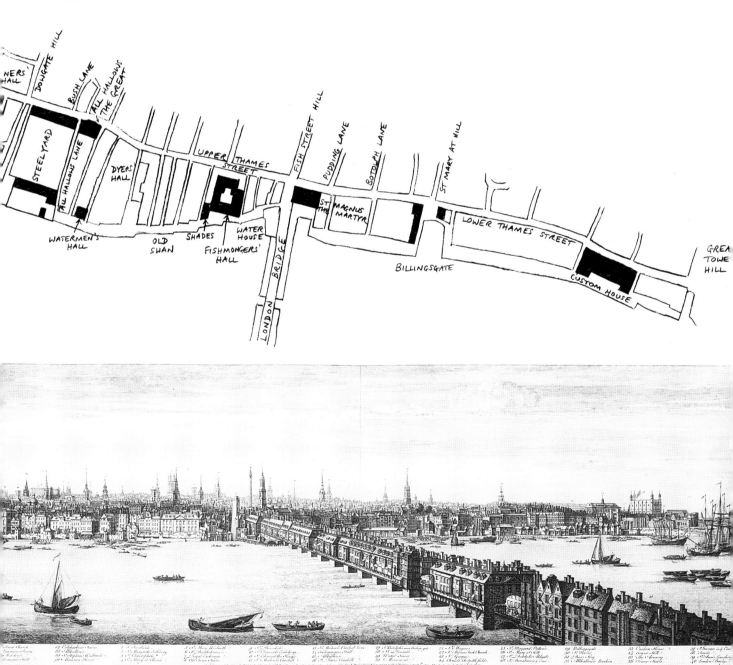

CUSTOM HOUSE

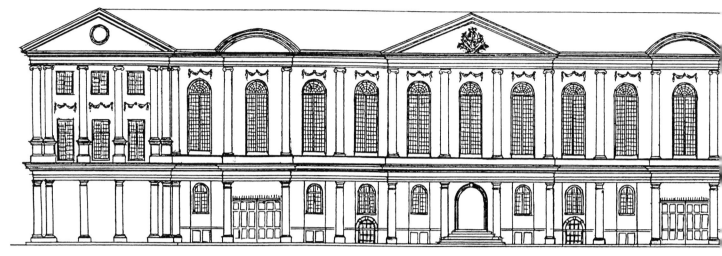

Custom House: river frontage (Custom House Quay)

The first London Custom House was built on Wool Wharf in the early 14th century for the collection of custom duty on imports and exports. Rebuilt twice in the later Middle Ages, it was destroyed in the Great Fire, and rebuilt, probably to Wren's design, a long two-storeyed brick frontage with return wings, articulated by alternating triangular and segmental pediments, from 1669 to 1671, at a cost of £10,000. The tall windows in the upper storey of the main block lit the Long Room, where merchants paid duty and obtained passes to clear their goods; Defoe described it as 'like an Exchange ... Nothing of the Kind in Europe is like it'. The west end of the building was damaged by the explosion of a gunpowder store in 1714, and the whole was rebuilt in a similar style to Thomas Ripley's design between 1717 and 1725 – this was in its turn burned down in 1814, and the present Custom House to David Laing's design (partly rebuilt by Robert Smirke in 1828) was then built on the adjacent site to the west; the site of the original is now occupied by the Sugar Quay office block. Since no accurate representation of Wren's Custom House survives, this reconstruction applies the details of Wren's building to the proportions of Ripley's – the resulting inaccuracies are probably minor. *(See plate 6, p.28.)*

BILLINGSGATE

Billingsgate, originally probably a water gate in the old City wall which ran along the river bank, was first mentioned in about 1000; it was probably named after a local property owner. It was first referred to as a dock as late as 1337, but had probably functioned as such from the earliest times. As the Middle Ages progressed it became an inlet on the waterfront as the adjoining properties encroached on the foreshore on either side of the public landing place. Billingsgate was originally much less important than the other main City landing place, Queenhithe, but eventually overtook its rival as the increasing size of sea-going ships meant that they could no longer pass through London Bridge. A provisions market developed on the bank by the 13th century, and the fish trade was well established by the fourteenth. (The sale of stale fish at Billingsgate in 1380 prompted the most serious of the medieval feuds between the textile guilds, led by the Drapers, and the provisions guilds, of whom the Fishmongers were the most important.) In the 17th century Billingsgate came to specialise as a fish dock (under the oligopoly of a small number of powerful fishmongers until it was constituted a free fish market in 1699), although it was also an important market for imported fruit and Kentish cherries, and for coal (especially before the Coal

Billingsgate dock and market: frontage of west side

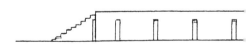

Exchange was established nearby in 1747), London's main fuel and the tax base for the rebuilding fund. In addition Billingsgate was much used for passenger traffic, being the main embarkation point for ports further down the River, and for people who did not wish to shoot the dangerous rapids which surged through London Bridge on the ebbing and flowing tides (they walked round and picked up a boat at Old Swan Stairs). Billingsgate was a particularly vibrant market. It was famous from early times for the variety of its fish. Dutch eel boats obtained a concession to sell live eels there in 1698. Large numbers of oyster boats sold their wares on deck in a floating extension of the market. The foul language of the market

Billingsgate Market: frontage of east side

men became proverbial, and the fishwives were noted for their sharp tongues. Numerous rough maritime taverns slaked thirsts. As the volume of trade increased Billingsgate changed from being a retail market (at which the citizens had the right every day to buy fish before the merchants) to predominantly wholesale. The view shows the colonnaded market space which was provided in the aftermath of the Great Fire, as shown in Bowles's print of 'The Humours of Billingsgate'. This was replaced by an iron market structure in the late 18th century. In 1850 pressure on space caused the filling in of the dock, with a new market building to the design of J.B. Bunning, itself replaced in the 1870s by Sir Horace Jones's extant

building. Billingsgate became effectively the clearing house for the whole of the fish trade of Great Britain, with special fish trains, and later road haulage, bringing fish from ports all over the country. The resulting congestion around the market eventually forced its closure in 1982, since when it has been operating from a new building in Poplar. It remains, however, the most important inland wholesale fish market in the United Kingdom. The old market building in Lower Thames Street was adapted as a dealing room by Richard Rogers in the 1980s property boom. *(See plate 7, p.28.)*

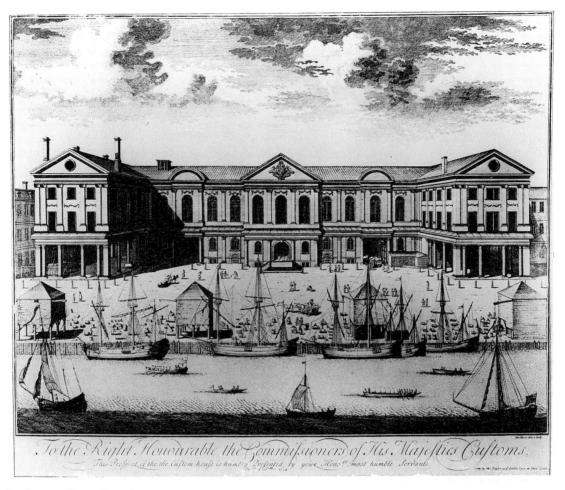

To the Right Honourable the Commissioners of His Majesties Customs.

This Prospect of the the Custom house is humbly Presented by your Honrs most humble Servants

6 Custom House from the River, John Harris, 1715. (Guildhall Library)

7 Billingsgate from Lower Thames Street, looking towards the River: 'The Humours of Billingsgate', A. Vanhaecken, 1736. (Guildhall Library)

THE VIEW AND HUMOURS OF BILLINGSGATE

ST MAGNUS THE MARTYR with ST MARGARET FISH STREET HILL

St Magnus's Church, dedicated to the Orcadian saint, stands on the south side of Lower Thames Street, on what was the corner of Fish Street Hill, the street which led onto old London Bridge. It was first mentioned in about 1133, though it was also referred to in a forged mid-12th-century charter which was dated 1067. St Magnus's was one the first churches to be gutted by the Great Fire in 1666. It was rebuilt in Portland stone by John Thompson to the designs of Wren from 1671 to 1678, and the 185-foot steeple was started in 1680-4 and completed in 1703-5 (by Samuel Fulkes). The overall cost was £12,000. Repeated alterations, restorations and repairs have changed St Magnus's original appearance greatly, but it is notable for the superb quality of its furnishings and, in spite of the many alterations it has undergone, is one of the best preserved of Wren's larger City churches. The church consists of nave and aisles; with a complete absence of correspondence between the columns and the windows. The view shows the original symmetrical north front; the two western bays of each aisle were demolished in 1762 as part of the widening of London Bridge to allow the footway to pass through the bottom of the steeple. At the same time repairs after a 1760 fire in the roof involved the removal of the pediment in the centre of the north front and of the transeptal cross-vault in the centre of the tunnel-vaulted nave (whose appearance is known from the drawing in the RIBA collection). The cross-axis was also marked by the grand entrance, now blocked, in the centre of the north front; Summerson speculated that

St Magnus the Martyr: Lower Thames Street frontage

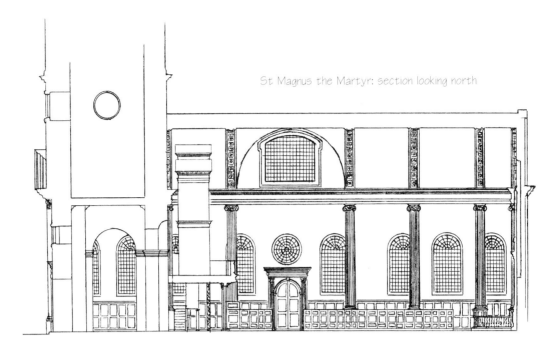

there may have been an abortive plan to establish a forum-like market-place between St Magnus's and the Monument – the existence of such an important entrance from the narrow Lower Thames Street certainly seems odd. The original large arched windows on the north side were replaced in 1782 with smaller circular ones to reduce the traffic noise in the church. The broad central bay in the interior was finally eliminated in a 1924 restoration with the insertion of an extra pair of columns. The steeple is possibly modelled on that of the church of St Charles Borromeo in Antwerp, and may have been influenced by Hooke; its square tower, projecting clock, octagonal upper stage, dome, and lead-covered concave spirelet provided an important landmark (juxtaposed with the nearby Monument) at the head of London Bridge in views both northward across the river and southward down Fish Street Hill, even after a new bridge was built at a higher level and 200 feet to the west in the 1820s, until it was largely obscured in the 1920s by the construction of Adelaide House, the first London skyscraper.

St Margaret Fish Street Hill was first mentioned in the early 12th century. After the Great Fire its site became Monument Yard, with the Monument standing where its west tower had been.

WATER HOUSE, London Bridge. The London Bridge Waterworks, built by Peter Morice in 1582, was the City's first pumped water supply (before then London's conduits were supplied by gravity). Waterwheels installed under the northernmost two arches of London Bridge exploited the rush of the tide through the narrow apertures (at some states of the tide the volume of water trying to push through caused cataracts, with a difference in water level of up to six feet) to pump the water into an adjacent water-tower on the west side of the bridge, from which it was supplied to Cornhill. The early destruction of the Water House in the first sweep of the Great Fire down Fish Street Hill was a crucial setback to the fire-fighting. The Water House was rebuilt from 1668 to 1669. Its plain tower was a prominent feature in views of the City from the River. New pumping machinery installed in 1720, able to raise three million gallons a day, was famous throughout the 18th century as a wonder of engineering. By the 1760s the waterworks had expanded to occupy four arches of the bridge; by the 1820s it was supplying four million gallons a day. The waterworks was finally cleared away along with the demolition of the old bridge in 1831.

Fishmongers' Hall: Upper Thames Street entrance

FISHMONGERS' HALL

In medieval London there were two fishmongers' guilds: the Saltfishmongers (who were the more numerous and powerful; the company was chartered in 1272) and the stockfishmongers. The Fishmongers were the most powerful of the medieval London victuallers' guilds (this is reflected in their current fourth place in the order of precedence of the livery companies), and were prominent in the bitter and sometimes violent disputes of the late 14th century between the victuallers and the textile guilds. Fish was a staple of the medieval diet, and the fishmongers monopolised the trade, even having their own court of law, the Leyhalmode, to police it. Each of the fishmongers' companies had at one stage three halls, including one each near the old fish market in Old Fish Street between St Paul's and the river. In the mid-14th century the Saltfishmongers acquired a large mansion near London Bridge and the new fish market in Fish Street Hill; it had previously been the residence of a succession of influential fishmongers, including Sir William Walworth, the Mayor who helped Richard II suppress the Peasants' Revolt in 1381 by stabbing Wat Tyler (the reputed origin of the dagger which appears in the City of London's coat of arms). In 1504 they made this their main headquarters. The two fishmongers' companies merged in 1536, when they rebuilt the London Bridge hall with a suitably grand river frontage. Architectural grandeur was again in the Company's mind when it came to rebuilding the Hall after its destruction in the Great Fire; this was done from 1668 to 1671 to the design of Edward Jerman and Thomas Lock in a brick-built pedimented Dutch style. Exploiting its magnificent riverside position, it was the most expansive and elegant of the post-Fire rebuildings of the livery companies' halls, and it dominated this part of the riverbank until it

was pulled down in the late 1820s to make way for the approach to the new London Bridge. The new Fishmongers' Hall, built from 1831 to 1835 by Henry Roberts in neo-Greek style, occupies most of the site of its predecessor. The Company continues to exercise an important role in the regulation of the London fish trade.

SHADES TAVERN

The Shades, first mentioned in 1549, was a tavern which occupied part of the vaults under Fishmongers Hall, and the adjoining house; it was rebuilt after the Great Fire as a narrow three-storeyed brick house of standard design. It was a fashionable tavern in the late 17th and 18th centuries, and was patronised by Joseph Addison and his circle. It was especially noted for the quality of its wines. The house was demolished in 1831 to make way for the rebuilt Fishmongers' Hall, but a Shades Tavern remains in nearby Martin Lane, occupying a much-restored but nevertheless rare survival of the City's late 17th-century houses.

DYERS' HALL, White Cock Alley, Dowgate. Dyers' Hall, close to the Thames, its site now occupied by Ebbgate House, was rebuilt after the Great Fire (and again after another fire in 1681); the later Hall is shown in the Bucks' panorama. The Company moved to its present location in Dowgate Hill in 1731. The most important of the 'minor companies', the guild was first mentioned in 1188 and chartered in 1471; it controlled the dyeing of wool, silk and leather until the early 18th century.

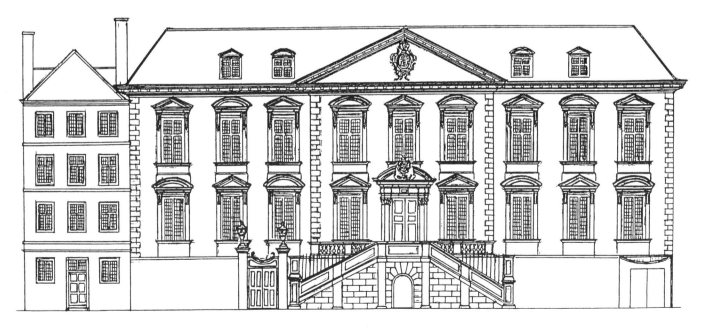

Fishmongers' Hall: river frontage (Fishmongers' Hall wharf); Shades Tavern to the left

WATERMEN'S HALL

The Company of Watermen built themselves a Hall on part of the site of Coldharbour (a large riverside mansion which had belonged to a succession of members of the nobility in the later Middle Ages) after the Great Fire. The Hall was completed in 1670 and rebuilt in 1720 with a grander river frontage; the view is derived from the depiction of the 1670 hall in Overton's panorama. In 1780 the Watermen moved to a new Hall in St Mary at Hill, Billingsgate; the original site is now covered by Mondial House. The Company of Watermen of the River Thames was established by various Acts of Parliament during the 16th century, and does not fall under the jurisdiction of the Lord Mayor, as do other City companies. The Lightermen (who ferried goods from ship to shore, whereas the Watermen carried passengers) were joined to the Watermen's Company by an Act of 1700. Because of the paucity of bridges and the congested streets, river transport was until the 19th century probably the most important and convenient means of getting around London; passengers would call for 'Oars' at one of the numerous stairs or wharves along the length of the Thames. Watermen also rowed the state barges of royalty and the City. They were notorious for their repartee and foul language. During the 19th century improvements in road transport, new bridges (which the watermen vigorously opposed), and steamer services virtually eliminated the watermen's trade, and the lightermen suffered from the development of enclosed docks. The Port of London Authority took over most of the Watermen's and Lightermen's Company's powers in 1908.

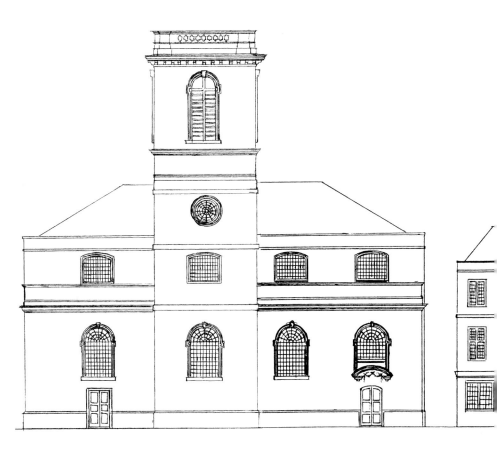

Watermen's Hall: river frontage (Coldharbour Stairs)

STEELYARD

German merchants were established in London by the 10th century, and gradually superseded the Danes as the mainstay of the English carrying trade. By the 13th century they were operating from a guildhall on the Upper Thames Street site; in the same century the Cologne merchants and the 'Easterlings' of Hamburg and Lübeck, who had been commercial rivals, combined to form the 'Merchants of Almaine', the Hanseatic League which dominated the medieval Baltic trade in grain, ropes, timber, pitch, tar, flax, linen, wax, and steel, and also provided substantial shipping for the carriage of English wool to the Continent and for the Mediterranean trade. The colony of German merchants expanded to cover a two-acre site on the south side of Upper Thames Street between Cousin Lane and All Hallows Lane. It was called the Steelyard, the name being either a corruption of 'Staelhof' (staple house), or a reference to the 'steelyard' weigh-beam. The German merchants enjoyed trading and customs privileges because of their importance to the English economy, and the Steelyard became almost a town within a town, with its own administration, customs, and currency. Such preferential treatment led to increasing resentment on the part of English merchants. The late medieval expansion of English mercantile shipping, and continuing pressure from English merchant adventurers, eventually led to Edward VI's revocation of the Hanse privileges in 1551, although German merchants in the Steelyard continued to compete effectively in the English cloth trade until

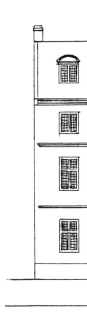

Upper Thames Street: south side between All Hallows Lane and
Cousin Lane, including Thames Street frontage of the
Steelyard and All Hallows the Great to the left (see page 41)

they were banished in 1598. Readmitted by James I, the Germans continued to operate from the Steelyard area into the 19th century. The Steelyard was completely destroyed in the Great Fire and rebuilt by the initiative of the wealthy merchant and 'House Master', Jacob Jacobsen, as a complex of brick houses and warehouses, with a more elaborate office building with a short tower-porch facing the River, river stairs flanked by pillars supporting carved German eagles, and a crane on the wharf whose baroque roof was a prominent feature of the London riverfront. Jacobsen and his nephews Jacob and

Theodore (the dilletante architect of the Foundling Hospital) ran the Steelyard until the Hanse towns took it in hand again in 1720. All was swept away in 1865 to make way for Cannon Street Railway Station, which still occupies the whole of the site, although commerce returned to the site in the 1990s in the form of the London International Financial Futures Exchange's trading floor above the station, much of whose success, aptly, was built on trading derivatives of German government bonds and Deutschmark interest rates.

Steelyard: river frontage (Steelyard Wharf)

QUEENHITHE GRANARY

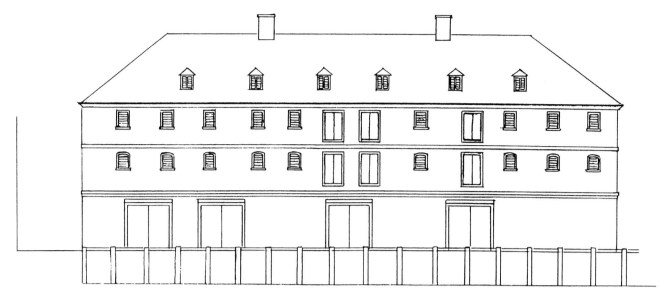

Queenhithe Dock and Granary: river (south) frontage

First mentioned in 898 as Aetheredshithe, presumably named after the late ninth-century Ealdorman of Mercia of that name, who was King Alfred's son-in-law, Queenhithe received its present name in the early Middle Ages from one of the queens to whom its tolls were successively granted. It was the most important dock of early medieval London, supplying fish to the Old Fish Street market, and other goods for Cheapside. The north bank represents roughly the original shoreline of the River, and the inlet was formed by successive encroachments of the riverbank on either side. Queenhithe was granted to the City in the mid-13th century. Its importance declined from the 15th century onwards as the increasing size of ships meant they could no longer pass through the narrow arches of London Bridge, and docked instead at Billingsgate. Thereafter Queenhithe's focus was the inland trade, and it developed a specialist role as the main dock for unloading grain which had been milled upriver. This recalled its medieval status as the only place in the City at which grain was allowed to be landed. A granary and market house was built in the mid-16th century on the open ground called Romeland on its north side. The Granary was burnt in 1666 and rebuilt in brick in a utilitarian style. It was demolished in the early 19th century to make way for the Smiths Wharf warehouses, themselves replaced in the 1970s by Queen's Quay House.

FITCH'S HOUSE

This, the grandest private house on the City waterfront, with its pedimented projecting centre and rusticated quoining, was built by the early 1680s, probably for Sir Thomas Fitch. Fitch was the contractor for Wren's and Hooke's improvements to the River Fleet. The house stood on the corner of the Fleet and the Thames, and was no doubt intended to set an example for the buildings which were to line the projected but never realised New Quay along the Thames shoreline. The house was occupied from the early 1690s until 1713 by the quack doctor William Salmon, evidence of the commercial success of his 'pill to cure all diseases' and his huge output of medical treatises. Later in the 18th century, with the deterioration of the Fleet and the entrenchment of fashionable society in the West End, the house became what was no doubt the grandest warehouse in London. It was removed as part of the developments for the approach to the new Blackfriars Bridge in the 1760s; the site is now covered by the Queen Victoria Street entrance to Blackfriars Station. *(See plate 57, p.176.)*

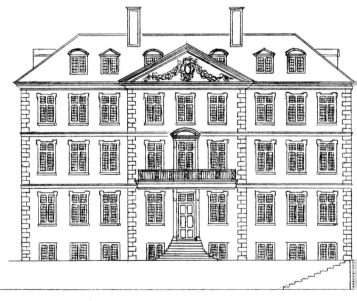

Fitch's House: river frontage (Blackfriars Stairs)

DUKE'S THEATRE

The Duke's Theatre, or Dorset Gardens Theatre, was built in 1671, reputedly to Wren's design but probably not, for the Duke of York's Company, which had in the early 1660s used the nearby Salisbury Court Theatre, burnt in the Great Fire. The colonnaded frontage, overlooking a carriage court and river stairs, was prominent in the view of the City from the River. Under the management of Lady Davenant, the Duke's Company produced plays by John Davenant, Richard Otway and John Dryden there, and Henry Purcell's operas. The theatre's decline began in 1682 when the Duke's Company merged with the King's Company and migrated to Drury Lane, reflecting the inexorable migration of fashionable society towards the West End. It became a venue for prize-fighting in 1698 and was demolished in 1720. The City of London was not to have another theatre until the Mermaid was established in Puddle Dock after the Second World War. The site was later occupied by the offices of the New River Company and then, continuing the utility theme, the Whitefriars Gas Works; it now lies beneath J.P. Morgan's offices, well back from the riverbank as a result of Joseph Bazalgette's reclamations for the Victoria Embankment.

Duke's Theatre, Dorset Gardens: river frontage (Whitefriars Stairs)

ST BENET PAUL'S WHARF WITH ST PETER PAUL'S WHARF

St Benet's is one of the few almost perfectly preserved City churches, lacking only its box pews. It was mentioned in the 12th century, and Inigo Jones was buried there in 1651. It was rebuilt after the Great Fire from 1678 to 1684 by Edward and Thomas Strong in a Dutch style, probably to Hooke's design. It is of brick with stone dressings, decorative brickwork, carved festoons, and a lead-covered square dome with cupola on the tower. The illustrated earlier design includes an attic with oval windows above the festoons, which would have given the church a much grander aspect. The transfer of St Benet's to the Welsh Episcopalian Church in 1879 saved it from planned demolition. It used to stand prominently on the north side of Upper Thames Street, on the corner of Benet's Hill, until radical replanning in the 1970s, when this part of Upper Thames Street was closed and the new White Lion Hill swept round its north-western side; it now faces onto Queen Victoria Street.

St Peter Paul's Wharf was mentioned in 1170; it was also called at various times St Peter the Less, St Peter Wood Wharf (this was the centre of the medieval wood trade, with Woodmongers' Hall nearby), St Peter Baynards Castle (after the adjacent fortification which guarded the western flank of London's riverbank), and St Peter on Thames. It was the main centre of Anglican liturgy in the City during the Civil War and Commonwealth. Burnt in 1666, it was not rebuilt; the churchyard survived on the east corner of St Peter's Hill and Upper Thames Street until as part of post-Second World War redevelopment of the Blitzed surroundings of St Paul's it was covered by the new Peter's Hill pedestrian way.

St Benet Paul's Wharf: unrealised design for Upper Thames Street frontage, with steeple as built

ST MARY SOMERSET with ST MARY MOUNTHAW

St Mary Somerset stood on the north side of Upper Thames Street, on the east corner of Old Fish Street Hill. The steeple survives, and the site of the church is occupied by the adjoining garden and Lambeth Hill behind it. The church was first mentioned in the mid-12th century. 'Somerset' may be either the name of an early benefactor, or refer to a nearby 'Somer's Hythe'. Burnt in 1666, it was rebuilt to the designs of Wren by Christopher Kempster from 1686 to 1694. The body of the church, a simple Portland stone rectangle which contained its original furnishings (funded by the Commissioners and not the parish, an indicator of the latter's poverty) and plasterwork, was demolished in 1872 under the Union of City Benefices Act, and the proceeds of sale were used to build St Mary Somerset in Hoxton (the pulpit survives at Holy Trinity Church in Hoxton). The Portland stone steeple, built on a new site at the south-west corner to exploit views along Upper Thames Street, and to whose design Hawksmoor may have contributed, was preserved by the efforts of Ewen Christian because of its remarkable crown, which represents the City steeple at its most baroque. It is effectively an inversion of the steeple of St Christopher le Stocks; at each corner of the parapet is an urn, and in the centre of each side is a much taller obelisk pinnacle. The result is a highly dynamic reversal of the conventional proportions of a pinnacled church tower, analogous to the steeple of St Bartholomew by the Exchange. *(See plate 9, p.38.)*

St Mary Mounthaw was first mentioned in 1275. It probably originated as the private chapel of the Mounthaut family, whose mansion adjoined. The site is marked today by the east corner of Queen Victoria Street and Lambeth Hill.

St Mary Somerset: Upper Thames Street and Old Fish Street Hill frontages (diagonal view)

St Mary Somerset: Upper Thames Street frontage

ST MICHAEL QUEENHITHE
WITH HOLY TRINITY THE LESS

St Michael Queenhithe: cross-section looking east

St Michael Queenhithe: Upper Thames Street frontage

St Michael Queenhithe: Little Trinity Lane frontage

St Michael's Church stood on the north side of Upper Thames Street opposite Queenhithe. Fur Trade House now occupies the site. Queenhithe had previously been Ethelredshithe, and this also was the original designation of St Michael's Church, which was first mentioned in the early 12th century. Burnt in the Great Fire, it was rebuilt by James Flory and Samuel Fulkes to the designs of Wren from 1676 to 1686. It was an impressive church for an important site, dominating Queenhithe and contributing to the view of the City from the River, as well as reflecting the prosperity of the grain merchants who were its parishioners. The monumental Portland stone south front, with two tiers of windows and rich carved ornament, was matched by a similarly elaborate east front up Little Trinity Lane. The lead-covered north-west steeple, added between 1685 and 1687, was another variant on the theme of transition from square tower to square

needle spire, in this instance via a series of diminishing steps which were reminiscent of the Mausoleum at Halicarnassus. The nautical location of the church was reflected in the ship-shaped weathervane which is now atop the steeple of St Nicholas Cole Abbey. St Michael's was demolished in 1876 under the Union of City Benefices Act; the proceeds of sale were used to build St Michael's Church in Camden Town, and many of the fittings are now at St James Garlickhythe. The view shows the reredos, probably Georgian, which was illustrated by Clayton; Hatton described a Gothick reredos painted in perspective, a curiosity in an otherwise entirely classical building. *(See plate 10, p.38.)*

Holy Trinity the Less was first mentioned in 1182. It was so called to distinguish it from the Priory of Holy Trinity in Aldgate. It was rebuilt after the Great Fire as the German Church (see page 138). The site of Holy Trinity Less was the south-east corner of Little Trinity Lane and Great Trinity Lane.

8 Queenhithe and St Paul's, photograph from the Prince Consort's collection, *c.*1859, showing the working waterfront and the steeples of St Benet Paul's Wharf, St Mary Somerset, St Mary Magdalen, St Nicholas, St Michael Queenhithe, and St Mildred Bread Street. (Guildhall Library)

9 St Mary Somerset and Upper Thames Street, Thomas Shepherd, 1829. (Guildhall Library)

10 St Michael Queenhithe, photograph, *c.*1870. (National Monuments Record)

ST JAMES GARLICKHYTHE

St James's Church was first mentioned in about 1170, and according to Stow was named after a nearby wharf where garlic was sold. In early times it was also called St James Vintry, St James Comyns, or St James by the Thames. It was burnt in 1666 and rebuilt in brick and ragstone by Christopher Kempster to Wren's design between 1676 and 1684. The plan is fairly elaborate, a nave with transepts set within an aisled basilica, and with a projecting chancel, its many and large windows making for a light interior. The elaborate steeple, on a square plan with diminishing stages, was added in Portland stone by Edward Strong the Younger, perhaps to Hawksmoor's design, from 1714 to 1717, one of the last of the City steeples. The view shows the original appearance of the north side, before alterations to the windows and blockage of the door which opened on the cross aisle. The fittings (which now include a number of pieces from St Michael Queenhithe, notably the spectacular pulpit) are among the best in the City.

St James Garlickhythe: Maiden Lane frontage

St James Garlickhythe: cross-section looking east

VINTNERS' HALL

The Vintry, the area of the waterfront to the east of
Queenhithe, was the centre of the Bordeaux wine trade,
one of the most important in medieval London.
Englishmen drank claret in large quantities, and the
protection of the trade was one of the most important
strategic factors behind the Hundred Years War. The
Vintners were one of the most important of the London
guilds, reflected in the Company's eleventh place in the
order of precedence – it was chartered in 1364 with a
monopoly of the Gascon trade. Although its commercial
power later declined, the Company acquired a new lease
of life in 1973 when it was given responsibility for
enforcement of European Community wine legislation in
the United Kingdom. The Company acquired its Hall in
1446. Burnt in the Great Fire, it was rebuilt by 1671 to the
design of Roger Jerman. Alterations in the 19th century
have changed the Hall's external appearance, but the
interiors, including the livery hall, court room, and
staircase, are largely unchanged, and constitute a rarely
well-preserved example of the opulence with which the
livery companies rebuilt after the Fire – the wood carving
of the staircase (by William Woodroffe), screens and
panelling is particularly fine. The Hall stood around a
courtyard which opened at its north end to Upper Thames
Street via a fine gateway. The exteriors were given new
classical facings in 1822 in association with the
development of the new Southwark Bridge and the
widening of Thames Street, and the courtyard was filled in
and new façades provided in 1910.

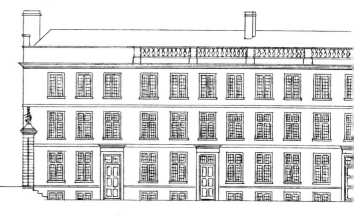

Vintners' Hall: frontage of east side of court

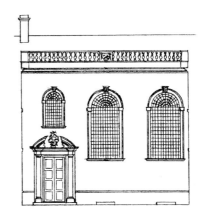

Vintners' Hall:
south frontage of court
(open to Upper Thames
Street) (livery hall)

Vintners' Hall: Gate to
Court from Upper Thames
Street

JOINERS' AND CEILERS' HALL

Joiners' Hall was rebuilt by about 1670, and again after
another fire in 1696, on a cramped site amongst the tangle
of warehouses between Upper Thames Street and the
River, just west of Dowgate. The Hall was burnt in 1811
and replaced by warehouses. The elaborately carved
gateway of 1670 with statues of mermen on its piers
survived until the 1940 bombing. The Thames Exchange
building occupies the site now. The guild was formed in
1375 and chartered as a company in 1571. Originally
subordinate to the Carpenters, it controlled the London
joinery and ceiling (i.e. wood carving) trades, and
members were therefore very active in the late 17th-
century rebuilding.

Joiners' Hall: Tennis Court Lane
entrance to courtyard

ALL HALLOWS THE GREAT WITH ALL HALLOWS THE LESS

All Hallows' Church stood on the south side of Upper Thames Street; the site is the pavement in front of Mondial House, where a kink in the street still marks where the church constricted it. All Hallows' was first mentioned in 1148. It was called 'the Great' to distinguish it from the nearby All Hallows the Less, which was not rebuilt after the Great Fire. Other medieval names of the church included All Hallows at the Hay (from the nearby Haywharf), All Hallows in the Ropery (this part of Thames Street was the centre of rope manufacture), and the Seaman's Church. A grammar school was established at All Hallows' by Henry VI in 1447. The church was burnt in 1666, and rebuilt in Portland stone by William Hammond to the designs of Wren from 1677 to 1682. The plain exterior, with its solid and sparsely decorated tower (a spire was apparently planned, but funds were not available for its execution), enclosed some of the finest decorative plasterwork and furnishings in the City, financed by the prosperous merchants (including Germans from the nearby Steelyard). The church endured a more piecemeal destruction than most in the City: the tower and north aisle were cleared away to widen Thames Street in 1876, and a belfry was built on the south side; the church itself was demolished (except for the belfry) under the Union of City Benefices Act in 1893, and the proceeds of sale were used to build All Hallows Gospel Oak; and the belfry was bombed in 1940. The churchyard was finally removed in 1969. Most of the finely carved furnishings by William Cleere and Thomas Powell survive, although widely dispersed – the elaborate screen, carved by Woodruffe and Thornton, with its royal arms and German eagle, is now in St Margaret Lothbury; other items are at Hammersmith, at the Fremlins Chapel at Halstead in Essex, and at St Michael Paternoster Royal.

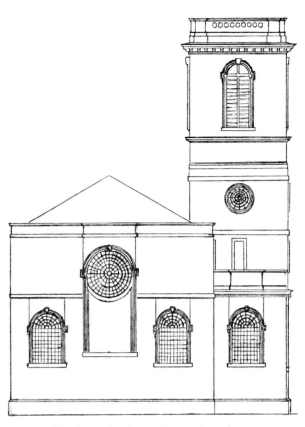

All Hallows the Great: Campion Lane frontage

All Hallows the Less was first mentioned in 1214. It stood on the south side of Upper Thames Street a short distance to the east of All Hallows the Great, opposite the entrance to Suffolk Lane; its churchyard remained until 1969 when it was taken into the widened street where it now passes in front of Mondial House.

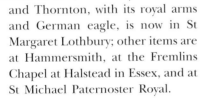

All Hallows the Great: cross-section looking east

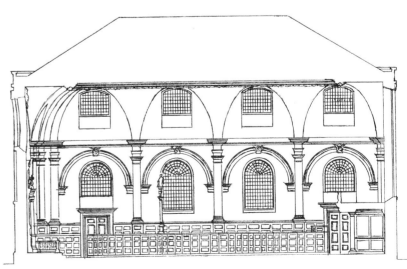

All Hallows the Great: section looking south

ST PAUL'S

WREN'S NEW CATHEDRAL presided over the skyline of the City from its hilltop site; around it clustered what little there was of a 'cathedral close' (London's has always been one of England's most 'urban' cathedrals), as well as a number of collegiate institutions, coffee houses (less commercial than their counterparts further east), and the publishing trade centred on Paternoster Row.

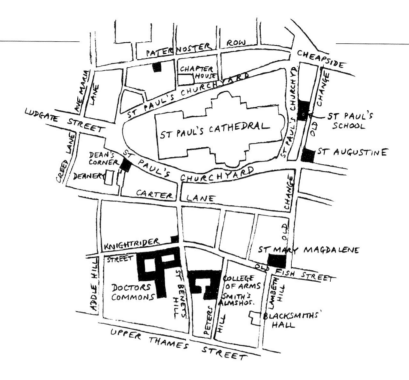

11 Interior of St Paul's Cathedral, Henry Overton, 1720. (Guildhall Library)

ST PAUL'S CATHEDRAL

Far too much has been written about St Paul's Cathedral to justify extensive treatment here. Wren's masterpiece, the culmination of a long and well-documented design process, was built between 1675 and 1710 by a number of outstanding masons – Joshua Marshall, Thomas Strong, both Edward Strongs, Christopher and William Kempster, Thomas Wise, and Jasper Latham. It is one of the great buildings of the world, the largest and most expensive of the post-Fire reconstruction projects, and one of the best-preserved. The main change from the original design, apart from the late Victorian choir mosaics, the numerous large monuments, and the high altar added in the 1950s, has been the removal of the original choir screen which, with the organ it supported, separated the choir visually from the rest of the church. The screen was removed in the late 19th century to provide a more open aspect; much of its woodwork was incorporated in doorcases in the transepts. The organ itself, built by Smith, with a superbly carved case by Grinling Gibbons, was relocated above the flanking choir stalls. The cross-section overleaf shows how the screen and organ originally appeared.

In the early 18th century, after the completion of the cathedral, Nicholas Hawksmoor produced designs for improvements to St Paul's Churchyard. Included in this scheme was a magnificent tall domed structure, presumably proposed to function as a baptistry on the model of those of several Italian cathedrals, which would have stood opposite the west front of St Paul's, at the south-west corner of the Churchyard and Ludgate Hill. The scheme was never realised, presumably because Parliament was not prepared to vote any more funds for a cathedral which had already cost three-quarters of a million pounds.

St Paul's Cathedral: Hawksmoor's unrealised baptistry: cross-section

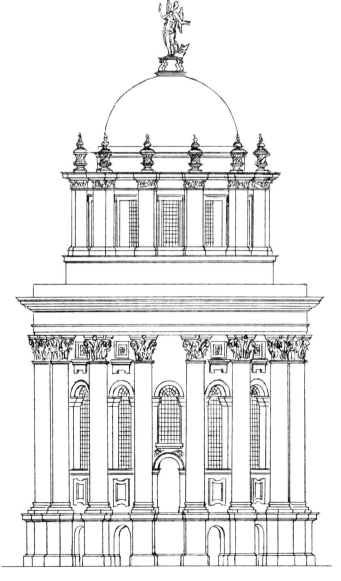

St Paul's Cathedral: Hawksmoor's unrealised design for baptistry

ST PAUL'S CHURCHYARD

St Paul's Cathedral: cross-section of west end of choir, showing west side of organ screen

Hawksmoor's scheme, worked out in some detail, for improvements to St Paul's Churchyard would have involved replacing all of the structures which asymmetrically surrounded the cathedral (except for St Paul's School) with an irregular but broadly symmetrical 'piazza' lined with houses which had arcaded walks at street level, giant pilasters separating the bays, and baroque 'caps' above the principal corners. At the west end was to be a semi-circular exedra opening into Ludgate Hill, with the 'baptistry' in its midst. The view shows the elevation of a short stretch on the north side. It is not clear to what extent this grand design, reminiscent of Covent Garden or continental 'places' and 'piazzas', was ever seriously proposed; presumably it was absence of funds and the vested interests of property owners which frustrated it, just as the elaborate fantasies for redesigning the entire City which were spawned in the period immediately after the Great Fire had to be abandoned.

St Paul's Churchyard: Hawksmoor's unrealised project: part of frontage of north side, showing opening to London House Yard

ST PAUL'S CHAPTER HOUSE, St Paul's Churchyard. The Chapter House (which before the Fire had stood in the middle of the cathedral's south cloister – a unique arrangement, perhaps the result of a shortage of space) was rebuilt on the north side of St Paul's Churchyard by Edward Strong to Wren's design from 1712 to 1714. It is of brick with rubbed brick and stone dressings, much restored in 1957 after being gutted in the Blitz, now the only 17th-century survivor in the Paternoster precinct.

12   Chapter House of St Paul's, photograph. (National Monuments Record)

PATERNOSTER ROW

Paternoster Row was a lane which probably developed originally in the 13th century, and ran along the north side of the precinct of St Paul's Cathedral. Its name may have derived from textwriters living there (a similar origin has been argued for Ave Maria Lane and Creed Lane); it became, with St Paul's Churchyard, a centre of the London book trade (it was the ignition of the stores of books which the booksellers took to the supposed safety of the crypt of Old St Paul's during the Great Fire that contributed substantially to the irreparable damage which the old cathedral suffered), and remained as such until its complete obliteration (again victim of the flammability of paper) in a fire-raid in 1940. No.47 was the last remaining 17th-century house in Paternoster Row, with a characteristic finely decorated main bay. It survived into the early 20th century, but was replaced well before the final immolation of 1940. Its site lies beneath the southern end of Paternoster Square.

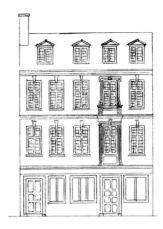

No.47 Paternoster Row

ST PAUL'S SCHOOL

John Colet, Dean of St Paul's, founded St Paul's School in 1512 for 153 boys (corresponding to the number of fishes in St Peter's miraculous draught), the largest school in England, and placed it under the government of the Mercers' Company. Erasmus took a great interest in the new school, and William Lilly was its first high master. Burnt in 1666, it was rebuilt in 1670 to the design of Edward Jerman with a central single-storeyed hall flanked by multi-storeyed wings. The building was demolished and replaced by a larger one in 1823, but pressure of space forced the school to move to Hammersmith in 1884, and it is now located at Barnes. The original site is now covered by St Paul's Churchyard and the new buildings of St Paul's Choir School. Boys were popularly referred to as 'Paul's Pigeons', and included John Milton, Samuel Pepys, the Duke of Marlborough, and Edmond Halley.

St Paul's School: St Paul's Churchyard frontage

ST AUGUSTINE WATLING STREET WITH ST FAITH UNDER ST PAUL'S

St Augustine's Church stood on the east corner of Old Change and Watling Street, just beneath the south-east corner of St Paul's. It was first mentioned in 1148, burnt in 1666, and rebuilt by Edward Strong the Elder to Wren's designs from 1680 to 1686, with the steeple completed in 1695-6, perhaps by Hawksmoor. St Augustine's was a small and plain church (partly of brick, but with Portland stone facings to the street frontages), but the lead-covered steeple, because of its proximity to St Paul's, was given spectacular treatment to provide a foil for the cathedral dome. It is unusual in incorporating both square and octagonal elements in the spire, and is also the only one of the City steeples (apart from St Michael Crooked Lane) to incorporate the bulbous spire which is such a characteristic feature of the baroque in central Europe. The interaction of verticals and convex and concave curves sets up a fine rippling effect, enhanced by the open lantern. The effect was spoiled in the 19th century when the bulbous spirelet was rebuilt with straight sides, but the original lines were restored in the rebuilding (in fibreglass) after the destruction of the church by bombing in 1940. St Augustine's steeple is therefore one of the very few gains for the City skyline arising out of the Second World War, and the view of it from Watling Street, with its ever-shifting relation to St Paul's dome beyond, is one of the great remaining baroque vistas of Wren's City. A preliminary design for the steeple by Hawksmoor incorporated a spire in the form of an elongated pine-cone, similar to Wren's pre-Fire design for the cupola of St Paul's dome. The site of the church itself is now occupied by the St Paul's Cathedral Choir School, and some of its furnishings survive at St Anne and St Agnes.

St Faith under St Paul's was first mentioned in the early 12th century. It originally stood under the east end of the Norman St Paul's Cathedral. The church was demolished in 1225 to make way for the eastward extension of the cathedral; thereafter the parishioners worshipped in the cathedral crypt until the Great Fire, after which they joined in the rebuilding of St Augustine Watling Street.

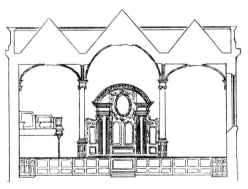

St Augustine Watling Street: Old Change frontage

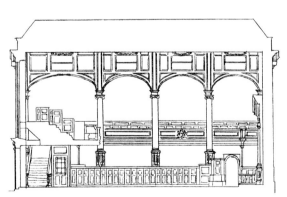

St Augustine Watling Street: section looking north

St Augustine Watling Street: cross-section looking east

DEAN'S CORNER

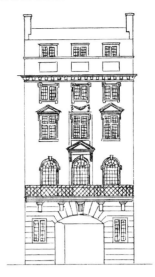

Dean's Corner: St Paul's Churchyard frontage

No.4 St Paul's Churchyard was a brick-built house with an elaborately decorated frontage which stood above the entrance to Dean's Court, which opens to the surviving Deanery. It was traditionally said to have been Wren's office during the rebuilding of St Paul's Cathedral. No.4 was demolished in 1895 as part of a scheme for redeveloping the south-west corner of St Paul's Churchyard. This part of the Churchyard was known as Dean's Corner, and it was said that there was always a wind blowing there, a circumstance which gave rise to a tongue-in-cheek City 'legend' to the effect that the Devil was riding the wind through the City and stopped off to visit the lawyers in Doctors Commons, leaving his mount to await his return in St Paul's Churchyard, but he found the lawyers' company so congenial that he took up permanent residence with them and the wind had been waiting for him at Dean's Corner ever since.

St Augustine Watling Street: Watling Street frontage, showing original design for steeple

DEANERY, Dean's Court, St Paul's Churchyard. St Paul's Deanery is the last survivor of the many brick mansions, houses 'of the greatest bigness', which once peppered the City. It is characteristic of them in being set behind a courtyard (albeit with a wall rather than houses screening it from the lane), in its fine rubbed brickwork, ample proportions, well-appointed doorcase and staircase, broad hipped roof, and generally Dutch baroque style. The house was rebuilt, perhaps to Wren's design, in 1670. The residence of the Dean of London was established on this site in 1145.

13 Deanery of St Paul's, photograph. (T.M.M. Baker)

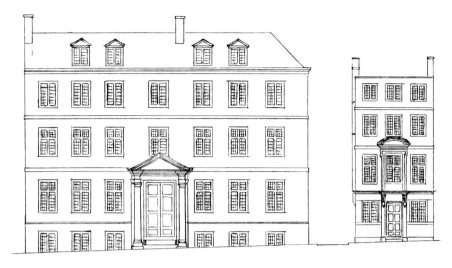

Doctors Commons: Benet's Hill frontage; No.7 Godliman Street to the right

GODLIMAN STREET

No.7 Godliman Street was a typical brick merchant's house of medium size which survived until the 1920s (and was thus one of the last of its kind), before being demolished for the development of Faraday House on its site.

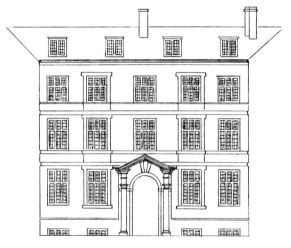

Doctors Commons: frontage of north side of College Court

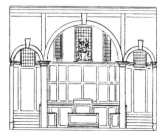

Doctors Commons: cross-section of court room, looking east

DOCTORS COMMONS

Doctors Commons was a college of advocates and doctors of law, first mentioned in 1532, which until 1666 was located in Paternoster Row. After the Great Fire it was rebuilt in brick by 1672 around two courtyards on the site of Mountjoy's Inn, a large mansion situated on the corner of Great Knightrider Street and Benet's Hill. It housed the Court of Arches (the highest court of the Archbishop of Canterbury, which heard mainly matrimonial cases); the Court of Audience; the Prerogative Court (where wills and testaments were proved); the Court of Faculties and Dispensations; the Consistory Court of the Bishop of London; the High Court of Admiralty; the Court of Delegates (which was formerly the highest court of appeal for civil cases); and accommodation for the advocates and proctors who practised in the courts. The college was chartered in 1768. It was satirised in Dickens's novels (he was employed at one time as a shorthand writer for the Proctors), and after a series of reforming acts in the 1850s, notably the 1857 Probate Act, the college was disbanded and its functions moved elsewhere; the building itself was demolished in 1867, partly to make way for Queen Victoria Street, and the site is now occupied mostly by the Faraday Building; some of the wood carving and panelling is now at Fulham Palace.

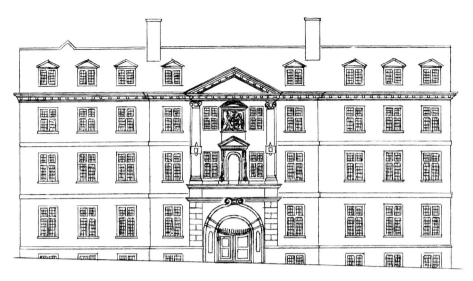

College of Arms: Benet's Hill frontage

COLLEGE OF ARMS

The College of Arms, responsible for the grant and administration of coats of arms, and also for organising state occasions such as coronations and the Opening of Parliament, originated in the Middle Ages as part of the royal household, was abortively chartered in 1484, and more successfully in 1555, when it took over Derby House, the town house of the Earls of Derby. Burnt in 1666, it was rebuilt from 1671 to 1688, probably to the designs of Maurice Emmett and Francis Sandford. The brick buildings surrounded a courtyard with its entrance on the west and Ionic pilastered frontispieces in the middle of the north, west, and east sides; these were shorn of their pediments during a later rebuilding. The south wing had to be demolished in 1867 to make way for Queen Victoria Street; this change also resulted in the College's moving its entrance to wrought iron gates on the open south side of the courtyard. The interior of the college retains much fine late 17th-century decoration, notably the woodwork of the Earl Marshal's Court Room. (*See plate 14, p.50.*)

SMITH'S ALMSHOUSES

Smith's Almshouses: Peter's Hill frontage

David Smith, Broderer (embroiderer) to Queen Elizabeth I, founded six almshouses in Peter's Hill in 1584. The site, just south of the College of Arms, was previously occupied by the Woodmongers' Hall. The almshouses were rebuilt in a humble style after their destruction by the Great Fire. The site is now covered by Queen Victoria Street where it passes in front of the College of Arms.

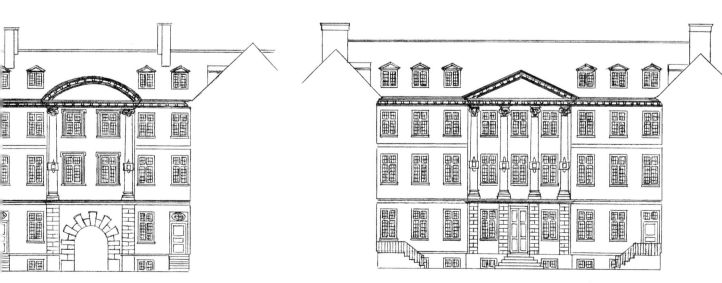

College of Arms: west frontage of court

College of Arms: north frontage of court

The COLLEGE of ARMS or HERALD'S OFFICE.

E. Cole Sculp.

14 Courtyard of the College of Arms, Benjamin Cole,
1750. (Guildhall Library)

BLACKSMITHS' HALL, Lambeth Hill, Queenhithe. A small company hall, rebuilt from 1669 to 1671 and abandoned in 1785; the site is now covered by the Salvation Army headquarters in Queen Victoria Street. The appearance of the Hall is not known. The Company existed by the late 15th century and was chartered in 1571, incorporating the Spurriers; it later also acquired a monopoly of tooth-drawing.

ST MARY MAGDALEN OLD FISH STREET
WITH ST GREGORY BY ST PAUL'S

St Mary Magdalen's Church stood on the north-west corner of Old Fish Street and Old Change, almost opposite St Nicholas Cole Abbey; the site is now occupied by No.2 Old Change Court. The church was first mentioned in the late 12th century, and may originally have been dedicated to St Wandrille. It was burnt in the Great Fire, and rebuilt by Edward Strong the Elder to the design of Wren from 1683 to 1687, with impressive Portland stone south and east fronts and slender north-west steeple, whose octagonal spire consisted of a lantern standing on diminishing stone steps, a variant of the steeple of St Michael Queenhithe; both may have been influenced by the Mausoleum of Halicarnassus. St Mary Magdalen's was damaged by fire in 1886 and demolished in 1890; a 1720 painting of the Transfiguration by Browne is now at St Martin Ludgate. Richard Harris Barham, author of the *Ingoldsby Legends*, was rector of St Mary Magdalen from 1824 to 1842.

St Gregory by St Paul's was first mentioned in 1010. It was attached to the south side of the west front of the Old St Paul's Cathedral, and its site is now represented by the south end of the steps at the west end of St Paul's.

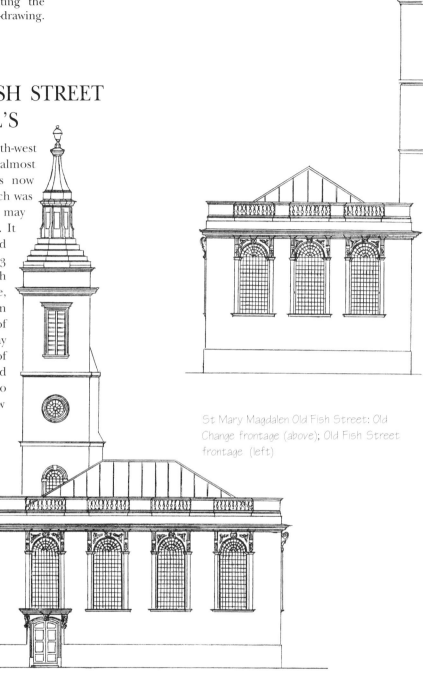

St Mary Magdalen Old Fish Street: Old Change frontage (above); Old Fish Street frontage (left)

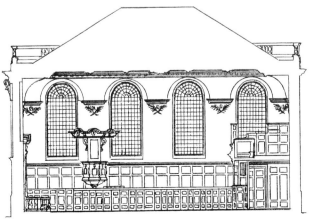

St Mary Magdalen Old Fish Street: section looking south

CHEAPSIDE

THE CITY'S broad High Street, one of its main shopping centres, was a place where ostentatious builders could show off their premises to greater advantage than almost anywhere in the rebuilt City, and where there was fierce competition between shopkeepers, with a resulting profusion of hanging signs. Many of the houses had balconies which served as viewing platforms for civic processions. The magnificent steeple of St Mary le Bow dominated all, to an even greater extent than today.

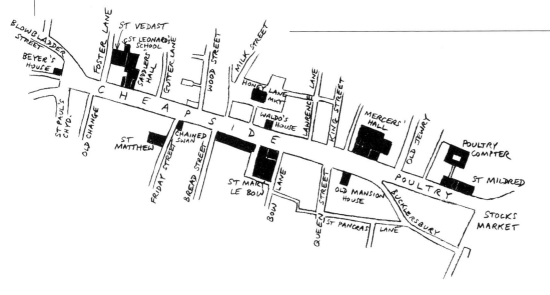

Cheapside: frontage of south side between Bow Lane and Bread Street, with the steeple of St Mary le Bow

CHEAPSIDE

For centuries Cheapside was the 'high street' of London, where the richest merchants and shopkeepers traded, and where much of the City, including its most fashionable residents, did their shopping. In medieval times 'Cheap' (the Old English word for 'market') was a general market which, stretching from Newgate to Cornhill and up the flanking streets and lanes, catered for virtually every necessity of life. With the improvements which followed the Great Fire the provisions markets were cleared away from the street itself onto purpose-built sites, but the mercers and drapers and goldsmiths, the most powerful and richest tradesmen of the City, remained in the shops which lined it, even as late as the 19th century, when the magnetism of the West End finally put an end to Cheapside's career as a fashionable shopping centre. In the late 17th century Cheapside was also a place where prosperous traders lived, and many of the houses which lined it were showpieces, exploiting the opportunity for ostentation which one of the broadest streets in London offered, and providing a suitably magnificent setting for the Cheapside processions which were, and remain, a feature of London ceremonial. Some of the most notable of the Cheapside houses – Mercers' Hall, Saddlers' Hall, the Old Mansion House, Waldo's House, Beyer's House, the Chained Swan – are here separately noted and illustrated. The more general Cheapside view shows the stretch of brick houses along the south side of the street on either side of the steeple of St Mary le Bow, from the corner of Bow Lane to the corner of Bread Street. All of these houses, along with most of Cheapside, were replaced during the later part of the 19th century by showy and much more substantial shops and warehouses which showed off the pride of the merchants of the City; almost all were in their turn destroyed during the fire raids of the Second World War, which were fuelled by the contents of the textile warehouses. The sites are now occupied by Bow Bells House and the Yorkshire Bank building on the corner of Bow Lane. The only remaining 17th-century houses in Cheapside are the tiny refronted shops on the west corner of Wood Street, in front of St Peter Cheap churchyard and its famous tree (the singing place of the thrush which inspired Wordsworth's 'Poor Susan's Reverie', 1800). *(See plates 15 & 16, p.57.)*

ST MARY LE BOW WITH ALL HALLOWS HONEY LANE AND ST PANCRAS SOPER LANE

The church of St Mary le Bow was in existence by the late 11th century, as evidenced by its partially surviving crypt, whose vaults gave it its name; it was also anciently called St Mary Newchurch, perhaps to distinguish it from the nearby St Mary Aldermary. It was in a sense the premier parish church of the City, partly as a result of its status as the seat of the Archbishop of Canterbury's Court of Arches, the senior ecclesiastical court of England; new Archbishops are still elected there. The medieval church was set back from the frontage of Cheapside, and seems not to have been particularly conspicuous except for the steeple which was built in 1512, and which consisted of four flying buttresses supporting a crowning lantern, a prominent feature of the City skyline which

St Mary le Bow: original design for steeple

St Mary le Bow: Cheapside frontage showing unexecuted loggia

St Mary le Bow: cross-section looking east

was echoed in Wren's rebuilding of St Dunstan in the East. The church was burnt in the Great Fire, and rebuilt by Thomas Cartwright and John Thompson to the design of Wren throughout the 1670s. Alone of all the City churches, it served three parishes. The body of the church is brick-built with Portland stone dressings; according to Wren's son its three-bay aisled design was inspired by the Basilica of Maxentius in Rome. Unsuccessful attempts were made to repair the medieval steeple in the late 1660s; in 1671 it was decided to start a new steeple well to the north – built in Portland stone, this was the first of the great baroque steeples of London, since it was far enough advanced to escape the moratorium on steeple building which was imposed in the mid-1670s (it cost £7,400, out of a total of £15,400 for

St Mary le Bow: section looking south

the whole church, the most expensive of the Wren churches). Deliberately brought forward to the Cheapside frontage, it dominates the street with its varied and strongly expressed diminishing stages, including the tower doorways set in baroque niches derived from Mansart's Hotel de Conti in Paris (a memento presumably of Wren's 1666 trip), the square belfry framed by doubled Ionic pilasters, pinnacles on the corners of the tower which suggest a Gothic effect by means of clusters of open volutes, a transparent circlet of columns, a ring of large volutes which echoed the crown of the old steeple, and a further columned stage on the plan of a Greek cross (rebuilt in a darker stone in a Victorian restoration) which carries an obelisk spire and weathervane in the form of a dragon. Facing Cheapside are a projecting clock and a balcony for viewing processions. The sections show the remarkable wooden free-standing spiral staircase which rose up the central core of the spire, and the galleried interior of the church

itself; all except the stone walls was destroyed by bombing in 1941, and the interior of the church was restored in a neo-Wren style by Laurence King in 1960.

A plan for a monumental two-bayed loggia, perhaps designed by Hawksmoor, extending from the steeple of St Mary le Bow to the corner of Bow Lane, foundered for lack of funds.

All Hallows Honey Lane was mentioned from about 1200. It stood in Honey Lane, behind the houses on the north side of Cheapside, and its site was taken into the new Honey Lane Market after the Great Fire. The church stood on the south side of what is now Russia Row, opposite the entrance to Russia Court.

St Pancras Soper Lane was mentioned from about 1100. It stood on the north side of Pancras Lane, on the corner of Gropecunt Lane (a haunt of prostitutes whose name meant just what it said); the churchyard remains.

CHAINED SWAN

No.37 Cheapside was a brick house with a stone sign of the Chained Swan which stood on the east corner of Friday Street. Although popularly believed to have predated the Great Fire, it was probably built shortly afterwards, and by the early 20th century was one of the very few late 17th-century houses remaining in Cheapside. It was demolished in 1928, its successor succumbed to the Blitz, and the site is now the pavement outside the northern entrance to New Change Buildings, the former Bank of England extension.

BEYER'S HOUSE

No.3 Cheapside stood on the north corner of Paternoster Row, facing eastwards down the length of Cheapside. With its pedimented windows, rusticated quoins, and balustraded parapet, it was one of the grandest of Cheapside houses. It was the shop and house of John Beyer, a draper who was reputedly the original of William Cowper's 'John Gilpin', the 'citizen of credit and renown' who, on a family outing to Edmonton, was borne by an uncontrollable horse all the way to Ware and back to Cheapside again. The house was replaced in the mid-19th century by a new warehouse, and the site is now occupied by the garden in front of 5 Cheapside.

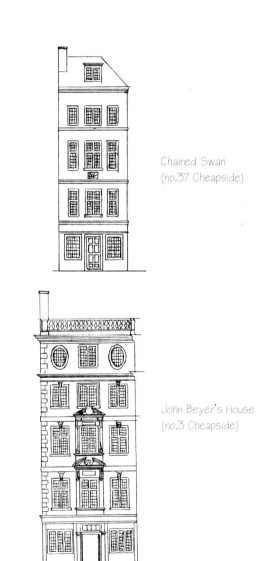

Chained Swan
(no.37 Cheapside)

John Beyer's House
(no.3 Cheapside)

15 Cheapside looking east, Thomas Bowles, 1751, showing the old shopfronts and hanging signs. On the left are Waldo's House, and in the distance the steeples of St Mildred Poultry and St Michael Cornhill; on the right the steeple of St Mary le Bow. (Guildhall Library)

16 Cheapside looking west across the rooftops, W. Duryer, 1823, showing the Old Mansion House, the dome of St Paul's, and the steeple of St Mary le Bow. (Guildhall Library)

ST VEDAST FOSTER LANE WITH ST MICHAEL LE QUERNE

St Vedast's Church was also called St Foster's, a corruption which survives in the name of the lane in which it stands. Vedast was a sixth-century Bishop of Arras, which suggests that the church may have been established by Flemish merchants. It was first mentioned in the mid-12th century. Burnt in the Great Fire, it was not so badly damaged that the parish was not able to restore it between 1670 and 1673 using much of the old fabric. This work was done outside the jurisdiction of the Commissioners by John Thompson, mason. Towards the end of the 17th century it became apparent that the restored church was structurally unsound, and it was rebuilt with Portland stone facings by Edward Strong the Elder to Wren's designs from 1695 to 1699 (again making use of the original south wall, much of which is still medieval). The body of the church consists of a rectangular nave with a south aisle. A new steeple was built at the south-west corner by Edward Strong the Younger between 1709 and 1712; built of Portland stone, it is the most advanced of all the City churches' in its sculptural treatment of the baroque, almost worthy of the great Roman architect Borromini himself with its interaction of complex concave and convex forms (impossible to convey in a two

dimensional elevation – a visit to the real thing is essential) – it is very possible that Hawksmoor had a substantial hand in its design. The church was gutted by fire bombs in 1941 and all of its fittings were destroyed, including the superbly carved reredos. The post-War reconstruction is very different from the original interior, and one of the most successful in the City, with furnishings brought in from other City churches, a college-chapel-style arrangement of the seating, and aluminium paint in lieu of gold leaf applied to the plasterwork of the ceiling.

St Michael le Querne was named after the corn market in Cheapside. First mentioned in the mid-12th century, it stood at the west end of Cheapside, where it curves away into Newgate Street, on the north corner of Paternoster Row; Beyer's house was built on its site.

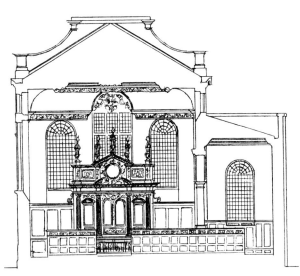

St Vedast Foster Lane: cross-section looking east

St Vedast Foster Lane: section looking south

ST LEONARD'S PARISH SCHOOL, Foster Lane, Cheapside. Standing in a courtyard on the north side of St Vedast Foster Lane, this is a small and heavily restored, but unique, survival of the City's 17th-century school buildings.

17   St Leonard's Parish School, photograph. (T.M.M. Baker)

SADDLERS' HALL

The main part of Saddlers' Hall was located in a court behind Cheapside; the view shows the frontage above the entrance passage, its narrowness a vivid demonstration of the value of Cheapside property. The Hall was rebuilt in 1670 after its destruction in the Great Fire. The Hall was again rebuilt after fires in 1815 and 1821, and again on its off-street site after its destruction by bombing in 1940; the site of the old Cheapside entrance now lies under Cheapside House, the headquarters of Lonrho. The Saddlers' Company is one of the oldest in the City – a guild of saddlers was referred to in 1160, although the first charter dates only from 1395. It had complete control over the London saddlery trade (which was concentrated in the nearby Foster Lane), and continues to exercise some influence in it.

Saddlers' Hall: Cheapside frontage and adjoining houses

WALDO'S HOUSE

No.108 Cheapside was one of the grandest houses in the City's 'high street'. Built for Sir Edward Waldo shortly after the Great Fire, it stood in a prominent position immediately opposite the steeple of St Mary le Bow. It was occupied in the late 17th and early 18th centuries by a succession of prominent City worthies, and its first floor balcony was traditionally the place from which sovereigns watched the Lord Mayor's Show. The interior was noted for the exceptional quality of its panelling and carved decoration and, when the house was demolished in 1861, the best room was removed to Gunrog in Montgomeryshire. Thus preserved from the wartime bombing of the Victorian warehouses which occupied the site, this room has now been returned to a nearby banking office. *(See plate 15, p.57.)*

MERCERS' HALL

The Mercers, the rich and powerful woollen and textile merchants who provided the backbone of London's medieval wealth, established themselves in a hall in Cheapside in 1407, in the district which was named the Mercery after them. Having built a new and larger hall in the early 16th century, the Company acquired the buildings of the dissolved Hospital of St Thomas of Acon (which had been founded about 1190 on the site of St Thomas Becket's birthplace by his sister Agnes, and was named from the saint's supposed miraculous involvement in the crusaders' recapture of Acre, Syria, in 1191) in 1541. Part of the hospital's conventual church, built in the mid-13th century, was set aside as the Mercers' Chapel, and the Hall remains the only one of the City livery

Sir Edward Waldo's House (no.108 Cheapside)

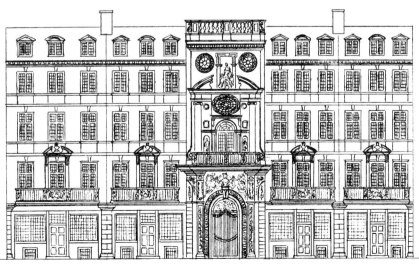

Mercers' Hall: Cheapside frontage and adjoining houses

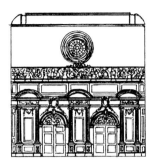

Mercers' Hall: livery hall, cross-section looking west

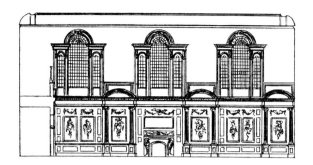

Mercers' Hall: livery hall, section looking north

Mercers' Hall: livery hall, cross-section looking east

companies' to have its own chapel. Mercers' Hall was destroyed in the Great Fire, and rebuilt between 1672 and 1682 by John Oliver and Thomas Cartwright to Edward Jerman's design. It followed the plan of the old hospital church, and was therefore set back from Cheapside, with a narrow-fronted porch linking it to the street. This façade, shown in the view, was built of Portland stone in a spectacularly undisciplined baroque style with elaborate carving by John Young, including foliage, cherubs, and the maiden's head emblem of the Company. When the Cheapside frontage was rebuilt in 1880 this was removed to Dorset, where it remains incorporated in the façade of Swanage Town Hall, possibly the finest remaining example of the post-Fire rebuilding of London's domestic architecture. The remainder of the 17th-century Hall, consisting of the chapel at the east end and the 'ambulatory' with the livery hall above it at the west end, was destroyed by bombing in 1941. The Hall was rebuilt, incorporating the salvaged remains of its original furnishings, in the 1950s. The Mercers' Company was established in the mid-14th century and received its first charter in 1394. It exercised only moderate control over the London mercery trade as such, and its real power, wealth, and influence derived from mercers' domination of the Fellowship of Merchant Adventurers, which originated in the Guild of St Thomas Becket established in 1296, and which controlled much of the English wool export trade, in competition with the Calais Merchant Staplers and the German Hanseatic League. The

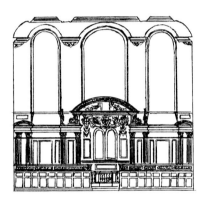

Mercers' Chapel: cross-section looking east

Merchant Adventurers were based in Flanders by 1360. They were chartered in 1505, thus becoming the first of the great London chartered trading companies. Their base was moved to Hamburg in 1567 (whence they came to be called the Hamburg Company). From 1598 to 1689 they monopolised the cloth export trade against fierce opposition from free traders (who eventually won the struggle), but thereafter the Hamburg Company declined in importance until it was finally extinguished by Napoleon's capture of Hamburg in 1807.

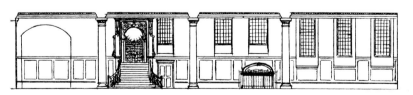

Mercers' Hall: ambulatory, section looking north

OLD MANSION HOUSE

No.73 Cheapside, with its aedicules and festoons, had the most richly-decorated frontage of any house in Cheapside, emulating Mercers' Hall opposite. It was unusual among new City houses in being entirely stone-fronted, and was built, reputedly but almost certainly not by Wren, for Sir William Turner, a draper and African and East India merchant who was Lord Mayor in 1668 and M.P. for the City from 1690 to 1693. It was occasionally occupied by Lord Mayors thereafter, and thence acquired its name after the completion of the new Mansion House in 1751. Most of the frontage of the house survived until 1927, when it was dismantled and stored by the City Corporation; it was given perhaps the bizarrest of all the transplantations of fragments of old City buildings in 1975, when it was incorporated in a municipal garden at St Margaret's Bay in Kent. Parts of the structure of the house were not demolished until redevelopment in the early 1990s. *(See plate 16, p.57.)*

Old Mansion House (no.73 Cheapside)

ST MATTHEW FRIDAY STREET WITH ST PETER CHEAP

St Matthew's Church stood on the west side of Friday Street a short distance south of Cheapside, where now is the courtyard of New Change Buildings, the old Bank of England Extension. First mentioned in the mid-12th century, it was burnt in 1666, and rebuilt by Edward Pearce to Wren's designs from 1681 to 1686. It was a small, plain church, the only exuberance being the Portland stone east end, which made the best of a narrow frontage with six closely spaced arched windows. This seems to have exhausted the available funds, for the tower was the plainest of all the City churches', without any elaboration or decoration at all; at £2,300 St Matthew was also the cheapest of them. It was demolished under the Union of City Benefices Act in 1881; some of the furnishings are now at St Andrew by the Wardrobe and St Vedast's Foster Lane, and the fine reredos is at Polesden Lacey in Surrey.

St Peter Cheap was first mentioned from the early 12th century. Musicians played on its roof during Cheapside processions. It stood at the west corner of Cheapside and Wood Street, where its churchyard still remains.

St Matthew Friday Street: Friday Street frontage

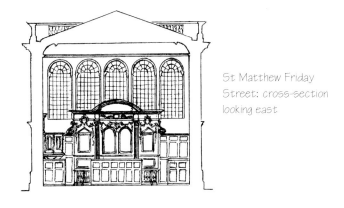

St Matthew Friday Street: cross-section looking east

HONEY LANE MARKET

Honey Lane Market was established after the Great Fire
on the site of the church of All Hallows Honey Lane to
accommodate provisions traders, including many butchers,
who were cleared away from Cheapside; it lay along the
south side of what is now Russia Row. The market building
was the smallest in London, and the details of its
appearance are not well documented. This imagined
reconstruction is based on Ogilby and Morgan's map, the
view in Morgan's 1682 map, and Leybourn's description.
The market house was occupied by a French Huguenot
congregation from 1691. It was rebuilt by George Dance
the Younger in the 1780s, and the market was noted for
the high quality of its provisions in the late 18th century. It
was cleared away in 1834 to provide a site for the new City
of London School.

Honey Lane Market: south frontage

POULTRY

Poultry is the eastward continuation of Cheapside,
linking it to Cornhill. It was named from the medieval
poultry market which was held in this part of the 'West
Cheap'. The view shows the houses which were rebuilt
on the north side westwards from St Mildred's Church
after the Great Fire, together with the entrance to
Poultry Compter. The house to the left of the entrance
was in the late 18th century the shop of Vernon & Hood,
booksellers – the latter's son, the poet Thomas Hood,
was born there in 1798. The site of these houses is now
occupied by Lutyens' old Midland Bank headquarters.

Poultry: north side, showing entrance to
Poultry Compter and St Mildred Poultry

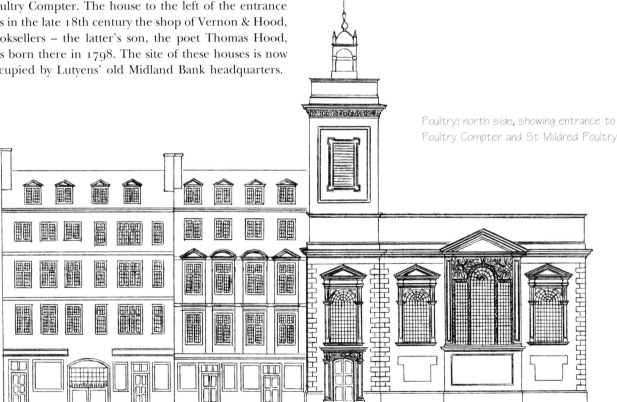

ST MILDRED POULTRY WITH ST MARY COLECHURCH

St Mildred's Church stood on the north side of Poultry opposite the junction with Queen Victoria Street, where now stands Lutyens' old Midland Bank headquarters (now part of HSBC). It was first mentioned in the early 12th century, and was also called St Mildred Walbrook (it stood on the east bank of the Walbrook stream). The church was burnt in the Great Fire, and rebuilt between 1670 and 1677 by Jaspar Latham to the designs of Wren. Although small, it received a particularly grand Portland stone south frontage, befitting its location on one of the City's main thoroughfares. There was an intention to build a spire, which foundered for lack of funds after the completion of the decorative but straightforward tower. St Mildred's was noted for the quality of its fittings. It was demolished under the Union of City Benefices Act in 1872, and the stones were acquired by John Fytche, a Lincolnshire antiquarian, for an ultimately abortive project to build a chapel at Thorpe Hall, Louth; some of the stones remain at Louth as garden ornaments. The only other surviving fragment appears to be the weathervane in the form of a ship which is now at St Olave Jewry; the fittings, removed to St Paul's, Goswell Road, which was built with the proceeds of sale, were destroyed when that church was bombed in 1941.

St Mary Colechurch existed by the 12th century, in the latter part of which Peter of Colechurch, the promoter of the new stone London Bridge, was its chaplain. The church was probably named after a benefactor. It stood on the north-west corner of Cheapside and Old Jewry.

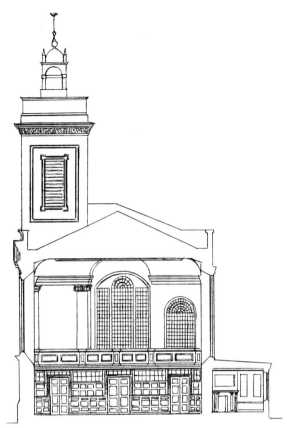

St Mildred Poultry: cross-section looking west

POULTRY COMPTER

Poultry Compter was the oldest of the London compters (sheriffs' prisons), established in the late 14th century. It stood behind the houses on the north side of Poultry, on a site now occupied by the old Midland Bank. After its destruction in the Great Fire, it was rebuilt by 1672 in brick around a small courtyard at the end of a long passage from Poultry; the view is a reconstruction extrapolated from Smith's engraving of its main entrance. Before its demolition in 1817 the Compter housed a number of notable prisoners, including James Somerset, a negro slave, confined and released in 1772, on whom was established the principle that a slave who set foot on English soil was automatically a free man. The Poultry Chapel, a Congregational chapel, was built on the site in 1829; it became a banking hall for the London Joint Stock Bank (later absorbed into the Midland) in 1872.

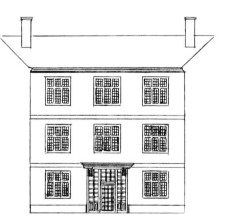

Poultry Compter: courtyard frontage

GUILDHALL YARD

NORTH OF CHEAPSIDE, the City's secluded centre of government was opened up to the world after the Great Fire by the new King Street and Queen Street which joined it to the River. Guildhall was hemmed about by a cluster of civic buildings and houses, and it faced down the cramped Guildhall Yard, lined by distinctive façades ranging from the plain Guildhall Offices and Blackwell Hall, London's cloth market, to the sole survivor today, the proud church of St Lawrence Jewry.

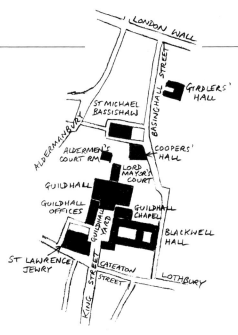

18   Guildhall Yard looking north: St Lawrence Jewry, the Guildhall Offices and Guildhall porch, Thomas Malton, 1783. (Guildhall Library)

GUILDHALL

Guildhall remains today, as it has been since at least the early 12th century, the seat of government and civic ceremonial of the City of London. It was always the largest of the great halls of the medieval City, expanding in the late Middle Ages to a length of 152 feet, and is today one of the best preserved. The Roman amphitheatre, which stood where Guildhall Yard is now, may have been used for civic gatherings in the early medieval period. Guildhall was first mentioned in 1128, although the arms of Edward the Confessor carved on the porch hint at an Anglo-Saxon origin. The earliest structure on the present site is the west crypt, built in the late 13th century; it supported a hall 90 feet long. Between 1411 and 1430 the existing hall was built by John Croxton, financed by several leading citizens including the executors of Richard Whittington. The crypt was extended eastwards, with fine surviving tierceron vaulting on Purbeck marble columns. The hall itself is Perpendicular gothic in style, with large windows in the gables and elaborate stone panelling on the inside of the walls; such panelling also covered the frontage of the porch, which was the only face that Guildhall presented to the world right up until the 1970s when redevelopment and extension of Guildhall Yard opened up to view parts of the hall which had until then been closely hemmed about by other buildings. Guildhall was gutted in 1666; Vincent described the slow burning of the great oak timbers of the roof, which made Guildhall look like 'a bright shining coal as if it had been a palace of gold or a great building of burnished brass'. Guildhall was rapidly restored by Peter Mills, incorporating much of the surviving medieval fabric, from 1667 to 1671; the cost of rebuilding the whole Guildhall complex was £37,000. The alterations to the structure included the raising of the walls, with large round-headed clerestory windows and a flat ceiling, a new cupola, and the addition of a baroque gable to the porch. The view shows the full length of Guildhall, whereas the frontage to Guildhall Yard was restricted to the porch; the lower parts of the rest were hidden by the adjacent Guildhall Offices and Guildhall Chapel. The furnishings were sparse except for the screen and panelling of the dais at the east end, and the elaborate porch leading to the Lord Mayor's Court Room; this was surmounted by a large clock (with plenty of scrollwork and statuary) on a bracket and huge wooden statues of Gogmagog and Corineus, the City giants, carved by Richard Saunders in 1708 to replace the statues which were carried in medieval civic processions, and had been stored in Guildhall and incinerated there in 1666. Nothing is now left of the 17th-century restoration of

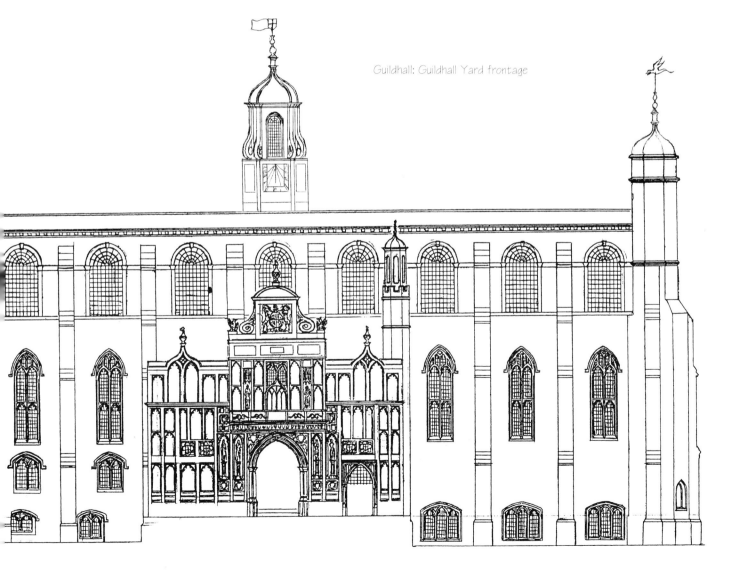

Guildhall: Guildhall Yard frontage

Guildhall. The porch frontage was replaced in Indo-Gothick style by George Dance in 1789; the furnishings were replaced early in the 19th century, and the clerestory and ceiling were replaced by a timber hammerbeam roof designed by Bunning in 1862. Finally the statues of the giants were destroyed when the Guildhall was gutted by fire-bombs in 1940. Guildhall in its present manifestation is a much restored medieval hall with a neo-Gothic stone, steel, and timber roof designed by Sir Giles Gilbert Scott and completed in 1953, containing new statues of giants carved by David Evans in the 1950s, and the original elaborate statues of worthies (William Beckford, William Pitt the Elder, William Pitt the Younger, Lord Nelson and the Duke of Wellington) installed in the late 18th and early 19th centuries. Guildhall has been since the earliest times the focal point of the City's administration and identity, and also of its relationship with the Crown and government in Westminster. In keeping with the traditional role of the great hall, feasts have long played a major part, and the City's entertainment of royalty and ministers, both at Guildhall and the Mansion House, is traditionally used as an important forum for the exposition of government policy, recognising the crucial role of the City in funding government expenditure and promoting London as a vital hub in international finance and trade. Anciently Guildhall also housed a number of courts, later removed to purpose-built courtrooms; Lady Jane Grey and Thomas Cranmer were among those tried there.

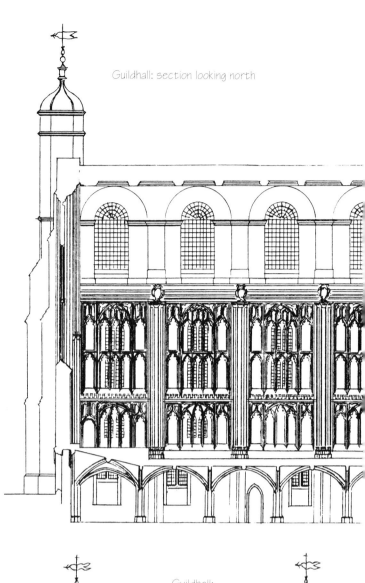

Guildhall: section looking north

Guildhall: cross-section looking west

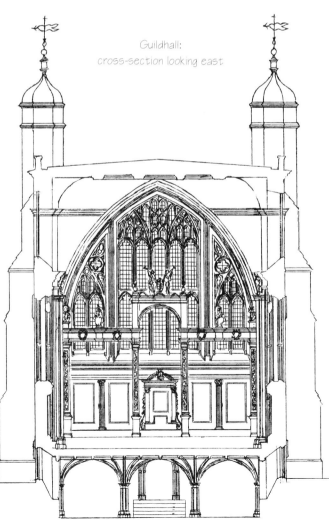

Guildhall: cross-section looking east

GUILDHALL OFFICES

The Guildhall Offices were built of brick after 1666 on the west side of Guildhall Yard to provide additional accommodation for the administration of the City. With their colonnaded 'piazza' filling the space between the Guildhall porch and the church of St Lawrence Jewry, opposite the Guildhall Chapel and Blackwell Hall, they added yet further to the civic grandeur (albeit a rather homely one) of Guildhall Yard. They were demolished in 1795 to make way for George Dance the Younger's Guildhall Justice Room, itself cleared away in the 1960s for the westward expansion of Guildhall Yard, which now covers the site. *(See plate 18, p.64.)*

Guildhall Offices:
Guildhall Yard frontage

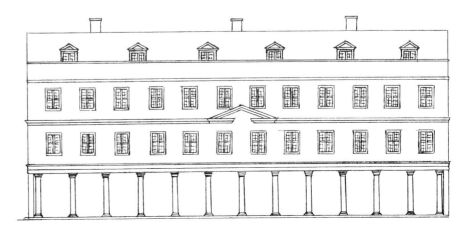

GUILDHALL CHAPEL

The Chapel of God, St Mary, St Mary Magdalen and All Saints was built in the 1290s on the south side of Guildhall, and rebuilt between 1435 and 1455 on a larger scale in Perpendicular style, with an elaborately panelled stone west front, by the benefaction of John Welles, Mayor in 1431. A college was established in the chapel in 1356 and dissolved in 1548, whereupon the City purchased the chapel for use on various civic occasions. Statues of Edward VI, Elizabeth I, and Charles I by Nicholas Stone, rejects from the Royal Exchange, were set up in niches on the façade in 1623; they are now kept at the Guildhall. The chapel was gutted in

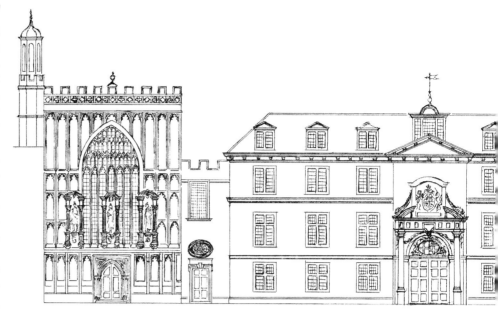

Guildhall Chapel, Blackwell Hall and No.23 King Street: Guildhall Yard frontage

the Great Fire but restored with most of its medieval fabric; it became the Court of Requests in 1782. It was demolished in 1822 to make way for a new Bankruptcy Court building, which was converted to house the Guildhall Art Gallery in 1886. This was in its turn destroyed by bombing in 1940, and the new Guildhall Art Gallery stands on the site.

BLACKWELL HALL

Blackwell Hall (the name was a corruption of Bakewell Hall), a mansion which was occupied by the Bakewells, a merchant family, in the 14th century, was acquired by the City in 1396 for use as London's main market for foreign merchants purchasing English woollen textiles. It thus provided the infrastructure for England's growing export trade, which was associated with the government-backed development of the English cloth manufacture and the associated decline in exports of raw wool, previously much in demand by European, especially Flemish, weavers. At Blackwell Hall factors, each specialising in particular types of cloth, sold manufacturers' wares, and the Drapers Company checked the quality of cloth and collected duties. The complex credit techniques employed by the merchants to finance the wool and cloth trade were one of the main strands in the development of the bill of exchange as a commercial instrument. Blackwell Hall's importance declined after England's loss of control over the Calais wool staple in the mid-16th century, but the market remained the centre of the Merchant Adventurers' control of the English cloth export, and was active enough to merit its rebuilding around two courtyards in 1588 and again, in brick, after its destruction by the Great Fire, by Peter Mills in 1672 (during the Fire £25,000 worth of cloth was destroyed). The view shows the impressive western entrance from Guildhall Yard. Blackwell Hall continued as the main London broadcloth market until it

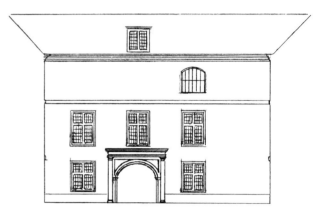

Blackwell Hall: frontage of west side of main courtyard

Blackwell Hall: frontage of east side of main courtyard

was demolished in 1820, making way for the new Bankruptcy Court – this building was bombed in 1940, and the site is now occupied by the new Guildhall Art Gallery. *(See plate 19, p.71.)*

KING STREET

King Street (named after Charles II) was a new street, cut through after the Great Fire together with Queen Street (named after Catherine of Braganza) to provide a direct route from Guildhall to Cheapside and the River at Three Cranes Stairs. As such it was an important processional route, and the house illustrated was of a size and grandeur commensurate with its position at the entrance to Guildhall Yard, opposite the spectacular east frontage of St Lawrence Jewry.

ST LAWRENCE JEWRY
WITH ST MARY MAGDALEN MILK STREET

The church of St Lawrence Jewry was first mentioned in the late 12th century. It was named from its position in the old Jewry of London (commemorated in the nearby street Old Jewry). The medieval church was large, and the rebuilding by Edward Pearce after the Great Fire to Wren's design was on the old foundations, except for the north-east corner which was taken into Guildhall Yard. Rebuilding (in Portland stone) began in 1671 and continued until 1680. At £11,870 it was one of the most expensive of the new City churches, mainly because of the sumptuousness of its fittings and decorations (the plasterer was Thomas Meade, the joiner William Cleere, and the carvers Edward Pierce and Richard Kedge). The church consists of a large nave with a north aisle and west tower with relatively simple lead-covered baroque spire (replaced in fibreglass after the Second World War). Neither the east nor the west end is square, and the east wall varies in thickness (this is ingeniously disguised by perspective effects from the inside) to provide a rectangular interior. The most elaborate external ornament is lavished on the east front, with its pediment, Corinthian order, and carved stone swags. The interior and fittings (of which the most spectacular was the organ gallery with its carved panels of musical instruments and Harris organ) were all completely destroyed by German bombing in 1940. The same raid also destroyed St Lawrence's vestry, whose richly ornamented plaster ceiling and wooden doorcases made it one of the finest rooms in London. The church was restored to the designs of Cecil Brown in the 1950s with new fittings in a sub-Wren style which fails to recapture the richness of the original. The importance of the church derives partly from its proximity to the Guildhall, and since 1782 it has officially been the church of the City Corporation. (See plates 18 & 20, pp.64 & 71.)

St Lawrence Jewry: cross-section looking west

LORD MAYOR'S COURT ROOM

St Mary Magdalen Milk Street was first mentioned in the early 12th century. It stood on the east side of Milk Street, where now is the corner of Russia Row, adjacent to the church of All Hallows Honey Lane, and its site was incorporated after the Great Fire in the new Honey Lane Market.

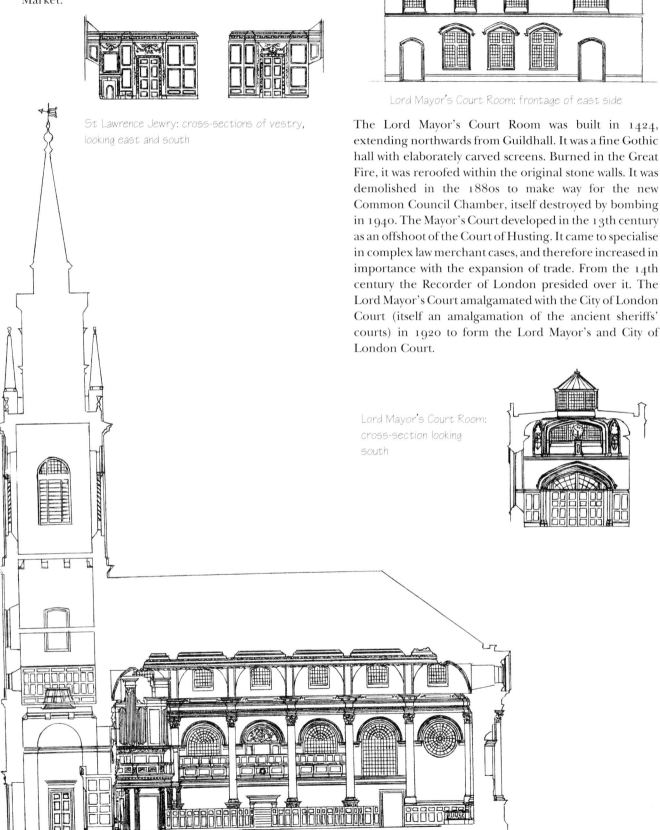

Lord Mayor's Court Room: frontage of east side

St Lawrence Jewry: cross-sections of vestry, looking east and south

The Lord Mayor's Court Room was built in 1424, extending northwards from Guildhall. It was a fine Gothic hall with elaborately carved screens. Burned in the Great Fire, it was reroofed within the original stone walls. It was demolished in the 1880s to make way for the new Common Council Chamber, itself destroyed by bombing in 1940. The Mayor's Court developed in the 13th century as an offshoot of the Court of Husting. It came to specialise in complex law merchant cases, and therefore increased in importance with the expansion of trade. From the 14th century the Recorder of London presided over it. The Lord Mayor's Court amalgamated with the City of London Court (itself an amalgamation of the ancient sheriffs' courts) in 1920 to form the Lord Mayor's and City of London Court.

Lord Mayor's Court Room: cross-section looking south

St Lawrence Jewry: section looking north

19 Blackwell Hall, George Shepherd, 1811. (Guildhall Library)

20 Vestry of St Lawrence Jewry, photograph. (National Monuments Record)

21 Aldermen's Court Room, photograph. (National Monuments Record)

22 Interior of Girdlers' Hall, photograph. (National Monuments Record)

ALDERMEN'S COURT ROOM

Aldermen's Court Room: cross-section looking east; cross-section looking south

The Aldermen's Court Room stood in the complex of administrative buildings on the north side of Guildhall, between Aldermanbury and Basinghall Street. It was rebuilt after the Great Fire between 1670 and 1680 with exceptionally rich decorations, including carved wood doorcases, an elaborate plaster ceiling, and ceiling and overmantel paintings by James Thornhill. The Court Room was destroyed by bombing in 1940 (its paintings alone survived – they are now in the Guildhall Art Gallery); its modern replacement stands on the west side of Guildhall Yard. The aldermen originated probably as hereditary lordships in the Anglo-Saxon period; in the early Middle Ages their role developed into one of elected territorial administrators, each of whom was responsible for one of the 24 wards into which the City was divided. It is probable that the Court of Aldermen took over the administrative function of the Court of Husting which was the original form of London local government. The aldermen's administrative role was largely taken over (not without some resistance from the aldermen themselves) by the Court of Common Council as the centuries passed, and their functions today are largely ceremonial, although they continue to be represented on the Common Council, are responsible for the City's magistrates' courts, and only aldermen can be elected Lord Mayor. *(See plate 21, p.71.)*

St Michael Bassishaw: Basinghall Street frontage

COOPERS' HALL

The first hall of the Coopers' Company was built in 1520; it was rebuilt at the fairly substantial cost of £5,000 in a plain classical style in 1670-1 after its destruction in the Great Fire; the Hall was again rebuilt in 1868, and finally destroyed by bombing in 1940. The site is now occupied by the square on the north side of the Guildhall Offices. The Coopers' Company was in existence by 1422 and chartered in 1501; it controlled the London barrel trade. Coopers' Hall was noted in the early 19th century as the scene of the draw for state lotteries (including the last one before the 1990s, in 1826).

Coopers' Hall: Basinghall Street frontage

ST MICHAEL BASSISHAW

St Michael's Church stood on the west side of Basinghall Street, on the site now occupied by the piazza in front of the Guildhall Offices. Both the street and the church were named after Basings Haw, the town mansion of the Basings, a powerful merchant family of early medieval London, which stood nearby. The church, first mentioned in the mid-12th century, was burnt in the Great Fire, and rebuilt in brick by John Fitch and James Flory to Wren's designs from 1676 to 1679. It had a traditional ground plan with nave and aisles, a huge segmentally pedimented east front, descending into concave side volutes, and a fairly simple lead-covered octagonal upper stage to the steeple (built from 1708 to 1712 by William Kempster) with a repeated concave motif in its buttresses and spire. The interior incorporated much fine plasterwork and woodwork. There were frequent problems with the structure, perhaps as a result of shoddy building; the clearance of the vaults in the late 19th century resulted in the weakening of the foundations, and the church was demolished in 1899.

St Michael Bassishaw: cross-section looking west

GIRDLERS' HALL

Girdlers' Hall was in existence by 1439; it was burnt in the Great Fire, and rebuilt by 1681. The livery hall was one of the best preserved in the City, with original panelling and elaborately carved screens; all was destroyed by bombing in 1940, and the new Hall, built in 1961, occupies roughly the same site. The Girdlers received letters patent in 1327 and their first charter in 1449. They were the makers of girdles, which had symbolic importance in medieval times. (*See plate 22, p.71.*)

Coopers' Hall: cross section of hall, looking west

Girdlers' Hall: cross-section of livery hall

Girdlers' Hall: Basinghall Street entrance

OLD JEWRY AND MOORGATE

NORTHWARDS out of the east end of Cheapside past the ostentatious merchants' mansions of Old Jewry ran the rather circuitous route towards the open spaces of Moorfields beyond Moorgate, which were presided over by the expansive buildings of the Bethlem Hospital.

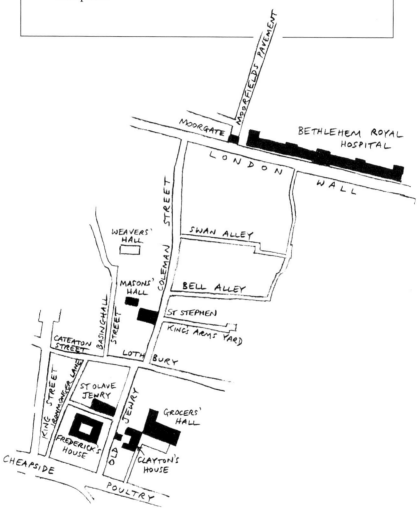

FREDERICK'S HOUSE

Sir John Frederick, an East India merchant, was Lord Mayor in 1661 and M.P. for the City from 1663 to 1679. He possessed a substantial courtyard house which opened off the west side of Old Jewry at its Cheapside end, just opposite Clayton's House, which he rebuilt in brick after its destruction in the Great Fire. The Excise Office acquired the house in 1747, and remained there until it moved to purpose-built premises in Old Broad Street in 1768. The Excise Office was established by Parliament in 1643 as a means of financing the Parliamentary effort in the Civil War. Excise duties were applied to luxury goods, notably tea and spirits, and gave rise to the flourishing smuggling trade of the 18th and early 19th centuries, against which the 'preventive' effort was organised from the Excise Office in London. The site of Frederick's House was developed speculatively by the Adam brothers in 1776 as Frederick's Place, most of whose houses survive as one of the best preserved Georgian enclaves in the City.

Sir John Frederick's House, Old Jewry: south, west, and north sides of courtyard

CLAYTON'S HOUSE

Old Jewry was clearly one of the most fashionable addresses in the late 17th-century City. The wealthy merchant Sir Robert Clayton built one of the grandest of the new mercantile palaces in the new London, at a cost of £1,669, in a courtyard opening off its east side, just north of Cheapside and opposite the equally substantial Frederick's House. Evelyn described Clayton as 'This prince of citizens, there never having been any who for the great stateliness of his palace, prodigious feasting and magnificence, exceeded him'. The house was noted particularly for the paintings of the Giants' wars on the walls of the dining room. Clayton, a scrivener, was Lord Mayor of London in 1679, and its M.P. from 1679 to 1681 and 1689 to 1707. He made a fortune from conveyancing after the Restoration, and was a pioneer of deposit banking, including the lending of money against property deeds. He was also one of the most prominent supporters of William of Orange in 1688, and a lavish benefactor of Christ's Hospital and St Thomas's Hospital, Southwark (in *The Second Part of Absalom and Achitophel* Dryden described him as 'As good a saint as usurer e'er made'). Clayton's house was occupied by the London Institution from its foundation in 1805 until 1812. Demolished shortly thereafter, its site is now occupied by the former office of the Commonwealth Bank of Australia at No.8 Old Jewry.

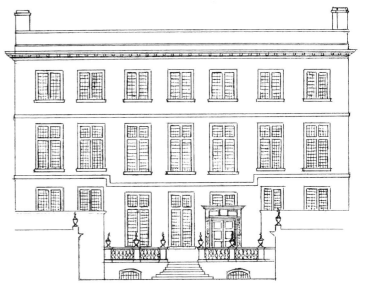

Sir Robert Clayton's House: west (courtyard) frontage

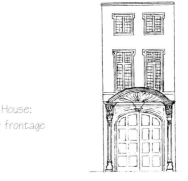

Clayton's House:
Old Jewry frontage

GROCERS' HALL

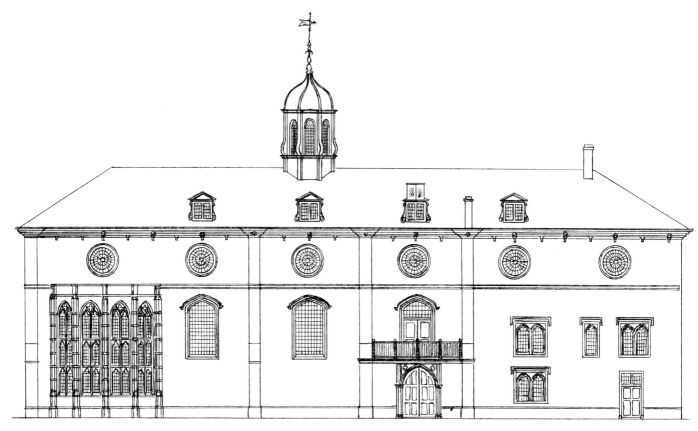

Grocers' Hall: Grocers' Hall Court frontage

The mansion of the Lords Fitzwalter was one of several houses used by the Grocers for their meetings in the 14th century. They acquired it in the early 15th century and built a large new Hall on the site in 1428. Grocers' Hall was badly damaged in the Great Fire, and rebuilt (retaining much of the original stone fabric) by the initiative of Sir John Cutler (a wealthy merchant who was four times Master Warden of the Grocers' Company) from 1668 to 1669. Its most prominent feature was the imposing Perpendicular gothic bay window at the west end of the livery hall. The Hall was repaired and enlarged by Sir John Moore in 1682, who set a fashion which was followed by several other Lord Mayors up to 1735 by residing at Grocers' Hall during his mayoralty. Grocers' Hall was also used as the office of the Bank of England from 1694 until 1734. It was rebuilt in neo-classical style by Thomas Leverton in 1802, then again in neo-Elizabethan style in the 1890s; this Hall was burnt down in 1965. Its south wing, which was not rebuilt, occupied the site of the original building; it lay along the south side of the court which opens off the west side of Princes Street (the original access to the Hall was however from Poultry). A London guild of pepperers was in existence by 1180, and ordinances date from 1345; the Company was chartered in 1428. The pepperers came to be known as grocers from the 14th century because of their predominantly wholesale dealings. They controlled the London spice trade, one of the most lucrative and prestigious in the medieval economy because of the expensive and capital-intensive nature of involvement in the oriental spice trade, spices being essential at that time for the preservation and flavouring of food. As a result of its wealth and prestige the Grocers' Company acquired second place in the order of precedence of the London guilds. The company was responsible for 'garbling' (inspecting and cleansing) spices on importation, and was also the guardian of the King's Weighbeam, which was used for weighing all imported goods for customs purposes.

ST OLAVE JEWRY WITH ST MARTIN POMARY

St Olave Jewry: Old Jewry frontage

St Olave's Church, dedicated to the martyred king-saint of Norway, stood on the west side of Old Jewry, in what was until the expulsion of the Jews in 1291 London's Jewish quarter. The church was first mentioned in about 1127, and was in early times also called St Olave Upwell, perhaps after a well which stood at its east end. In the Middle Ages the bells of St Olave's were rung to mark the opening and closing of trading in the cloth market at nearby Blackwell Hall. The church was burnt in the Great Fire, and rebuilt by John Shorthose with Portland stone facings to the designs of Wren between 1670 and 1679. The grandest of the church's frontages overlooked Old Jewry at the east end. St Olave's was demolished under the Union of City Benefices Act in 1888, although the simple tower was preserved. St Olave's Church in Stoke Newington was built with the proceeds of sale, and some of the furnishings from St Olave Jewry are still there; others are dispersed among a number of City churches. (See plate 23, p.79.)

St Martin Pomary was mentioned in the late 12th century. It may have been named after a nearby orchard. Its site is now covered by the churchyard of St Olave Jewry, on the east side of Ironmonger Lane.

St Olave Jewry: cross-section looking east

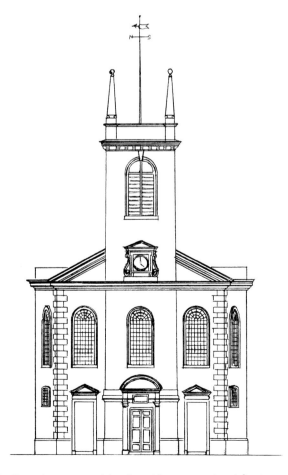

St Olave Jewry: west (churchyard/Ironmonger Lane) frontage

St Olave Jewry: cross-section looking west

ST STEPHEN COLEMAN STREET

The church of St Stephen stood on the west side of Coleman Street, opposite the opening into King's Arms Yard. First mentioned in the late 12th century, and possibly originally dedicated to St Colman, St Stephen's became a parish church only in 1456, having previously been a chapel of ease in the parish of St Olave Jewry. In the early 17th century it was a Puritan stronghold, with a committee of 13 (including two of the regicide judges) who decided whether parishioners were virtuous enough to receive communion. Oliver Cromwell was said to have lived in Coleman Street, and it was here that the five members of the House of Commons hid after Charles I's attempt to arrest them. The church was rebuilt between 1674 and 1677 by Joshua Marshall, to the design of Wren, after its destruction in the Great Fire. It was a small stone and brick church on an irregular plan, with a fairly plain stone steeple, but an exuberant Portland stone east front (shown in the view; according to Hatton in 1708 there were carved festoons beneath the pediment) and a fine wooden relief carving of the Last Judgement above the churchyard gate. In the mid-19th century the elaborate baroque curvature of the eastern pediment was replaced with a more severe straight-sided one, and its main artistic interest became confined to the interior – St Stephen's retained its high-quality furnishings (William Cleere was the joiner), including an unusually long and low reredos, in a good state of preservation until the church was completely destroyed by a direct hit in 1940.

St Stephen Coleman Street: Coleman Street frontage

MASONS' HALL

The Masons' Company occupied a small hall on the north side of St Stephen Coleman Street churchyard from the mid-15th century. Burnt in 1666, it was rebuilt from 1668 to 1670, with this gateway marking the alleyway leading to it. It was demolished in 1865; the site lay to the south of Masons Avenue. Curiously, considering the trade which it regulated, the Company never had an ostentatious hall. Master Masons were responsible for inspecting the condition of the City walls by the late 13th century. Regulations for the London Masons existed by the middle of the 14th century, and the guild controlled the medieval stonemasonry trade, although it was not chartered as a Company until 1677. Freemasonry developed out of the traditions of the guild in the early 17th century.

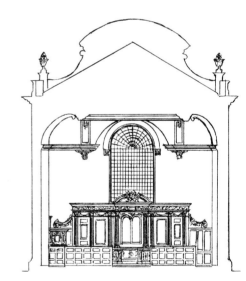

St Stephen Coleman Street: cross-section looking east

Masons' Hall: Basinghall Street entrance

WEAVERS' HALL, Basinghall Street. A small company hall, rebuilt to Jerman's design from 1667 to 1669 and demolished in 1856. It stood just off Basinghall Street on the east side, where the south-west corner of the new Woolgate Exchange building is now. The Weavers are the oldest documented company in the City, in existence by 1130 and chartered in 1155. The company controlled the London weaving trade, in the Middle Ages principally wool, though shifting in the 16th and 17th centuries towards silk.

23 Interior of St Olave Jewry, John Crowther, 1887. (Guildhall Library)

24 Bethlehem Royal Hospital viewed from Moorfields, Robert White, 1676. (Guildhall Library)

MOORGATE

Moorgate was originally built in 1415 by Thomas
Falconer, a London mercer, replacing a postern gate
which gave access to Moorfields (then one of London's
main recreation grounds) through the City wall. It was not
touched by the Great Fire, which stopped several houses
away down Coleman Street, but was rebuilt by Thomas
Cartwright in a characteristic baroque style in 1672, with a
higher arch so that the London trained bands could
march through it with their pikes upright. Moorgate was
an awkward piece of medieval town-planning: while
Moorfields Pavement was constructed in 1527 to run
northwards from it towards Finsbury, there was no
thoroughfare leading directly to it within the City wall –
Coleman Street opened into London Wall 200 feet to the
west. Paradoxically it was not until 78 years after

Moorgate: Moorfields
Pavement frontage

Moorgate's demolition in 1762 that Moorgate (the street)
was cut through from Lothbury to link with what by then
was Finsbury Pavement, as part of the street improvements
associated with the new London Bridge. The site of
Moorgate is the carriageway of Moorgate just north of the
junction with London Wall.

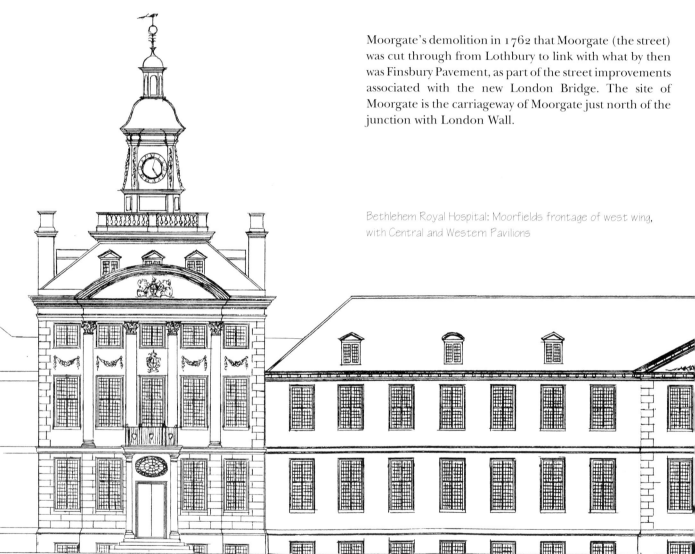

Bethlehem Royal Hospital: Moorfields frontage of west wing,
with Central and Western Pavilions

Bethlehem Royal Hospital: Moorfields
frontage of main gateway

THE CITY AFTER THE GREAT FIRE

BETHLEHEM ROYAL HOSPITAL

The Bethlehem Hospital moved from its old cramped quarters on the west side of Bishopsgate (the site is now covered by the Great Eastern Hotel) to Moorfields in 1676. The new building, designed by Robert Hooke and built from 1675 to 1676, extended along the south edge of Lower Moorfields (a public park which is now covered by Finsbury Circus and its surrounding buildings), backing onto the old City wall. The site of the Hospital is now represented by the entire north side of London Wall between Moorgate and Blomfield Street. Both the old and the new site were beyond the area destroyed by the Great Fire (indeed the new site, above the City ditch, had never been built on before), but the new Hospital very much partook of the spirit of improvement and magnificence which drove the rebuilders of London. It cost £17,000, and at some 530 feet long it was one of the largest structures in the City. Its long frontage, built of brick with stone dressings, faced north across Lower Moorfields, and was strongly articulated to avoid monotony. At the centre and either end were tall pavilions with segmentally pedimented frontispieces, hipped roofs, and cupolas. Between them stretched two plainer wings, each with a pedimented centrepiece. The main gate, which stood in front of the central pavilion, consisted of pillars capped by a broken pediment, on each side of

Mary of Bethlehem. By 1329 it incorporated a hospital, and by the late 14th century it specialised in the care of the insane. The Priory came under the patronage of the City in the mid-14th century, by when it was already popularly known as 'Bedlam', in which form its name entered the English language. The City acquired the premises when the Priory was dissolved in 1547, and reestablished the Hospital as a lunatic asylum; it was joined under the same management with Bridewell in 1557. From an early date until 1775 the patients were on public display, and Bedlam was one of the sights of London, frequently mentioned in contemporary accounts and literature – Hogarth famously depicted it in 'The Rake's Progress'. The patients were exhibited chained in their cells, which opened off long galleries. The penal reforms of John Howard, developments in the understanding of insanity, and public sympathy for the madness of George III, led to improvements in treatment and conditions in the late 18th and early 19th centuries. The Moorfields

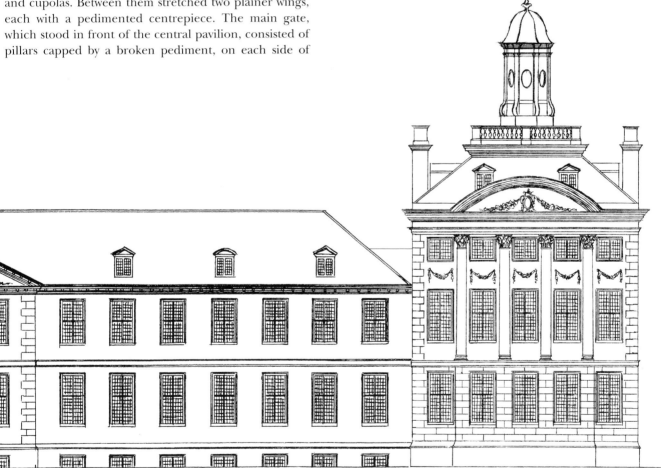

which reclined Caius Gabriel Cibber's famous statues of Madness and Melancholy – they were reputedly modelled on Oliver Cromwell's porter Daniel, who was admitted as a patient in 1656, and are now preserved in the Hospital's existing building in Beckenham. The Hospital had been established in Bishopsgate in 1247 as the Priory of St

building was demolished in 1815 when the Hospital moved to new premises in Lambeth, now the Imperial War Museum. The Hospital moved to Addington, Surrey in 1930, and later to Beckenham, Kent, where it continues to play a leading role in the treatment of and research into mental illness. *(See plate 24, p.79.)*

CORNHILL AND THREADNEEDLE STREET

THE HEART OF LONDON'S commercial life, the Royal Exchange, London's grand purpose-built merchants' trading-floor cum shopping-centre, stood between Cornhill and Threadneedle Street, and round it crowded a warren of taverns, shops, and coffee houses that derived business from and supported its trade.

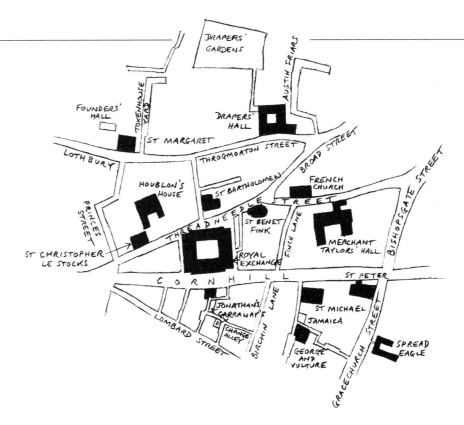

ROYAL EXCHANGE

Richard Gresham, merchant adventurer and Lord Mayor in 1538, originally proposed the establishment of an exchange in London, in imitation of the Antwerp Bourse, to provide an enclosed area where London's merchants, who did business in the streets or their own shops, could meet and trade. His scheme foundered for want of a suitable site, and it was Gresham's son Sir Thomas (a London mercer and the Royal agent in Flanders) and his Antwerp factor Richard Clough, spurred by the Spanish threat to Flanders' status as a trading centre, who eventually instigated the building of the Exchange between Cornhill and Threadneedle Street, in the heart of the commercial City, in 1566. The Exchange was built in a Flemish style by Flemings with arcaded 'piazzas' surrounding a central courtyard, and two floors of shops

(the 'pawns') above, which soon became a fashionable shopping centre. Queen Elizabeth designated the Exchange 'Royal' when she visited in 1570. On his death in 1579 Gresham bequeathed the Exchange to the City and the Mercers' Company jointly, and it has been administered ever since by the Joint Grand Gresham Committee which was then established. The importance of the Exchange to the commercial life of the City of London was demonstrated by Wren's giving it equal prominence to St Paul's in his 1666 proposal for rebuilding the City after the Great Fire, and by the speed with which it was actually rebuilt, between 1667 (the foundation stone was laid by Charles II on 23 October) and 1669, at a cost of £62,000; after St Paul's Cathedral the most expensive new building in the

Royal Exchange: Cornhill frontage

City. The architects were Edward Jerman, the City Surveyor, and Thomas Cartwright, the Master of the Masons' Company. The format was similar to Gresham's building, and the style was an up-to-date Dutch baroque, with round-headed arcades to the 'piazzas', a baroque interplay of round and elliptical curves in the façades of the first-floor 'pawns', and grand two-storey façades to Threadneedle Street and Cornhill, the latter with a monumental central frontispiece (with statues of Charles I and Charles II by Bushnell), surmounted by a 150-foot tiered steeple, which was itself capped by a grasshopper weathervane, a reference to Sir Thomas Gresham's heraldic emblem. All the façades were faced with Portland stone. The tower clock played popular tunes every three hours, and the courtyard façades were, like their Elizabethan predecessors, lined with statues of English monarchs in niches, many of them carved by Arnold Quellin; a statue of Charles II by Grinling Gibbons stood on a pedestal in the middle of the courtyard. The new Exchange opened for business in 1669, and its shops were occupied by 1671. The Royal Exchange thrived as the centre of England's booming international trade, and particular parts of the courtyard were occupied by the merchants who dealt in particular commodities or

Royal Exchange: west frontage of court

Royal Exchange: Threadneedle Street frontage

Jerusalem Coffee House), and the other London commodity exchanges. Lloyd's moved back into the Royal Exchange in 1774, occupying the north pawn, and there was a general process in the late 18th century of the pawns being taken over by company offices as fashionable shops followed the movement of population to the West End. In spite of the spawning of specialist exchanges the Royal Exchange continued to thrive as a meeting place for merchants into the 19th century; its most famous user was Nathan Meyer Rothschild, who regularly transacted business standing in front of one of the courtyard columns, which was referred to as Rothschild's column. The clock tower was rebuilt in neo-classical style in the 1820s, but the entire building was gutted by fire in 1838, after which the existing Exchange was built on a larger scale to the design of Sir William Tite. Throughout the late 19th and early 20th centuries business on the Exchange subsided as the specialist exchanges became more autonomous and powerful, and London's traders built ever grander offices for themselves; trade finally ceased on the floor of the Royal Exchange in 1939. It enjoyed a brief revival of its glory days as the trading floor of the new London International Financial Futures Exchange from 1982, but that too moved out to a purpose-built trading floor because of lack of space in 1990. The building until recently served as offices for the Guardian Royal Exchange; the Royal Exchange Assurance Company was established in one of the pawns in 1720, one of the only two insurance companies permitted by the Bubble Act. All that remains of the physical fabric of Jerman's and Cartwright's building are the 'Turkey stone' pavement (some of which may date from Gresham's exchange) and a few of the statues which survive either at the Royal Exchange itself or at the Central Criminal Court in Old Bailey (Queen Anne is at Finchcocks, Goudhurst, Kent). *(See plates 25 & 26, p.93.)*

with particular parts of the world. Pressure on space provided an opportunity for the coffee houses, which sprang up in profusion in the surrounding streets, to provide supplementary facilities, and eventually the coffee houses took on a life of their own as exchanges in their own right. This was the origin of the Stock Exchange (stock and share brokers met at Jonathan's Coffee House from 1698), the Lloyd's insurance market (Lloyd's Coffee House was established as the centre of marine insurance by the mid-18th century), the Baltic Exchange (which originated in the Virginia and Baltic Coffee House), the London Metal Exchange (which grew out of the

Royal Exchange: north frontage of court

CORNHILL

Cornhill was probably named after an early medieval grain market which was held in the street. Being the eastward extension of Cheapside towards the City's main eastern gate at Aldgate (the direction from which most of London's corn came) it was one of the principal thoroughfares of the City, and broad enough for Londoners to try to use it as a firebreak during the Great Fire. Later in the Middle Ages Cornhill came to be inhabited by important drapers, and from the 16th century it was much frequented by merchants and brokers whose activities centred on the Royal Exchange. The illustration shows two fine examples of the type of four-storeyed brick houses which were built under the Rebuilding Act to front the principal streets and which survived until the mid-19th century. They stood on the south side of Cornhill opposite the main entrance to the Royal Exchange, where now is the old Commercial Union headquarters. No.24 Cornhill was for much of the 18th century the Union Coffee House. The coffee houses of Cornhill and its adjoining courts absorbed much of the overflow from the crowded Royal Exchange during the commercial boom from the late 17th century onwards. Some of the Cornhill and Threadneedle Street coffee houses developed independent existences as specialised exchanges, with trade in particular commodities moving to them and away from the Royal Exchange itself. Between

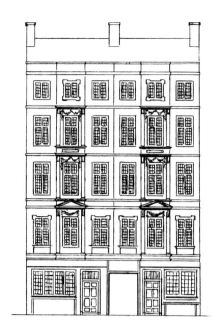

Nos. 24 and 23 Cornhill (with entrance to Change Alley)

Nos 23 and 24 was one of the Cornhill entrances to Change Alley, and immediately behind them was Jonathan's Coffee House. Also in Change Alley nearby was Garraway's Coffee House.

GARRAWAY'S COFFEE HOUSE, Change Alley, Cornhill. Garraway's was established in 1669 and one of London's main auction houses for commodities in the late 17th and 18th centuries; from it emerged the main London commodity exchanges. In 1670 it became the first house in England to retail tea.

JAMAICA COFFEE HOUSE, St Michael's Alley, Cornhill. St Michael's Alley saw the first two coffee houses in London, the Pasqua Rosee's Head and Bowman's, both established in 1652. The Jamaica was established in the 1670s and named after the Jamaica merchants who patronised it; from the 18th to the mid-19th centuries it was the main meeting place for West India merchants, and a centre of information on West Indies trade. In the 18th century it was noted for the best rum in London. The site is now occupied by the Jamaica Wine House, established in 1869.

JONATHAN'S COFFEE HOUSE, Change Alley, Cornhill. Jonathan's Coffee House was established in 1680, much patronised by stock jobbers, and the focus in 1719 and 1720 of the South Sea Bubble, one of the first and most serious of the financial crises which have punctuated London's career as one of the great capital-raising centres of the world. The South Sea Company, one of the great London joint-stock trading companies, established in 1711 with a monopoly of trade to Spanish America, was frustrated in its objectives by diplomatic difficulties. Needing to pay a return to its investors, it proposed instead a scheme by which it would buy up most of the National Debt. This scheme, with a leavening of fraud, led to a frenzy of speculative trading in the stock of the South Sea Company and numerous other bubble stocks, many of them for wholly fictitious enterprises (including reputedly one for 'an undertaking of great profit, but nobody to know what it is'), which were marketed on the back of the South Sea speculation. Change Alley seethed with people desperate to buy into rapidly soaring stocks. The Bubble Act of 1720, passed in an effort to control speculation, precipitated the collapse of the market, causing widespread ruin among those who had invested large sums in worthless investments, but also bringing fortunes to those who were able, or merely fortunate, to sell at the top of the market. In 1722 a group of 'respectable' stockbrokers tried to reserve Jonathan's for their exclusive use, and in 1773 a group of brokers established New Jonathan's in Threadneedle Street, the direct forerunner of the Stock Exchange (the name was changed almost immediately to the Stock Exchange Coffee House).

George and Vulture Inn: George Yard frontage

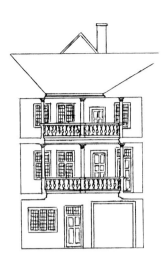

Spread Eagle Inn, Gracechurch Street:
frontage of west side of yard

A hostelry by the 16th century, according to Stow the George had once been the London mansion of the Earls Ferrers. It acquired its vulture appellation presumably by amalgamation with a neighbouring house. Burnt in the Great Fire, it was rebuilt in brick at the north end of George Yard, on the east side of the passageway which leads through to St Michael's Alley. A favourite venue for dinners and meetings during the 18th and 19th centuries, and more famous than any of the City inns because of its fictional association with Charles Dickens' *Pickwick Papers*, it narrowly escaped the 1748 Cornhill fire and was finally demolished in 1855, to be replaced by the New City Club. At that time the George and Vulture reopened as a tavern in an adjacent Georgian house in Castle Court, where it continues today.

The Spread Eagle was one of the last survivors of the galleried inns which were built throughout the City in the aftermath of the Great Fire. It was demolished in 1865, and drawings made at the time are sufficient for an attempt at a reconstruction of its appearance. It stood around a yard on the east side of Gracechurch Street, and backed onto Leadenhall Market (the site is between the existing main entrance to the market and Ship Tavern Passage). It provided coach and carrier services to the south-east, and was owned in the early 19th century by the great innkeeper John Chaplin.

ST PETER CORNHILL

St Peter's Church claimed precedence in the Middle Ages over all of the London parish churches on the strength of its claim (which may have dated at least to the eighth century) that it was established under the Romans. Its senior status extended even to 1860, when it was specifically exempted from the Union of City Benefices Act. After its destruction in the Great Fire the church was rebuilt in brick by Thomas Humphry, Joshua Marshall and Abraham Story, to the design of Wren and Hooke, from 1677 to 1684. It consists of a tall barrel-vaulted nave and aisles, with a grand two-tiered east frontage to Gracechurch Street and a brick west tower with an obelisk spire (originally covered with lead, now with copper) standing on a small dome. Except for its pewing and dark Victorian stained glass, the interior is one of the best preserved of the City churches, with fine plasterwork by Henry Doogood and John Grove and carved wooden furnishings by William Cleere, notably the reredos, pulpit, west gallery, and the rare chancel screen.

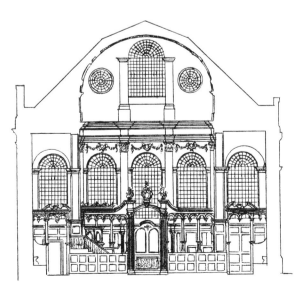

St Peter Cornhill: cross-section looking east

ST MICHAEL CORNHILL

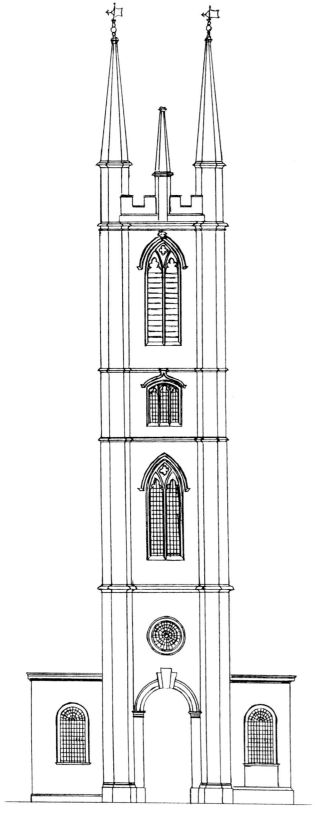

St Michael Cornhill: Dickinson's unrealised design for steeple

St Michael's Church is situated behind the houses on the south side of Cornhill. It was first mentioned in 1055, and was historically one of the most important of London's churches, with many associated chantries and fraternities, and what was said to be the finest ring of bells in England (they were cast in the 1420s). St Michael's also boasted in its stonework the alleged clawmarks from a visitation of the devil when the bells were being rung in a storm; this perhaps is the origin of the 'Cornhill Devil' which sits in terracotta on top of an adjoining gable. The rich medieval church was burnt in the Great Fire, and rebuilt under the aegis of the parish authorities by Nicholas Young (without, so far as is known, any input from Wren or the Commissioners) from 1670 to 1672 in a plain classical style with nave and aisles and a groined vault resting on Tuscan colonnades. A replacement for the old tower (which was patched up in the late 1660s) was begun by Samuel Fulkes to the design of William Dickinson (under Wren's direction) in 1715-17 (probably incorporating old fabric), but discontinued because the coal fund ran out of money. The steeple was completed under the 1711 Fifty New Churches Act by Edward Strong the Younger to Hawksmoor's design between 1718 and 1722 in a forthright Gothick style; it was constructed of Portland stone. Funding for the completion of the tower was sparingly given, and St Michael's was the last of the great City steeples to be finished. St Michael's was heavily Victorianised by Sir Giles Gilbert Scott between 1857 and 1860; this involved the replacement of almost all the fittings in Gothic style, a new and elaborate Gothic porch, and filling the windows with Venetian tracery, so that, even though it was undamaged in the Second World War, the church retains (its tower excepted) probably the least of its 17th-century character of all the City churches.

ST CHRISTOPHER LE STOCKS

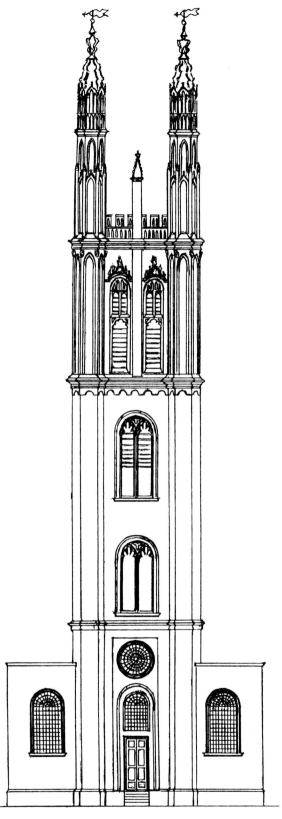

St Michael Cornhill: St Michael's Alley frontage

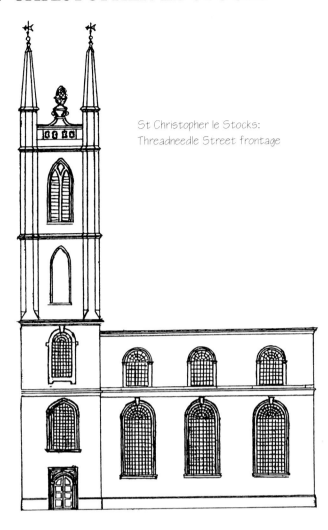

St Christopher le Stocks:
Threadneedle Street frontage

The church of St Christopher le Stocks stood on the north side of Threadneedle Street, almost opposite the Stocks Market, after which it was named. It was first mentioned in the late 12th century, and rebuilt in 1462. The steeple was rebuilt in 1506. The church was burnt in the Great Fire, but much of the fabric remained in usable condition and was incorporated by John Thompson in the parish's rebuilding (in which Wren and the Commissioners were probably not involved) between 1670 and 1671 – St Christopher's was the first of the restored City churches to be finished, and one of the cheapest. The church retained the aisled medieval plan when it was again substantially rebuilt by Edward Strong the Younger to the design of Wren, after the fabric had shown signs of deterioration, in 1711-12, and the new Gothic pinnacled tower, also completed in 1712, probably retained its medieval appearance fairly accurately, albeit with the addition of a baroque flourish in the pedestals and urns in the centre of each parapet. Troops were stationed on the tower to protect the adjacent Bank of England during the Gordon Riots in 1780, and the church was demolished in 1782 to improve the security of the Bank and provide it with space for expansion. St Christopher's thus became the first of Wren's City churches to disappear, although some of its furnishings remain in St Margaret Lothbury and St Vedast Foster Lane.

HOUBLON'S HOUSE

Sir John Houblon, a merchant from an influential and successful Huguenot family, and a member of the Grocers' Company, was Lord Mayor in 1695, M.P. for the City from 1698 to 1700, and the first Governor of the Bank of England on its foundation in 1694. His brick-built house (which is featured, along with a portrait of Houblon, on the £50 note) was one of the finest and largest of the City merchants' houses built shortly after the Great Fire. It was demolished in 1732 to provide the site for the Bank of England's first purpose-built office, designed by George Sampson. The site is now approximately occupied by the central courtyard of the Bank.

Houblon's House, Threadneedle Street: courtyard frontage

ST BARTHOLOMEW BY THE EXCHANGE

St Bartholomew's Church stood on the east side of Bartholomew Lane, where now stands the Royal Bank of Scotland. First mentioned in the early 12th century, it was known as St Bartholomew the Less (to distinguish it from St Bartholomew the Great in Smithfield) until Sir Thomas Gresham built the Royal Exchange on the opposite side of Threadneedle Street in 1566. The church was burnt in the Great Fire, and rebuilt in brick and stone by John Thompson to the designs of Wren from 1674 to 1681 on its medieval aisled plan (retaining some of the old walls), with a south-west tower which was conventional in design except for its extraordinary parapet, a baroque conceit which blurred the boundary between the building and the sky, and, with its openwork arched 'windows', almost gave the impression that the structure was unfinished. An extra baroque touch was provided by the absence of corner pinnacles, which reversed the conventional proportions of the top of a church tower; a similar effect was achieved with different elements at St Mary Somerset. St Bartholomew's was demolished in 1840, along with St Benet Fink, as part of the improvements associated with the new Royal Exchange which was then building. The furnishings were removed to a replica of the church which was built in Moor Lane and later, when that too was demolished in 1902, to a new St Bartholomew's Church at Stamford Hill. (See plate 27, p.94.)

St Bartholomew by the Exchange: Bartholomew Lane frontage (diagonal view)

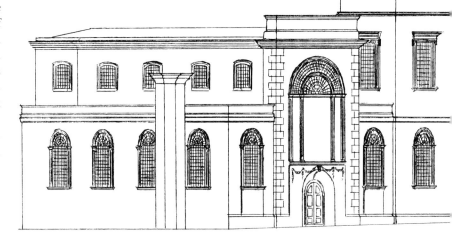

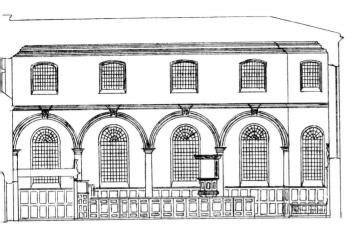

St Bartholomew by the Exchange: section looking north

St Bartholomew by the Exchange: cross-section looking east

St Bartholomew by the Exchange:
Bartholomew Lane frontage

St Benet Fink: Threadneedle Street frontage (diagonal view)

ST BENET FINK

The church of St Benet Fink was one of the first of the Commissioners' new City churches to be built, and one of the first to disappear, demolished in 1842 as part of the widening of Threadneedle Street which accompanied the building of the new Royal Exchange. Its site is in the roadway on the south side of Threadneedle Street at the junction with Old Broad Street. It was first mentioned in the early 13th century but probably dated from at least the

11th, and according to Stow was named after Robert Fink, who built it. Burnt in the Great Fire, it was rebuilt by Thomas Cartwright, with Portland stone facings to its brick walls, to the designs of Wren or (perhaps more probably, given its Dutch elements) Hooke from 1670 to 1681. As at St Antholin's, the curve of the street was exploited to produce a daring plan: an elongated decagon, enclosing a hexagonal central nave surmounted by an elliptical dome with a hexagonal lantern – another variation in the evolution of geometrical forms which was characteristic of Wren's domed churches, evident at St Antholin's and St Stephen Walbrook, and of the expression of tension between longitudinal and centralised plans. The fact that the dome rested on arches opening into barrel-vaulted 'nave' and double 'transepts' (by contrast with St Antholin, where it rested on an entablature) must have made the interior of this small church extraordinarily impressive. George Holman, a Roman Catholic parishioner, contributed £1,000 towards the cost of the church. The street frontage was decorated with ornamental festoons, as was the tower with its square lead-covered dome and lantern, sited to exploit views up Old Broad Street and along Threadneedle Street. The proceeds of sale of the church were used to build St Benet Fink Church at Tottenham; none of the fittings appears to have survived except for the paintings of Moses and Aaron from the reredos, which are now at Emmanuel School in Wandsworth. *(See plate 28, p.94.)*

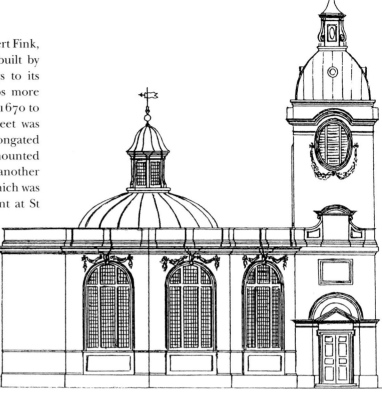

St Benet Fink: Threadneedle Street frontage

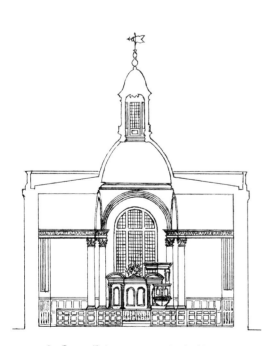

St Benet Fink: cross-section looking east

St Benet Fink: section looking south

25 Cornhill and the Royal Exchange, Philippe de
Louterberg, 1788. (Guildhall Library)

26 Courtyard of the Royal Exchange, Philippe de
Louterberg, 1788. (Guildhall Library)

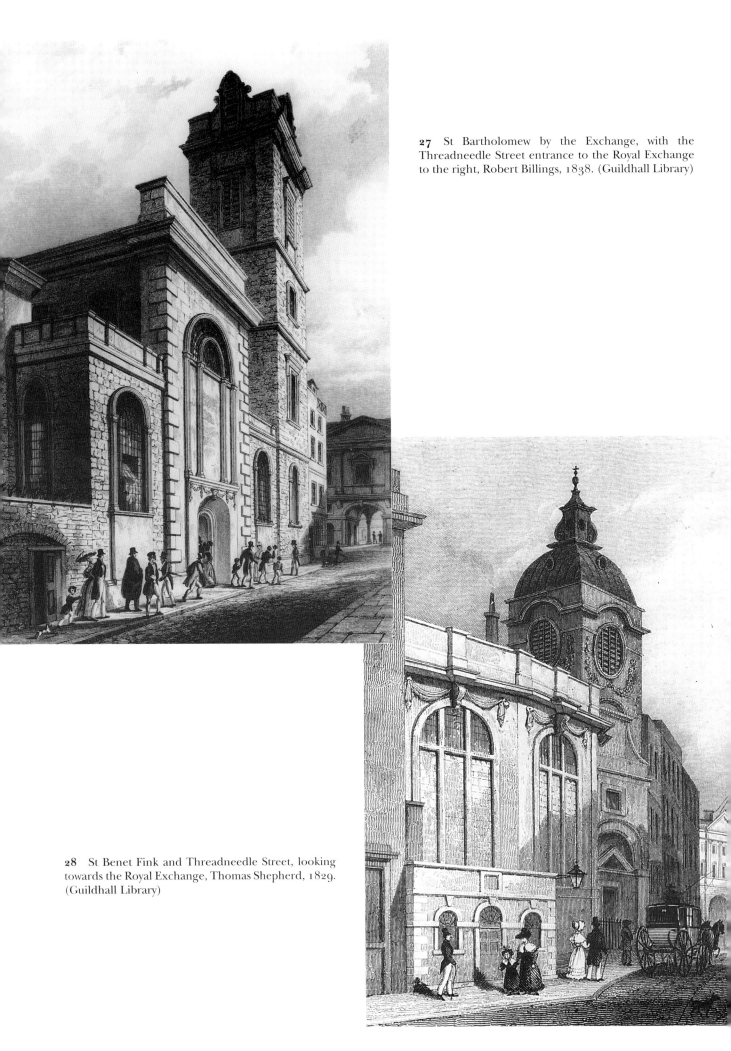

27 St Bartholomew by the Exchange, with the Threadneedle Street entrance to the Royal Exchange to the right, Robert Billings, 1838. (Guildhall Library)

28 St Benet Fink and Threadneedle Street, looking towards the Royal Exchange, Thomas Shepherd, 1829. (Guildhall Library)

FRENCH CHURCH

French Church: Threadneedle Street frontage

French Church: section looking south

A hospital of St Anthony of Viennois was established in Threadneedle Street in 1243 to treat victims of St Anthony's Fire. During the 15th century almshouses and a grammar school were added to the foundation; the school was (along with that of the Hospital of St Thomas of Acon) the most important of the medieval City – its boys were referred to as 'St Anthony's Pigs', an appellation which derived from the City's grant of all pigs which were deemed unfit for human consumption to the hospital. The hospital was dissolved in 1540 because of its monastic association. The school subsequently declined, and the hospital chapel was granted in 1550 to the congregation of French Calvinist protestants in London. It was burnt in 1666 and rebuilt, possibly incorporating some of the medieval fabric, with a row of circular windows to light its galleries and a central lantern. The church was demolished in 1840 and the site occupied successively by the Hall of Commerce (an abortive commercial club which was intended to rival the Royal Exchange and the great coffee houses), whose building later became the office of Parr's Bank, and the existing building which was formerly occupied by the Westminster Bank. The congregation moved to St Martins le Grand, then in the 1880s to Soho Square.

MERCHANT TAYLORS' HALL

The Tailors' Company acquired the house of John Yakesely, the king's tentmaker, in 1349. The great hall was rebuilt in the late 14th century – it was the largest of the City companies' halls, and is the only one which retains medieval fabric (parts of the kitchen and livery hall), in spite of extensive destruction in both the Great Fire and the Blitz. The Hall was rebuilt from 1671 to 1673 to the designs of Jerman, including an elaborate gatehouse on Threadneedle Street. The livery hall received its finely carved screen, designed by Hooke, in 1673; it was destroyed in 1940. The Company of Tailors and Linen Armourers was chartered in 1327; linen armourers made the padded linen tunics which were worn under medieval armour, and members of the company also included tentmakers. The Company became the inspecting authority for cloth measures in London. A curiosity of City history was the dispute between the Tailors and the Skinners over civic precedence, which was eventually resolved by the Mayor's according the sixth and seventh position in the order of precedence to each company alternately; this remains the case today, and is said to be the origin of the expression 'at sixes and sevens'. The London Tailors increasingly expanded into merchanting in the later Middle Ages, and this was recognised by the change of the name of the Company in Henry VII's reign; it had virtually lost control of the tailoring trade by the 17th century. Merchant Taylors' Hall is alleged to have witnessed the first performance of 'God Save the King', by John Bull at a banquet for James I in the early 17th century.

DRAPERS' HALL

The Drapers' Company moved into Thomas Cromwell's mansion in Throgmorton Street on his attainder in 1543. Drapers' Hall was burnt in the Great Fire and rebuilt by Thomas Cartwright to the design of John Gorham between 1667 and 1671, with the rooms surrounding a central colonnaded courtyard; some of the structure from this building survives today. The Hall was damaged by fire in 1772, and it was then that Gorham's baroque frontage was rebuilt to a neo-classical design in the Adam style. Most of the existing fabric, including the street front and the livery hall, is now the result of 19th-century rebuildings. An association of London drapers existed in the 12th century and the Company was chartered in 1364. It has third place in the order of precedence, a measure of the importance of the drapery trade in the Middle Ages. Drapers were involved in the manufacture and later the import and export of woollen cloth, an industry which was developed by the Crown in the 14th and 15th centuries specifically to exploit the world-famous quality of English wool, and to cut out the Flemings who dominated the north European cloth-making and cloth-dealing trade. In the later Middle Ages the Drapery was

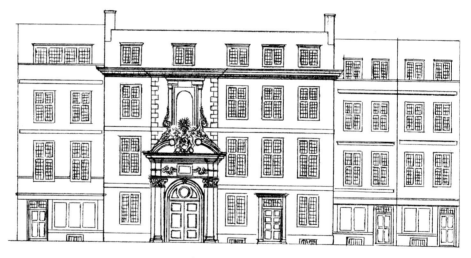

Merchant Taylors' Hall: Threadneedle Street frontage

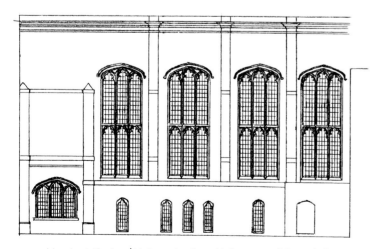

Merchant Taylors' Hall: garden (south) frontage of livery hall

Merchant Taylors' Hall: cross-section of hall, looking east

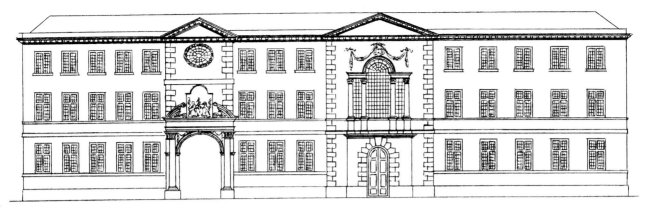

Drapers' Hall: Throgmorton Street frontage

concentrated in the main weaving area around Cannon Street (the old Drapers' Hall was in St Swithin's Lane, in the heart of the Drapery). The Company was responsible for checking the quality and measurements of cloth at the London fairs. Its control over the London trade declined gradually during the course of the 16th and 17th centuries.

ST MARGARET LOTHBURY

Lothbury was a broad street (by medieval standards) running from east to west to the north of Poultry. A variety of explanations have been offered for its name, the most picturesque being John Stow's suggestion that it was named after the loathsome noise made by the founders and coppersmiths who occupied it in the Middle Ages; more prosaically it probably means 'the manor of Lotha'. Lothbury was noted in the 17th century for its bankers and merchants, and Dr Johnson used the word as a shorthand for the commercial City. The church of St Margaret, first mentioned in the late 12th century, stands on its north side. Burnt in 1666, it was rebuilt in Portland stone by Samuel Fulkes to the design of Wren from 1683 to 1692; the steeple was added from 1698 to 1700. The church consists of nave and south aisle, with a south-west steeple with lead-covered spire. The view shows the street frontage as it was originally, fronted by a row of shops. The rich collection of 17th-century woodwork includes many furnishings brought in from other City churches, including the superb chancel screen from All Hallows the Great; the result is one of the most genuine surviving evocations of the late 17th-century City.

FOUNDERS' HALL, Lothbury. The Founders rebuilt their Hall from 1669-72 (appearance unknown), and rebuilt in 1845; the building is now the office of Brown Shipley & Co., merchant bankers. The guild received ordinances in 1365 and was chartered in 1614. It controlled the founding of bronze, brass and latten until 1831.

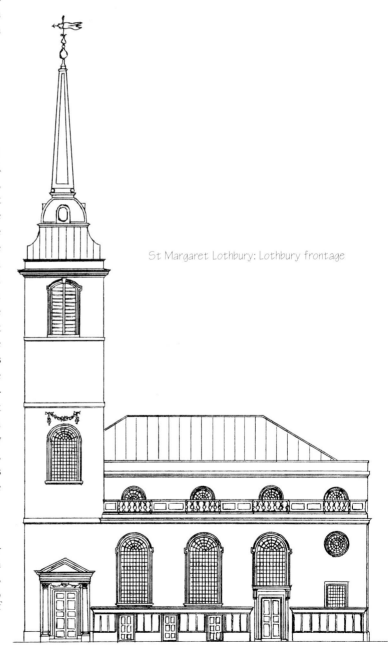

St Margaret Lothbury: Lothbury frontage

THE STOCKS AND LOMBARD STREET

THE STOCKS MARKET, one of the City's largest market places, stood between Cheapside and the commercial heart of London to the east, where Lombard Street, the centre of the banking trade, ran eastwards towards Fenchurch Street and the unburnt part of the City.

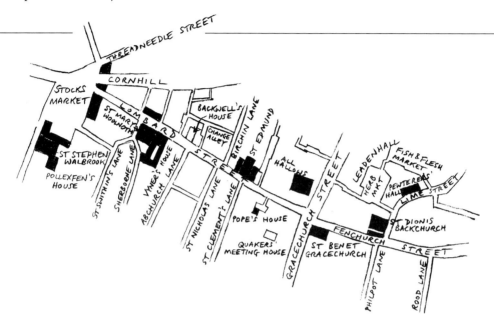

Stocks Market: frontage of east side (with conjectural reconstruction of first rebuilding of St Mary Woolnoth steeple beyond

STOCKS MARKET

The Stocks Market, named after the stocks which stood there, was established as a fish and flesh market by Henry le Waleys, Mayor, in 1282, on a restricted site at the junction of Lombard Street, Cornhill, and Poultry. A substantial stone market building was built in 1410, and burnt in the Great Fire. The Stocks Market was re-established after the Fire as a general market, specialising in fruit and vegetables, on an extended site which stretched southwards across the site of the church of St Mary Woolchurch Haw (whence it was also known as Woolchurch Market) as far as the north side of St Stephen Walbrook, whose dome and steeple dominated it from the south, as shown here in the illustration of that church. In 1672 Sir Robert Vyner (a goldsmith banker who became Lord Mayor in 1675 and whose house was in Lombard Street nearby) erected an equestrian statue of Charles II trampling Oliver Cromwell on a tall pedestal at the north end of the marketplace; it had started life as a statue of the Polish King Jan

Sobieski trampling a Turk – Vyner acquired it second-hand and installed Charles II's head in place of Jan's, but no alterations were made to the victim, so Cromwell appeared turbanned. In the late 17th and early 18th centuries the Stocks was the most important vegetable market in London, but it was cleared away in 1737 to make way for the new Mansion House. The traders were removed to Fleet Market in Farringdon Street, while the statue was taken to Lincolnshire, and has now ended up at Newby Park in Yorkshire. The view also shows the Oxford Arms, the shop on the acute corner between Lombard Street and Cornhill, which was Thomas Guy's bookshop between 1668 and 1724. Guy used the fortune which he amassed from a monopoly on Bible printing and judicious South Sea speculation to found Guy's Hospital, Southwark, in 1721. In the early 19th century this was 'Lucky Corner', one of several Cornhill lottery agents. *(See plates 29 & 30, p.100.)*

Stocks Market: frontage of south side, with St Stephen Walbrook beyond

29 Cornhill and Lombard Street (detail), looking east from Poultry and the Stocks Market, showing the hanging signs and, from left to right, the steeples of St Christopher le Stocks, the Royal Exchange, St Peter Cornhill, St Michael Cornhill and St Edmund Lombard Street, Thomas Bowles, 1751. (Guildhall Library)

30 The Stocks Market, with St Stephen Walbrook and the spire of St Swithin Cannon Street beyond, Nicholls and Boydell, 1746. (Guildhall Library)

ST STEPHEN WALBROOK with ST BENET SHEREHOG

St Stephen's Church stands on the east side of Walbrook, a street which commemorates the stream that divided the two hills upon which the City of London was built, and which still flows in an underground culvert to the Thames at Dowgate. The church, which took its name from the river, was built (probably in the late 11th century) on its west bank. A magnificent rebuilding on a new site on the east bank between 1429 and 1439 by Henry Chichele, a former Mayor of London, resulted in one of the largest churches in the City, some 125 feet long. After its destruction in the Great Fire St Stephen's was rebuilt in stone between 1672 and 1679 by Christopher Kempster, Thomas Strong, and Edward Strong the Elder, under the patronage of the Grocers' Company and to the design of Wren, with reduced dimensions. The church represents in the restrained baroque complexity of its interior the summit of achievement amongst those built to replace the losses in the Great Fire. The rectangular space is filled with columns which can be read, depending on the position of the observer, and blending into each other, as nave and aisles, nave and transepts, or domed octagonal central space with ambulatory. There is also a vertical progression in the central space – the square formed by the central twelve columns is emphasised by its being carried up into the clerestory, but is superimposed on the octagon of the central eight columns, whose eight arches support the pendentives on which rests the circular cornice and richly ornamented dome, with plasterwork by John Grove and Henry Doogood. Such a progression of geometrical forms from the square to the circular, found also in other domed City churches, was emblematic in the baroque idiom of an ascent from the earthly to the divine, a visual embodiment of the intercessory role of the church. It was even more pronounced when the church was filled with square box pews, later cut down in a Victorian restoration, but has now been weakened by the centralised Henry Moore altar stone and its accompanying circular arrangement of the seating. The church retains many original fittings superbly carved by Jonathan Maine, William Newman and Thomas Creecher. The Portland stone west steeple, with its delicate diminishing lanterns, was added in 1713-14 by Edward Strong

St Stephen Walbrook: cross-section looking east

St Stephen Walbrook: Stocks Market frontage, showing unexecuted porch

POLLEXFEN'S HOUSE

the Younger, perhaps with input from Hawksmoor as well as Wren to its design. The total cost of the whole masterpiece was a mere £9,500. The view on page 99 shows the north frontage of the church, unaltered but obscured since the mid-18th century behind the bulk of the Mansion House. With its graceful dome it was designed to preside over the Stocks Market (the steeple of St Swithin Cannon Street provided a distant accent behind it), perhaps in the style of a Roman basilica dominating the 'forum', with the oval windows in the north wall allowing space beneath for the market's 'piazza'. It was originally intended that the steeple should be attached to this frontage, facing the market; a later proposal was for a grand entrance to the church on this side – neither project came to fruition. The 'piazza' shown in the view on page 101 is a conjectural reconstruction based on Leybourn's plan, Boydell's view of the market, and the drawings of the proposed north portico in the RIBA collection – this may be an idealisation based on the concept of the Stocks Market as a Roman forum.

St Benet Sherehog was originally dedicated to St Sithe, a corruption of St Osyth. The church gave its name to Sise Lane, opposite the north end of which it stood, on the north side of Pancras Lane. A sherehog was a ram which had been gelded after its first shearing, and the name may have some reference to the London wool trade. The churchyard survived until recently removed for Lord Palumbo's controversial new office block to James Stirling's design at 1 Poultry.

Pollexfen's House, Walbrook: courtyard frontage

The Pollexfens were a prosperous merchant family whose mansion in Walbrook adjoined St Stephen's Church on the south side. Before the Great Fire the church's vaults seem to have extended under the house, for the Pollexfens were celebrated for being buried under their own roof. The mansion was rebuilt in brick according to the usual fashion, replicating the medieval arrangement, with the main house at the back of a court which was flanked by warehouses and offices. Pollexfen's House survived until late in the 19th century, but its appearance is known only from a print (from which this reconstruction is derived) in the Crace Collection. The site is now occupied by Bond Court.

LOMBARD STREET

Lombard Street was named after the Lombard merchants who settled there in the 12th century, and who displaced the Jews as the principal bankers of London. For long afterwards Lombard Street was the centre of London banking. Here were the offices of the great Italian banking families of the Middle Ages, of Gresham, Vyner, Backwell, and other great merchants and goldsmith bankers of the 16th and 17th centuries, and of many of the great private banks which dominated London's financing trade in the 18th and 19th centuries. The prosperous brick houses in the view were those opposite St Mary Woolnoth Church, on the site now occupied by Lloyds Bank, as depicted in an early 19th-century watercolour by George Shepherd. Behind the house at the right, in a house in Pope's Head Alley, a group of marine underwriters established the New Lloyd's Coffee House in 1769. They did so in order to escape the poor reputation of the original Lloyd's Coffee House, on the other side of Lombard Street, whose patrons were extending their insurance business in the direction of gambling and speculation. The promulgation of rules for the conduct of insurance business at New Lloyd's Coffee House in 1771 marked

the start of the career of Lloyd's as London's prime insurance market. Lloyd's moved to ampler premises in the Royal Exchange in 1774. The old houses in Lombard Street were replaced during the 19th century by grander offices to accommodate the booming business and prestige of the banks.

Lombard Street: frontage of north side from Cardinal's Hat Alley to Pope's Head Alley

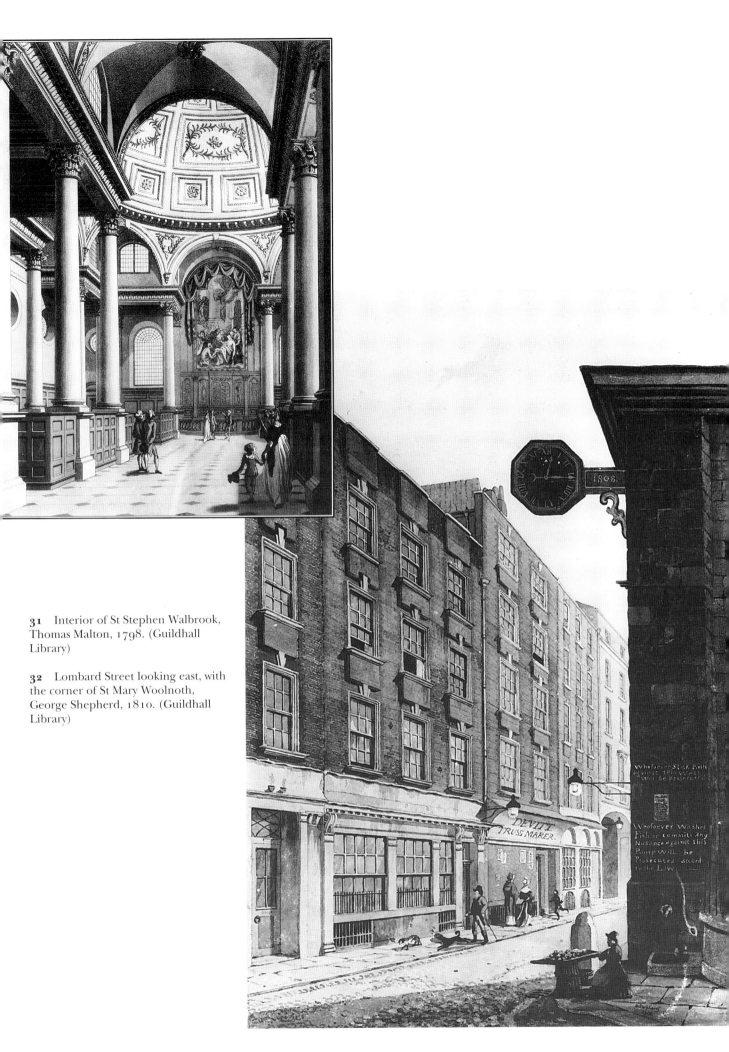

31 Interior of St Stephen Walbrook, Thomas Malton, 1798. (Guildhall Library)

32 Lombard Street looking east, with the corner of St Mary Woolnoth, George Shepherd, 1810. (Guildhall Library)

BACKWELL'S HOUSE, Lombard Street. The house of Alderman Edward Backwell, one of the greatest of the London goldsmith bankers, who financed Cromwell and Charles II, and who contributed substantially to the development of banknotes and the modern banking system, had a large house at the sign of the Unicorn, on the north side of Lombard Street opposite the entrance to Abchurch Lane. One of the best documented of the post-Fire property speculators, he amassed a large estate for redevelopment between Lombard Street and Cornhill. The appearance of the rebuilt Unicorn is however not recorded. Like many goldsmiths, he was bankrupted by the stoppage of the Exchequer in 1672, although the business recovered and was eventually absorbed into Williams & Glyn (now part of Royal Bank of Scotland).

ST EDMUND KING AND MARTYR WITH ST NICHOLAS ACONS

St Edmund King and Martyr:
Lombard Street frontage: first state

St Edmund King and Martyr: Lombard Street frontage

St Edmund's Church was first mentioned in the mid-12th century, although the dedication to the popular East Anglian saint suggests an earlier foundation. It was burnt in the Great Fire, and rebuilt in Portland stone on its original site, oriented towards the north, by Abraham Story and John Waters to the design of Wren and Hooke between 1670 and 1679. It consists of an aisleless nave and a short projecting chancel, which was originally surmounted by a semi-circular lantern, removed in the early 19th century – it was necessary to provide light on

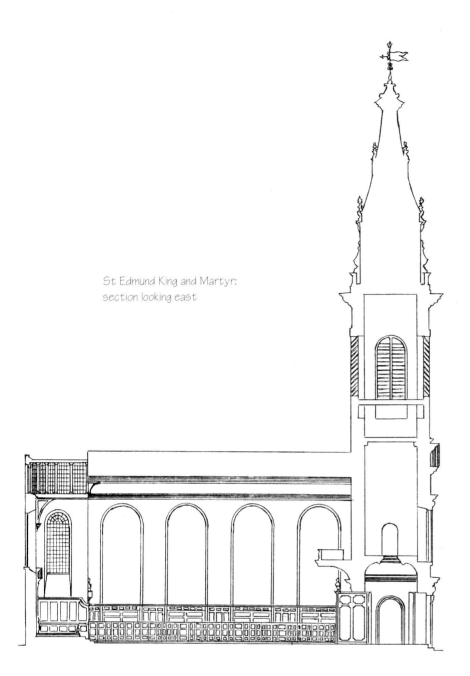

St Edmund King and Martyr:
section looking east

this cramped site. The grand frontage faces south onto Lombard Street, with its huge volutes flanking the tower; the volutes originally carried carved stone garlands, and the tower a short cupola (which is, however, not shown in Morgan's 1682 panorama). The garlands were removed and the present lead-covered concave-sided spire (perhaps by Hawksmoor) added in 1708; the pedestals on the spire originally carried flaming urns, which were removed in the early 20th century. The interior of the church retains most of its late 17th-century furnishings, and St Edmund's thus remains, in spite of the many structural alterations it has undergone, one of the most authentic of the City churches.

St Nicholas Acons was named after one Haakon, probably a Danish merchant. It was built in 1084 by Malmesbury Abbey on the west side of Nicholas Lane, where a garden between Lombard Street and King William Street used to mark the site of its churchyard.

ALL HALLOWS LOMBARD STREET

All Hallows' Church stood in its churchyard north-west of the junction of Gracechurch Street and Lombard Street, without a street frontage. It was indeed known as 'the church invisible' because it was so closely hemmed about by buildings. All Hallows' was first mentioned in the mid-11th century, and was anciently also called All Hallows Gracechurch – Gracechurch Street may have been named after either All Hallows' or St Benet's. According to Stow, the appellation derived from a nearby grass market;

All Hallows Lombard Street:
entrance to churchyard from Lombard Street

alternatively it may have referred to the fact that the early church was thatched. Burnt in the Great Fire, it was initially patched up, but later found to be too badly damaged and rebuilt by John Thompson in Portland stone to Wren's design from 1686 to 1694. Since the church was hidden from the street, the style was plain throughout. John Wesley preached his first extempore sermon (he had forgotten to bring his script) in the church in 1735. All Hallows' remained one of the best preserved of the Wren City churches until it was removed in 1939 to make way for the expansion of the headquarters of Barclays Bank. It was the last of the City churches to be 'moved' to the suburbs; the tower was re-erected at All Hallows' at Twickenham, and all of the superb furnishings by William Cleere and John Miller (including some from St Benet Gracechurch) are preserved in the new church there, along with the wooden Lombard Street entrance to the churchyard, carved with skulls, bones, hourglasses and other *mementi mori*.

The church of St Mary of the Nativity was said to have been named after Wulfnoth, a Saxon prince who was supposed to have founded it on the site of a Roman Temple of Concord. St Mary Woolnoth was first mentioned in 1273, and rebuilt in 1442. It was damaged by the Great Fire and repaired, perhaps to Wren's design but probably on the initiative of the parish, with substantial financial backing from Sir Robert Vyner, between 1670 and 1675, probably incorporating much of the medieval fabric, and retaining the original square tower. Little is known of its appearance – the north front had 'Tuscan windows', while the rest of the church was restored in 'modern Gothick' style; the reconstruction of the steeple in the view of the Stocks Market on page 99 is based on Morgan's 1682 panorama of London. The structure was however not sound, and St Mary Woolnoth was demolished in 1716, to be replaced by Hawksmoor's existing building, erected from 1716 to 1727 by Thomas Dunn, the most baroque of all the City churches with its dynamic contrasts between north, south and west fronts, its double tower, and its small but dramatic square interior. It and St Michael Cornhill's steeple were the only City churches to be rebuilt under the 1711 Fifty New Churches Act. St Mary Woolnoth cost £16,500, the most expensive of all the new City churches. With the completion of the church the 60-year campaign to make good the destruction wrought by the Great Fire of London was effectively concluded. The cutting of King William Street in the early 1830s exposed St Mary Woolnoth on an important corner site at the new Bank junction. The Victorians were indifferent or hostile to Hawksmoor's unconventional baroque architecture, and no less than six attempts were made to remove the church, each frustrated by its status as the Lord Mayor's parish church. Bank Station was built in its vaults in 1897, and the station entrance obscured its south front, but it continues to survive all vicissitudes as one of the finest of Hawksmoor's works.

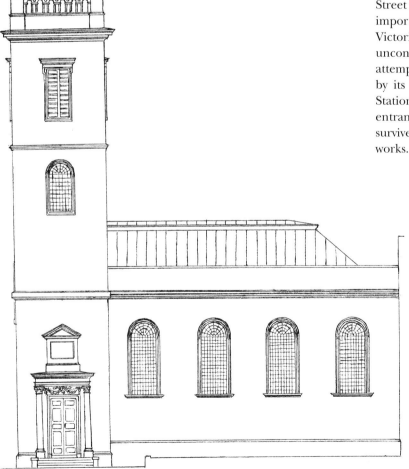

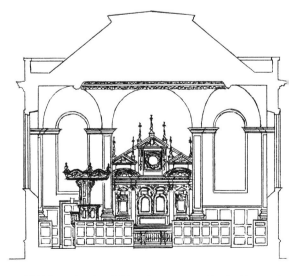

All Hallows Lombard Street: south (churchyard) frontage

All Hallows Lombard Street: cross-section looking east

St Mary Woolnoth: south (churchyard) frontage

St Mary Woolchurch Haw stood at the south-east corner of Walbrook and Lombard Street. It was first mentioned in the early 12th century, and named after a weighbeam, used for weighing dutiable wool, which stood in its churchyard until it was removed to the Custom House in 1383. The Stocks Market was expanded to cover the site of the church after the Great Fire, and it is now covered by the Mansion House.

VYNER'S HOUSE

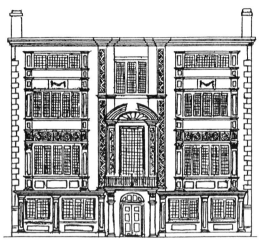

Sir Robert Vyner's House: Lombard Street frontage

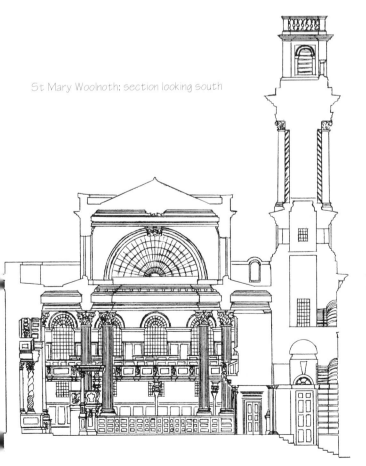

St Mary Woolnoth: section looking south

Sir Robert Vyner's House: frontage of south side of courtyard

Sir Robert Vyner, goldsmith banker, maker of the new royal regalia after the Restoration, financier to Charles II until the stoppage of the Exchequer in 1672 bankrupted him, and Lord Mayor in 1674, built a large house for himself next to St Mary Woolnoth immediately after the Great Fire. It had one of the most elaborately decorated frontages of the new City merchants' houses, and a long courtyard behind. Vyner entertained the King there several times. The General Post Office moved into the house in 1678 and remained there until it transferred to its new St Martins le Grand headquarters in 1819; a branch post office remains on part of the old site. (See plate 33, p.111.)

POPE'S HOUSE

No.1 Plough Court, tucked away behind the corner of Lombard Street and Gracechurch Street, was a modest brick house rebuilt in the aftermath of the Great Fire. Its appearance was recorded in the 19th century because it was the birthplace in 1688 of Alexander Pope, the son of a linen draper. It later became the Plough Court Pharmacy, which subsequently expanded to become Allen & Hanbury, chemists. The house was demolished in the late 19th century.

QUAKERS' MEETING HOUSE, White Hart Yard, Gracechurch Street. The first Quaker meeting house in London, which stood in a courtyard off the west side of Gracechurch Street, just south of the Lombard Street junction. William Penn and George Fox talked there, and the latter was arrested there in 1670.

Pope's House
(no.1 Plough Court)

ST BENET GRACECHURCH WITH ST LEONARD EASTCHEAP

St Benet's Church stood on the south-east corner of Gracechurch Street and Fenchurch Street, its corner steeple dominating street views both up and down the main thoroughfare north from Old London Bridge. St Benet's was first mentioned in 1181, and according to Stow was named after a nearby grass market; other possible derivations of the name are grass growing around the church, or from its roof's being covered with grass turves. It was burnt in the Great Fire, and was rebuilt by Thomas Wise to Wren's design from 1681 to 1687. It was a small, single-aisled church, which was given distinction by its lofty interior, its elaborately decorated plaster barrel vault by John Grove and Henry Doogood, the grand Portland stone north frontage which befitted its important site, with two tiers of windows as at St Michael Queenhithe, and sumptuous furnishings by William Cleere, including an elaborate reredos and an east wall painted to resemble gold and crimson curtains. The prominent lead-covered steeple was a variant on the common theme of a spire resting on a dome; in this case

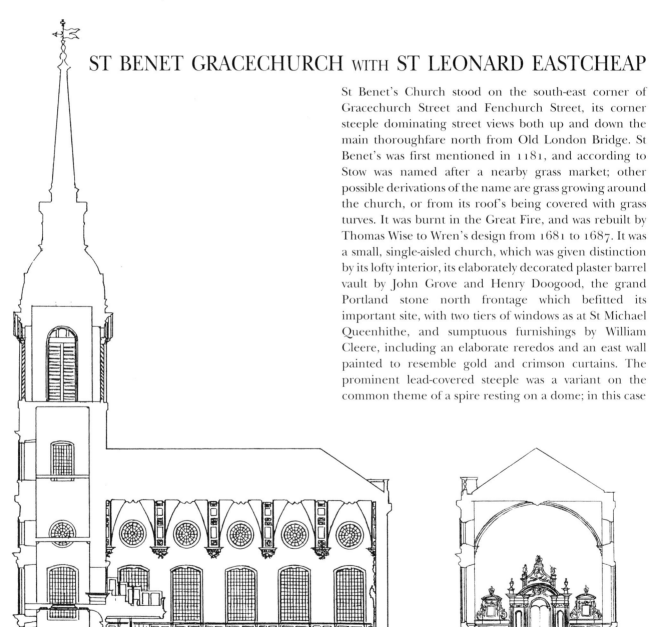

St Benet Gracechurch: cross-section looking north

St Benet Gracechurch: cross-section looking east

St Benet Gracechurch:
Fenchurch Street frontage

the dome was octagonal, whereas the spire was square in plan, a reversal of the usual geometrical progression of the City churches' baroque steeples. The church was closed in 1864 under the Union of City Benefices Act of 1860, and demolished in 1867; it was thus the fifth of Wren's City churches to disappear, and the first as a result of the new legislation to reduce the number of churches in the City. St Benet's Church in Mile End Road was built with the proceeds of sale. Some of the furnishings are now at St Olave Hart Street and at All Hallows Twickenham. *(See plate 34, p.111.)*

St Leonard Eastcheap was also called St Leonard Milkchurch (probably after William Melker, a late 13th-century benefactor). It was first mentioned in 1180, and stood on the south-east corner of Eastcheap and Fish Street Hill, its site now taken into the street opposite the entrance to Monument Underground Station.

ST DIONIS BACKCHURCH

St Dionis's Church was situated on the west side of Lime Street, just north of Fenchurch Street. The name may derive from its location, set back from the street (the nearby St Gabriel Fenchurch, which stood until 1666 in the middle of Fenchurch Street, was also called St Gabriel Forechurch), or alternatively from an early benefactor; Dionis was a corruption of St Denys. The church was first mentioned about 1100. It was burnt in the Great Fire, and rebuilt in Portland stone by John Thompson to Wren's design between 1670 and 1677, with nave and aisles, a fine pedimented east front facing Lime Street, superb fittings, and a plain west tower with lantern, completed in 1685. The church was built on the foundations of its irregular predecessor, resulting in none of its walls meeting each

St Dionis Backchurch: cross-section looking east

other at right angles. Uniquely among the City churches, there was a proposal in 1857 for a Victorian gothic rebuilding, to a design by G.E. Street. St Dionis was demolished in 1878 under the Union of City Benefices Act, and the proceeds of sale used to build St Dionis Parsons Green, where some of the original furnishings survive; the monuments are now at All Hallows Twickenham.

St Dionis Backchurch: Fenchurch Street frontage

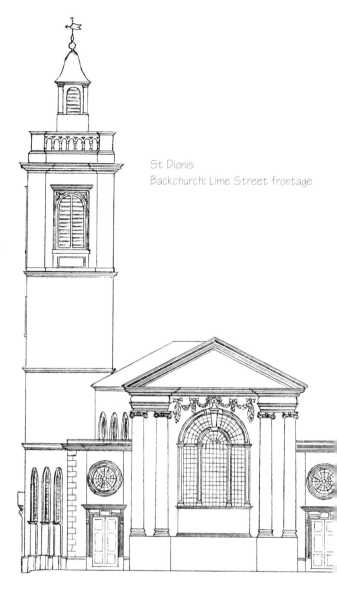

St Dionis Backchurch: Lime Street frontage

PEWTERERS' HALL

The Pewterers' Company built its first hall on the north side of Lime Street in the late 15th century. Burnt in 1666, it was rebuilt by John Wildgos between 1668 and 1670. The illustration shows the houses which fronted the street, with the characteristic elaborate entrance to the courtyard, where the Hall itself stood – parts of it survived until their demolition in 1932. Pewterers' Hall was particularly noted for its fine decorative plaster ceilings, of which the most spectacular, in the Parlour, has been incorporated in replica in the reinstatement of that room at the Geffrye Museum in Shoreditch. After the Second World War the Company moved to a new Hall in Oat Lane, Aldersgate, which also retains some 17th-century panelling. The Company was in existence by the mid-14th century; it controlled the pewter trade until its influence declined in the 17th century.

Pewterers' Hall: Lime Street frontage

33   Courtyard of Sir Robert Vyner's house, Sutton Nicholls, 1720. (British Museum)

34   St Benet Gracechurch, looking down Gracechurch Street towards the Monument and the steeple of St Magnus the Martyr to the right, George Shepherd, 1811. (Guildhall Library)

TOWER STREET

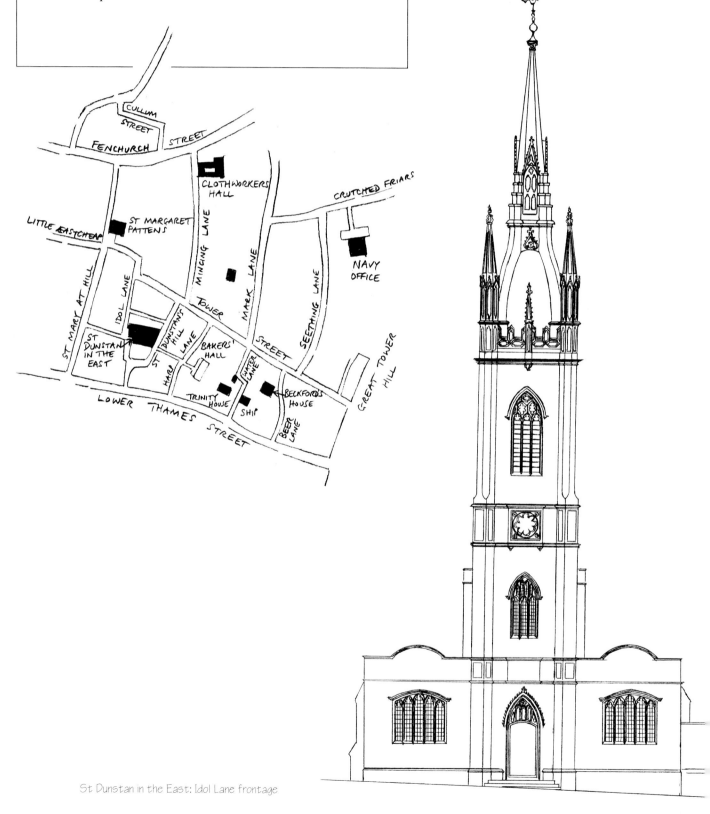

BEHIND THE MAIN PART of the City's riverfront port, narrow lanes climbed past merchants' houses and warehouses and taverns to Tower Street, the main artery eastwards out of Eastcheap.

St Dunstan in the East: Idol Lane frontage

St Dunstan's Church, dedicated to the 10th-century archbishop of Canterbury, was first mentioned in about 1100. It was rebuilt in the 13th century, and a south aisle was added in 1381-2 to the design of Henry Yevele, one of the greatest of the medieval English architects. St Dunstan's steeple was one of the loftiest in London, and a prominent landmark. The church was gutted by the Great Fire, but the outer walls (including those of Yevele's aisle) were sufficiently sound to be retained in the rebuilding of 1668-71 (unlikely to have been Wren's) which was funded by a gift of £4,000 by Lady Dyonis Williamson. The interior, however, was rebuilt with Corinthian arcades supporting a clerestory with primitive Venetian windows, and the overall effect must therefore have been similar to the juxtaposition of classical and gothic in the extant St Sepulchre Newgate Street. The church was restored from 1695 to 1702, and the steeple was replaced from the ground in Portland stone between 1695 and 1701 by Ephraim Beauchamp to Wren's design (tradition held that his daughter also had a hand in it; it is also possible that it was an early work of Hawksmoor). It is 'modern Gothick' in style, the tower with its four pinnacles carrying a steeple whose four flying buttresses support a tall needle spire – although in a gothic style, and inspired no doubt by the similar but squatter early 16th-century steeple of St Mary le Bow, it retains baroque undertones in the sinuous lines of the buttresses and the transparency both beneath the buttresses and through the lucarnes. The views are attempts at a reconstruction of the 17th-century church, based on 18th-century prints. The fabric of the body of the church itself had deteriorated markedly by the early 19th century, and it was rebuilt in a Perpendicular gothic style to the design of David Laing in 1817. This was gutted by bombing in the Second World War, and all that remains today is the aisle walls and Wren's steeple, still an important element in the view of the City from the River.

St Dunstan in the East:
south (churchyard) frontage

ST MARGARET PATTENS with ST GABRIEL FENCHURCH

The church of St Margaret Pattens was first mentioned in the mid-12th century. According to Stow it was named after pattenmakers who lived nearby; alternatively Patin may have been the name of a founder or benefactor. The church was burnt in the Great Fire and rebuilt by Samuel Fulkes to Wren's designs between 1684 and 1689, incorporating some surviving medieval walls. It is faced in Portland stone, with a wide nave and north aisle containing a gallery; many of the original furnishings are still there. The steeple was added from 1698 to 1702. At 200 feet it is the third tallest of the City church steeples, with a tall lead-covered spire which still forms a prominent feature in the view of the City from the River. The urns with which it was adorned were later removed.

St Gabriel Fenchurch was first mentioned in the early 12th century – throughout the Middle Ages it was dedicated to St Mary or All Hallows, and became St Gabriel's only in the 16th century. It stood in the middle of Fenchurch Street (which was named after it; the name itself may refer to a nearby grass market) midway between its junctions with Rood Lane and Cullum Street.

St Margaret Pattens:
Rood Lane frontage

BAKERS' HALL, Harp Lane. The Bakers' Company rebuilt their Hall by 1676. It was burnt again and rebuilt in 1715, then destroyed by bombing in 1940 (the appearance of the early 18th-century hall is known, but not its post-Fire predecessor's). A new Bakers' Hall, part of a new office block, continues on a site slightly further east. A guild of bakers existed by the mid-12th century. The white bakers were chartered as a company in 1486, and a further charter of 1569 incorporated the brown bakers. The company controlled the bread trade via the Assize of Bread until 1804 – the Assize determined the weight of a penny loaf, which varied according to meal prices.

TRINITY HOUSE

The Fraternity of Trinity House in Deptford Strond was chartered in 1514. It developed from the Deptford Guild of Mariners, one of several seamen's guilds around the English coast. The fraternity was responsible for defence and pilotage of the Thames and Deptford Dockyard. The fraternity became a corporation in 1547, and in 1566 Parliament authorised it to set up buoys and levy dues on shipping all around the English coast. In 1593 its revenues were boosted with the acquisition of rights of ballastage (dredging navigation channels and selling the spoil as ship's ballast), beaconage, and buoyage on the Thames. During the 17th century its functions expanded to

Trinity House:
Water Lane entrance

Ship Tavern: Water Lane frontage

SHIP TAVERN

The Ship was rebuilt plainly in brick after the Great Fire, except for its richly decorated doorway with splendidly carved sign of a ship in full sail in the hood. The tavern was patronised by Essex farmers and corn factors, and it was there in 1747 that they decided to formalise their trading arrangements by establishing a Corn Exchange (opened in Mark Lane in 1749). The Ship was demolished in the 19th century; its site is now covered by the extension of Byward Street down to Lower Thames Street. *(See plate 35, p.116.)*

BECKFORD'S HOUSE

No.34 Great Tower Street was a large brick merchant's house, incorporating a warehouse in its basement, which stood in Beckford Court, set back behind the street on its south side. It was built in about 1670 and was later probably the house of William Beckford, Lord Mayor in 1762 and 1769, M.P. for the City from 1754 to 1768, controversial supporter of John Wilkes in opposition to King George III, and father of the eccentric Gothick novelist and builder William Beckford. By the early 20th century the house was the best-preserved late 17th-century merchant's house remaining in the City, retaining its original interiors with fine panelling and staircases. It was destroyed by bombing in the Second World War, and the site now lies under the extension of Byward Street down to Lower Thames Street. *(See plate 36, p.116.)*

Beckford's House (no.34 Great Tower Street):
Beckford Court frontage

MARK LANE

This was one of the most palatial of the City merchants' houses whose appearance is known, its Corinthian pilastered frontage, built of brick with stone dressings, and its elaborately carved wooden doorcase, giving it a grandeur which belied its size. Standing in a courtyard off the west side of Mark Lane, on the very boundary of the area destroyed by the Great Fire, it was built in the late 17th or early 18th century. In the early 19th century Shepherd called it the Old Spanish Ambassador's House. It was one of the last survivors of the grand City merchants' mansions, finally destroyed in the Blitz. The stately and elaborately carved wooden pedimented entrance to its courtyard from Mark Lane was removed in the 1920s, and is now preserved in the Victoria & Albert Museum.

include licensing Thames pilots, providing lighthouses, raising wrecks, and suppressing piracy. Trinity House acquired a headquarters in the City, in Water Lane, Great Tower Street, in 1660. Burnt in the Fire, it was rebuilt by 1670 in brick and stone, adorned with busts. Its detailed appearance is not known because it burned down again in 1714; the view shows the frontage of the entrance gate in Water Lane. Through the later 17th, 18th, and 19th centuries Trinity House continued to accumulate responsibilities, including the testing in navigation of boys of Christ's Hospital Mathematical School, the provision of lightships, and a monopoly of lighthouses (acquired in 1836). The Corporation moved to its current premises on Tower Hill in 1796; Old Trinity House was replaced by warehouses in the mid-19th century, and the post-war extension of Byward Street crosses its site.

No.33 Mark Lane (Old Spanish Ambassador's House): courtyard (east) frontage

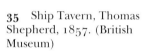

35 Ship Tavern, Thomas Shepherd, 1857. (British Museum)

36 Beckford's house, photograph. (Guildhall Library)

CLOTHWORKERS' HALL

The Clothworkers' Company was formed in 1528 by the merger of the Fullers (who fulled, tentered, and teazelled woollen cloth) and the Shearmen (who sheared or set it – the finishing process); both companies had originated in the 14th century with the development of a native clothworking industry (England had previously exported raw wool to Flanders). The new company occupied the former Shearmen's Hall, which was in Mincing Lane in the 1470s. The Hall was rebuilt twice before its destruction in the Great Fire, after which a new Hall was completed in 1668; it was brick-built on a modest scale, but an element of grandeur was provided by the Corinthian columns on the exterior of the livery hall, the interior of which had fine plasterwork and wood carving. Clothworkers' Hall was replaced by a much grander classical building in the late 1850s; this was destroyed by bombing in 1941, and the site is now occupied by the latest Clothworkers' Hall, built in the late 1950s.

Clothworkers' Hall: Mincing Lane frontage

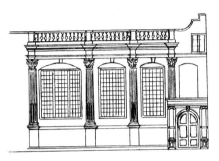

Clothworkers' Hall: east frontage of court (livery hall)

NAVY OFFICE

Henry VIII established the Navy Board in 1546, under the jurisdiction of the Lord High Admiral, to provide for the efficient administration of his reformed Royal Navy; it managed the royal dockyards, and the building and servicing of ships. A new office was built on the site of Sir John Allen's mansion (itself on the site of the garden of the Friary of the Holy Cross, Crutched Friars) in 1654; with its need for proximity to the docks it was one of the very few offices of national government located in the City. Accommodation for officers was incorporated, and it was from his roof in this complex that Samuel Pepys (who was Clerk of the Acts of the Navy from 1660 to 1673, and Secretary of the Navy from 1673 to 1679) observed the start of the Great Fire in Pudding Lane in the early morning of 2 September 1666. The Navy Office survived the Great Fire, but succumbed to its own little fire in 1673. It was rebuilt to Wren's or Hooke's design by 1683, with a pedimented central office block surmounted by a tall weathervane, flanked east and west by blocks of accommodation for officers. Nelson's uncle, Captain Maurice Suckling, lived there as Comptroller of the Navy, and Nelson stayed with him in 1777 when he was taking his lieutenancy examination. The buildings were demolished in 1778 when the Navy Office moved to Somerset House (and thence later to Spring Gardens, Whitehall); the East India Company built a large complex of warehouses on the site, which is now covered by the north-west corner of the old Port of London Authority Building (now the headquarters of the insurance brokers Willis Corroon), at the corner of Pepys Street and Seething Gardens.

Navy Office:
north (courtyard) frontage

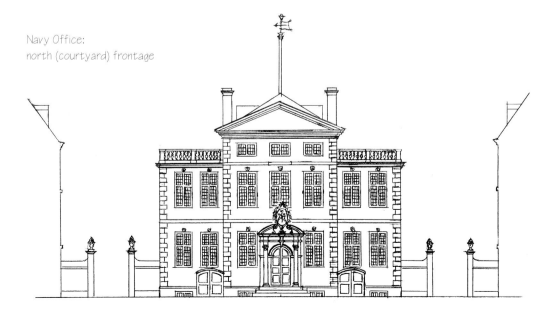

EASTCHEAP AND CANNON STREET

T HE FIRST PART of London to be burned, this was one of the chief hubs of communication on the south side of the City, where one of the main west-east routes crossed Fish Street Hill, the principal north-south street that plunged downhill past the Monument to the Great Fire and out over London's only bridge across the Thames.

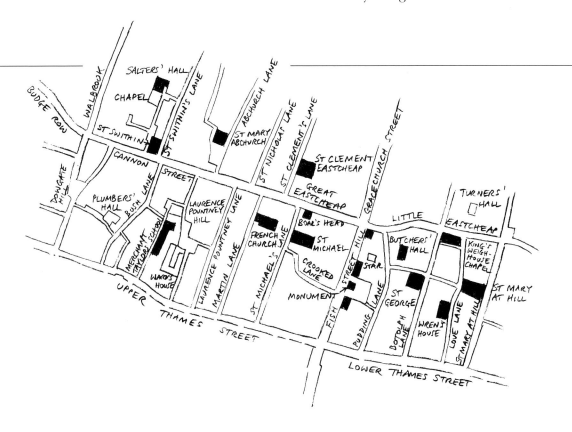

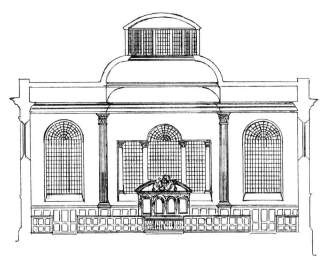

St Mary at Hill: cross-section looking east

ST MARY AT HILL WITH ST ANDREW HUBBARD

St Mary at Hill Church stands on the west side of the lane which bears the same name, on the steep hill leading down from Eastcheap to Lower Thames Street. According to Stow it was the steepness of this hill which prompted the appellation 'at Hill'. St Mary's stands in what was the earliest part of the City to be resettled in the ninth century, but the church itself was first mentioned in about 1177. It was damaged in the Great Fire, but substantial parts of the medieval fabric were able to be reused in Joshua Marshall's rebuilding, to Wren's design, of 1670 to 1674. Of the late 17th-century church only the stone east front (later rendered over – originally it was adorned with carved festoons) with its three arched windows and the general appearance and arrangement survive (the plan is classic example of Wren's baroque economy – a cross inside a square, with a central dome). Crace's section shows however that the shallow dome with its broad shallow lantern differed markedly from what is there now. The medieval west tower (on which Wren placed a lantern in 1695 which, though small, deployed a virtuoso succession of convex and concave curves) was replaced by a plain brick tower in 1787. There was substantial rebuilding of parts of the church in 1826 (replacing the surviving Gothic windows in the north and south walls with new windows in the Wren style), and the interior had to be restored, in a style which was remarkably faithful to the 17th-century original, after a fire in 1848. Nor were the church's vicissitudes over then, and another extensive and faithful rebuilding had to be undertaken after a fire in 1988. The result is a unique palimpsest among City churches – much of the medieval walls survives beneath the rendering and plaster, and St Mary at Hill is the only one of Wren's City churches where parts of the church itself survive (more or less) but the steeple does not.

St Andrew Hubbard was first mentioned in 1108, and probably named after an early benefactor. It stood on the south side of Eastcheap, between Love Lane and Botolph Lane. The King's Weighhouse, later rebuilt as the King's Weighhouse Chapel, was built on its site.

KING'S WEIGHHOUSE CHAPEL

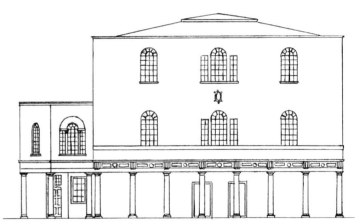

King's Weighhouse Chapel: Little Eastcheap frontage

The King's Weighhouse was situated in Cornhill until its destruction in the Great Fire. It was afterwards rebuilt in Little Eastcheap on the site of the church of St Andrew Hubbard. By this time the Weighhouse was, however, falling into desuetude. It housed the King's Weights and the Great Beam, which were used for weighing the merchandise of foreign merchants. From the late Middle Ages the Weighhouse was administered for the Crown by the Grocers' Company. The King's Weighhouse Chapel was established in the Weighhouse in the late 17th century by a Presbyterian congregation. They rebuilt the Chapel in 1694 with an arcaded ground floor towards Little Eastcheap. The Chapel was demolished for street widening in 1834, and a new Weighhouse Chapel was built in Fish Street Hill; the congregation now has a chapel in Duke Street, Mayfair. The site of the original chapel lies under Eastcheap between Botolph Lane and Lovat Lane.

St Mary at Hill: St Mary at Hill frontage

WREN'S HOUSE

No.32 Botolph Lane was a fine late-surviving example of the merchants' houses of the 'greatest bigness'. It was built of brick, with a pedimented Portland stone centrepiece, shortly after the Great Fire, with a substantial frontage overlooking a court which opened off the eastern side of Botolph Lane near its southern end. It contained fine interiors, including one room whose panelling, plaster ceiling, and Chinoiserie paintings of 1696 by Robert Robinson, are now at the Sir John Cass School in Aldgate. There was a tradition, almost certainly unfounded, that Wren lived in the house, hence its name. It was demolished in 1906.

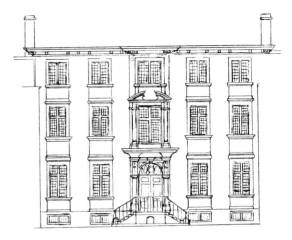

Wren's House, Botolph Lane: courtyard frontage

ST GEORGE BOTOLPH LANE WITH ST BOTOLPH BILLINGSGATE

St George Botolph Lane: Botolph Lane frontage

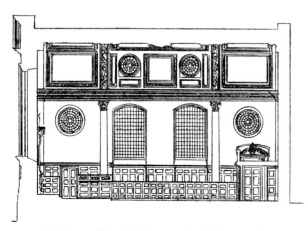

St George Botolph Lane: section looking south

The church of St George stood on the west side of Botolph Lane, where Farynor House (named after Thomas Farynor, the King's baker in whose house, close by in Pudding Lane, the Great Fire of London began) now stands. Botolph Lane was part of the very first resettlement of the old Roman city of London in the ninth century; the first mentions of St George's Church date from the 12th century. Burnt in the Great Fire, the church was rebuilt by Nicholas Young to the designs of Wren between 1671 and 1679, reportedly incorporating rubble from Old St Paul's, but with Portland stone facings. The view shows the east front, pedimented to exploit the oblique views along Botolph Lane, with the north-west tower behind facing onto St George's Lane. The interior of the church was a subtle baroque superposition of a centralised Greek-cross plan and a longitudinal barrel-vaulted nave, supported on four Composite columns. When the church was demolished in 1906 some of the furnishings went to the nearby church of St Mary at Hill and to St George's Church in Southall, Middlesex, which was built with the proceeds of sale of the site.

St Botolph Billingsgate was probably founded in the late 11th century, and first mentioned in the mid-12th. It stood on the south side of Lower Thames Street, opposite the entrance to Botolph Lane.

37   Wren's house, Philip Norman, *c.*1900. (Museum of London)

38   St Michael Crooked Lane and the Monument, George Scharf, 1830. (Guildhall Library)

BUTCHERS' HALL

Butchers' Hall: Pudding Lane entrance

Before the Great Fire the Butchers' Company had its Hall in Butcher Hall Lane (now King Edward Street) close to the Shambles of Newgate Street. After its destruction the Butchers built a new Hall between 1667 and 1677 on the site of their old Scalding House (where Eastcheap butchers scalded carcasses in order to remove their hides) on the east side of Pudding Lane, between St George's Lane and Eastcheap. The view shows the entrance from Pudding Lane into its courtyard. ('Pudding' was the butchers' offal which in the later Middle Ages was carted along Pudding Lane from the butchers' stalls in Eastcheap for disposal in the Thames.) Butchers' Hall was burnt and rebuilt in 1830, and finally demolished in 1882 for the construction of the District and Circle Underground lines; the Butchers built a new Hall in Bartholomew Close in West Smithfield. Stow mentioned the existence of a Butchers' Hall in 975, and an adulterine guild of butchers was in existence by 1179; the guild received ordinances in 1331, but was not chartered as a company until 1605. It controlled the slaughter and sale of meat in the City, and retains a close connection with Smithfield Market.

TURNERS' HALL, Philpot Lane, Eastcheap. This small company hall stood in a courtyard between Philpot Lane and Rood Lane. It was rebuilt in 1670, and the Turners moved out to College Hill in 1737. The Company, which obtained ordinances in 1478 and a charter in 1604, controlled the trade in turned wood, furniture, and later machine tools.

PUDDING LANE, Billingsgate. Pudding Lane is part of the grid of lanes which marks the original Alfredian *burh* at the north end of London Bridge. It was made forever notorious when the Great Fire started in Thomas Farynor's house on the east side (where Monument Street now runs down to Lower Thames Street) in 1666. The lane's name (which in fact referred to butchers' offal, not pudding in the modern sense) did not help, especially when coupled with the myth that the Great Fire was finally put out at Pie Corner (now the north corner of Giltspur Street and Cock Lane, West Smithfield); the 'golden boy', a late 17th-century statue which still stands at Pie Corner, explicitly made the connection between the Fire and Londoners' 'sin of gluttony' (Pie Corner was in fact named after the Pie Inn, whose sign was a magpie). Pudding Lane was plainly rebuilt after the Fire, and its appearance is not known. Its distinguishing feature was the inscribed stone where Farynor's house had stood, put there by Lord Mayor Patience Ward after the foiling of the Popish Plot in 1681; it reiterated the myth that the Fire was the work of French Catholic agents (even though Hubert, who was hanged after he confessed to firing London, was in fact a Huguenot). Removed by James II, the stone was reinstated after the Glorious Revolution, and finally taken down in the middle of the 18th century; it is now in the Museum of London.

Fish Street Hill: frontage of east side, on either side of Monument Yard; No.48 Fish Street Hill is on the far left

FISH STREET HILL

Fish Street Hill led down to old London Bridge from Eastcheap, and was commonly called Bridge Street until about 1500. From the late 13th century it came increasingly to be known as Fish Street or New Fish Street, after the fish market which was held there and which gradually took over the role of London's main fish market from Old Fish Street (above Queenhithe to the west) as the Middle Ages progressed. The market's growth reflected that of Billingsgate as the main landing place for fish, and the surrounding area was inhabited by many notable fishmongers; nearby the powerful Fishmongers' Company had its main Hall. Pudding Lane runs a short distance to the east of Fish Street Hill, which was therefore one of the first streets to be burned in the Great Fire. On its east side stood the church of St Margaret Fish Street Hill, the first City church to be burned down. It was not rebuilt, and on its site the City erected the Monument to the Great Fire, which with the steeple of St Magnus's church at the bottom of the hill dominated views southwards along Gracechurch Street and northwards from London Bridge. The view of Fish Street Hill shows how the Monument, now dwarfed by surrounding office blocks, dominated its original domestic context, with Cibber's sculpted panel of Charles II relieving the stricken City on the west side of its pedestal almost as big as the houses.

MONUMENT

The Monument, a giant fluted Doric column (at 202 feet the tallest free-standing column anywhere), surmounted by Robert Bird's gilt bronze flaming urn (Wren wanted to put a statue of Charles II there), was built of Portland stone by Joshua Marshall to the design of Wren and Hooke between 1671 and 1677. It commemorates the Great Fire with inscriptions and sculpted relief panels by Caius Gabriel Cibber around its base; one early proposal for the Monument, illustrated here, even had bronze flames leaping from the sides of the column itself, with a phoenix on top.

STAR INN, Fish Street Hill. The Star stood between Fish Street Hill and Pudding Lane, just north of London Bridge (its street entrance is shown to the left of Monument Yard in the view of Fish Street Hill). The ignition of the hay stored in its yard was a critical stage by which Farynor's house fire got out of control in 1666. The Star was subsequently rebuilt with galleried ranges around its yard, and coaches ran from it to Kent in the 17th and 18th centuries.

BOAR'S HEAD TAVERN

Boar's Head Tavern: Great Eastcheap frontage

The Boar's Head was the most famous of the Eastcheap taverns of the late Middle Ages, immortalised as Mistress Quickly's establishment, which was patronised by Sir John Falstaff and his cronies in Shakespeare's history plays. It was burnt in the Great Fire, and rebuilt in brick in 1668, with a new stone sign which is now in the Museum of London. Maitland recorded that there was also a sign which read 'This is the chief tavern of London'. During the 18th and early 19th centuries commemorative Shakespeare dinners were held there. The building ceased to be a tavern in the early 19th century and was rebuilt as tenements, before all disappeared in 1831 with the construction of King William Street, the approach to the new London Bridge. The site of the Boar's Head is under the street just opposite the entrance to Monument Underground Station on the corner of Cannon Street and King William Street.

Monument: unrealised design

ST MICHAEL CROOKED LANE

The church of St Michael stood on the east side of Crooked Lane, and was demolished in 1831 to make way for the approach to the new London Bridge, the second, and one of the best, of Wren's churches to be destroyed. It was first mentioned in the early 13th century, and extended twice by fishmonger mayors, in the 1360s by John Lovekyn, and in the 1380s by William Walworth, who made it collegiate. Burnt in 1666, it was rebuilt in Portland stone by William Hammond to Wren's designs between 1684 and 1687, with the tower completed in 1698 by John Clarke (with pyramidal pinnacles), and the steeple added by Edward Strong from 1709 to 1714. St Michael's was typical in that the body of the church itself was quite plain, with a simple rectangular nave, but the steeple, with its prominent position close to the river and London Bridge, was brilliantly elaborate, one of the very finest of Wren's genre of tiered spires (Hawksmoor may have had some input). Constructed of lead-covered wood, it had a core of diminishing cylindrical stages, surrounded at each of three levels by complex and ever-changing corner buttresses, volutes and urns, the whole structure developing a sophisticated baroque convex-concave movement in all dimensions (which cannot be fully conveyed in two), supplemented by the transparency of the pierced buttresses in the bottom stage, and the sinuous curvature of the onion-shaped spirelet which surmounted it. It was seen to particularly good effect looking up Crooked Lane (as in Shepherd's drawing and engraving) and from the River and London Bridge, and was recorded in detail by George Scharf just before it was pulled down. The site lies under the pavement on the west side of King William Street, between Eastcheap and Arthur Street. *(See plate 38, p.121.)*

St Michael Crooked Lane: Crooked Lane frontage

French Church (St Martin Orgar): Martin Lane frontage of tower

FRENCH CHURCH (ST MARTIN ORGAR)

St Martin's Church was first mentioned in the 12th century when Orgar the Deacon granted it to the Canons of St Paul's. It was also called St Martin Morgan. The church was burnt in the Great Fire, and not rebuilt by the parish. The ruins of the west tower and nave were instead granted to a French Huguenot congregation, who patched them up and continued to use the church until it was demolished in 1820. The view is a reconstruction based on 19th-century prints. The site is now occupied by the rectory of St Clement Eastcheap, built in 1851, whose Italianate tower retains the projecting clock of its predecessor.

ST CLEMENT EASTCHEAP WITH ST MARTIN ORGAR

St Clement's Church was mentioned in the 12th century and possibly in the 11th. It was burnt in the Great Fire, and rebuilt in brick (now rendered over) by Edward Strong to Wren's design from 1683 to 1687. It is a relatively plain church consisting of a rectangular nave with tapering aisle and simple south-west tower. Many of Jonathan Maine's furnishings survived Butterfield's restoration in 1872, although the reredos had to be put back together again by Sir Ninian Comper in 1933. The view shows the original box pews and south aisle gallery.

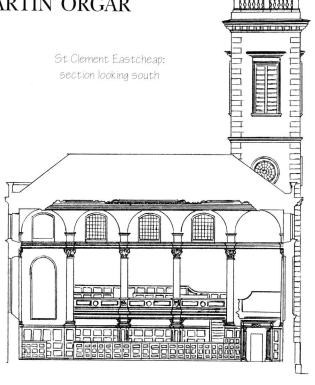

St Clement Eastcheap: section looking south

ST MARY ABCHURCH WITH ST LAURENCE POUNTNEY

The church of St Mary Abchurch was mentioned in the late 12th century. It was anciently also called St Mary Upchurch; the name could have arisen either from its position on rising ground above the river, or from the name of a founder or benefactor. A medieval crypt remains, but the church was completely rebuilt in brick between 1681 and 1686 by Christopher Kempster to the design of Wren or Hooke after its destruction in the Great Fire. It is one of the very finest of the surviving City churches, and certainly the best post-War restoration, having suffered severe bomb

St Mary Abchurch: unrealised design for Abchurch Lane frontage, with steeple as built

damage. The view shows an imaginary composite, juxtaposing the existing steeple (whose lead-covered spire consists of a lantern and spire resting on an ogee dome, a whimsical variant on the type of St Benet Gracechurch or St Peter Cornhill) with an early design by Hooke for a larger church which would have had an octagonal domed centre surrounded on three sides by aisles. The final design has a dome (painted by William Snow in 1708 with the Worship of Heaven) covering almost all of the space. The furnishings are of the highest quality and almost complete – only the box pews are wanting. Pride of place is taken by the reredos, the only documented work by Grinling Gibbons in any of the City churches; it took five years to put back together again after it was smashed to pieces in the Blitz. Also spectacular are William Grey's pulpit and sounding board, and the doorcases and other furnishings by William Emmett. The west gallery, tucked away in an aisle, was formerly used by the boys of Merchant Taylors' School, for whom the church functioned as a school chapel.

St Laurence Pountney existed by the mid-12th century. It was originally called St Laurence next the Thames, St Laurence Candlewick Street, or St Laurence London Stone, and was renamed after Sir John de Poulteney, Mayor four times in the 1330s, who rebuilt it as a collegiate church from about 1334. The spire was one of the tallest in the medieval City, a prominent landmark when viewed from the River. Flemish weavers traded in the churchyard from the late 14th century. The site of the church and its churchyard survive as gardens in Laurence Pountney Hill – dramatic demonstrations of how interments raised the ground.

ST SWITHIN CANNON STREET WITH ST MARY BOTHAW

St Swithin's Church stood on the north side of Cannon Street, between St Swithin's Lane and Salters Hall Court, on the site now occupied by No.111 Cannon Street. Dedicated to the Winchester saint, it was first mentioned in the late 12th century, and was called St Swithin London Stone from its proximity to London Stone, a lump of Clipsham limestone which may date from Roman times, but was standing in the Middle of Cannon Street by about 1100, had a symbolic importance as the 'centre of the City' (Jack Cade struck it with his sword during his 1450 rebellion to mark his capture of the London), and which remains in the same position as when it was built into the south wall of St Swithin's in 1798. The church was destroyed in the Great Fire, and rebuilt (incorporating stones from the nearby church of St Mary Bothaw) to Wren's design by Joshua Marshall and Samuel Fulkes between 1677 and 1683, exploiting the small site with an octagonally domed square interior; the dome itself had superb plaster festoons by John Grove and Henry Doogood. The Portland stone south and east frontages were richly decorated with carved stone festoons. Beyond the church, at the north-west corner, rose the steeple, added in 1686, a variant (as at St Antholin's) on the theme of transition from square tower to octagonal spire – at St

St Swithin Cannon Street: Cannon Street frontage

St Swithin Cannon Street: Cannon Street and St Swithin's Lane frontages (diagonal view)

Swithin's this was achieved by a concave cutting-away of the top corners of the tower, so that the main cornice at its top was itself octagonal; the spire was lead-covered. St Swithin's was gutted by bombs in 1941, and the surviving ruins were cleared for redevelopment in 1962.

St Mary Bothaw was first mentioned in the mid-12th century. It may have been named after a nearby boatyard. The site is the forecourt of Cannon Street Station.

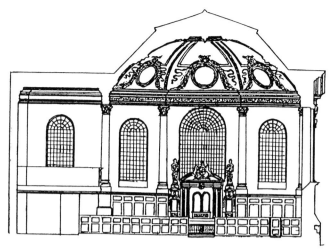

St Swithin Cannon Street: cross-section looking east

SALTERS' HALL

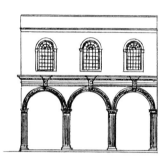

Salters' Hall: Salters' Hall court frontage

The Salters' Company moved from Bread Street (where they had first acquired their Hall in 1454) to Oxford House, which had previously been the town house of the Earl of Oxford, in 1641. It was burnt in 1666, rebuilt in 1668 by John Wildgos, and extended in 1695. The main features were the three-bay loggia on the east side and the large garden where, in the days when the property was owned by the Abbots of the Sussex priory of Tortington, Henry VII's unpopular ministers Empson and Dudley, whose houses adjoined, met to discuss policy. Salters' Hall was rebuilt in a splendid Grecian style by Henry Carr from 1824 to 1827, and it was this Hall that was destroyed by bombing in 1941. The site is now occupied by St Swithin's House. The Salters' Company, which is ninth in the order of precedence, grew out of a fraternity of salters which was established in 1394, the company itself receiving its first charter in 1559. In medieval times it controlled the trade in salt, which was vital for preserving meat and fish, as well as other commodities such as flax, hemp, and potash.

SALTERS' HALL CHAPEL, Salters Hall Court, Cannon Street. A Presbyterian congregation, established in College Hill in 1652, built a chapel just south of Salters' Hall in 1687. One of the most important non-conformist meeting houses in the City, it was demolished in 1822 for the new extended Salters' Hall; the site is now covered by St Swithin's House.

PLUMBERS' HALL, Chequer Yard, Dowgate. Rebuilt by 1671, its Georgian successor was demolished in 1863 for Cannon Street Station. The guild obtained ordinances in 1365, and was chartered in 1611. The trade embraced glazing, roofing, cisterns, and lead weights. Members were prominent in the reconstruction of the churches and public buildings of the City.

LAURENCE POUNTNEY HILL, Cannon Street. Nos. 1 and 2, built in 1703 (replacing houses built shortly after the Fire) are two of the finest City houses surviving from the post-Fire period. They are a pair, of brick, with finely carved cornices and doorcases – in the hood of one is a relief of boys playing marbles. Three other late 17th-century houses remain nearby: one, much altered in the 19th century, overlooking St Laurence Pountney churchyard; another, behind the Laurence Pountney Hill houses in Suffolk Lane, with some finely decorated plaster ceilings; and the Old Wine Shades wine bar in Martin Lane, also much altered.

39 1 and 2 Laurence Pountney Hill, photograph. (National Monuments Record)

MERCHANT TAYLORS' SCHOOL

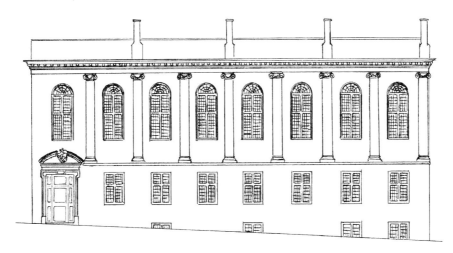

Merchant Taylors' School: Suffolk Lane frontage

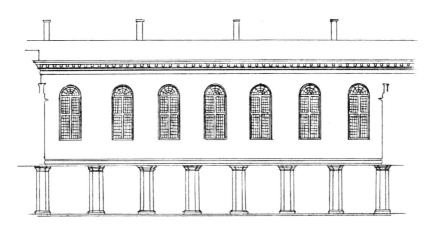

Merchant Taylors' School: west frontage of court

Merchant Taylors' School was founded by the Merchant Taylors' Company in 1561, and established in part of the Manor of the Rose, a large mansion which was built by Sir John Pulteney, one of the greatest merchants of early 14th-century London and four times Mayor, in 1341. The school has had close links with St John's College, Oxford, since its foundation in 1565. In the late 16th century it was, with its strong humanist tradition and its 250 pupils, the largest school in England. The school was burnt in the Great Fire and rebuilt by 1675 in brick to Hooke's design, with a long pilastered frontage to Suffolk Lane, a cloister on its inner side, and a long first-floor schoolroom. The school moved to the Charterhouse in 1875, after which its old building was demolished, and finally to Northwood, Middlesex, in 1935. Old boys include Edmund Spenser, Robert Clive and Titus Oates (who was expelled).

WARD'S HOUSE, Laurence Pountney Hill. Sir Patience Ward (reputedly so named because his father, who already had six sons, was hoping for a daughter), Lord Mayor in 1680, owned a large house on the west side of Duxford Lane which occupied the site of the Manor of the Rose, the palatial residence of Sir John de Pulteney, who was Mayor four times in the mid-14th century. Ward was an opponent of Charles II and James II, a supporter of William of Orange, and M.P. for the City from 1689 to 1690. A vehement Protestant, he was responsible for the anti-Catholic inscriptions placed on the Monument and the site of Farynor's house in Pudding Lane.

WATLING STREET

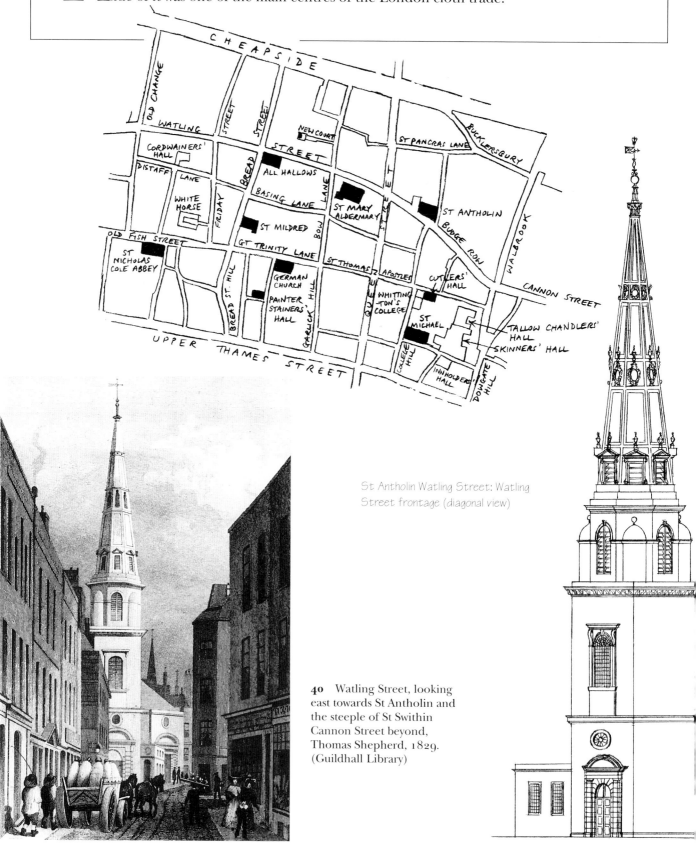

R UNNING EASTWARDS from St Paul's Churchyard and parallel to Cheapside, Watling Street was one of the principal streets of the City. The closely packed district to either side of it was one of the main centres of the London cloth trade.

St Antholin Watling Street: Watling Street frontage (diagonal view)

40 Watling Street, looking east towards St Antholin and the steeple of St Swithin Cannon Street beyond, Thomas Shepherd, 1829. (Guildhall Library)

ST ANTHOLIN WATLING STREET WITH ST JOHN WALBROOK

Also called St Antholin's Budge Row, the church stood, where now stands Temple Court, the headquarters of Legal & General, on the north side of Watling Street and Budge Row, which was until the extension of Cannon Street in the mid-19th century one of the principal east-west thoroughfares through the City. St Antholin's was first mentioned in the early 12th century. The dedication was a corruption of St Anthony, as was the other common early appellation, St Antling's. Rebuilt at the end of the 14th century, the church became in the late 16th and early 17th centuries a major stronghold of Puritanism – the St Antholin's lectures (instituted in 1559) began at 5 o'clock in the morning, and 'St Antling's bell' was a byword at the time for Puritan zeal. It was therefore not surprising that the Commissioners from the Church of Scotland lodged in an adjoining house during their negotiations with Charles I in 1640. Burnt in the Great Fire, the church was rebuilt in brick with Portland stone facings by Thomas Cartwright to the designs of Wren between 1678 and 1683, with the stone spire added in 1686-7. It was one of Wren's most masterly designs, ingeniously exploiting both the awkwardness and dramatic location of the site. Budge Row curved away southwards in front of the church; this provided an

opportunity for the steeple to dominate the view eastwards along Watling Street (in juxtaposition with the more distant spires of St Swithin Cannon Street and St Mary Abchurch), an opportunity which the architect exploited with one of his most magnificent designs. St Antholin's steeple was, like St Swithin's, a variant on the theme of the baroque transition from square tower to octagonal spire, here with a convex note provided by the domed semi-cylindrical buttresses at the corners of the octagonal top stage of the tower. The steeple was so impressive that even when the body of the church was demolished under the Union of Benefices Act in 1875 there was an intention to preserve it as a landmark; it was only in the following year that commercial interests prevailed, and the steeple came down. The curve of Budge Row presented Wren with a diagonal frontage, a difficulty which was exploited by giving St Antholin's an elongated octagonal plan – an octagonal domed nave, surrounded by an octagonal aisle (with the eastern corners squared off), all under a huge octagonal tent-like roof. As a result the interior showed the City churches' characteristic baroque tension between centralising and longitudinal accents, as well as representing in simplified form the same vertical progression from the square, through the octagonal,

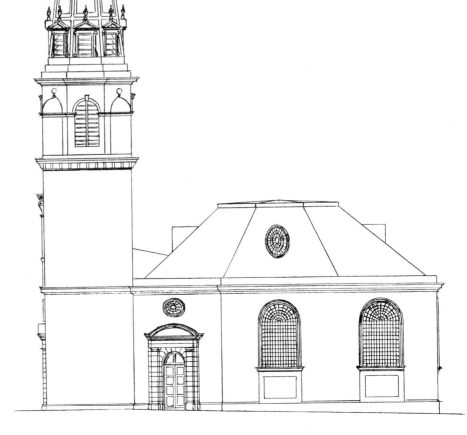

St Antholin Watling Street:
Watling Street frontage

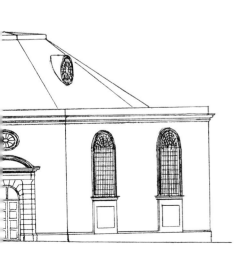

to the elliptical dome, which emerged in its most fully developed form at St Stephen's Walbrook, and which was emblematic in the baroque idiom of the ascent from the worldly to the divine. The dome was enriched with superb plasterwork festoons by Henry Doogood. Also illustrated here is an earlier design for a more conventional church with a less elaborate steeple. On demolition some of the furnishings were removed to St Mary Aldermary and St Antholin's Nunhead, the former of which was 'restored', and the latter built, with the proceeds of sale. The pulpit is now at Blandford Forum, Dorset. The topmost stage of the spire, from the third tier of lucarnes upwards, was rebuilt as a garden ornament at Forest Hill, where it remains today. *(See plate 41, p.136.)*

St John the Baptist Walbrook, mentioned in the early 12th century, stood on the north corner of Cloak Lane and Dowgate Hill; a 19th-century memorial marks its site.

St Antholin Watling Street: unrealised design, showing steeple and cross-section

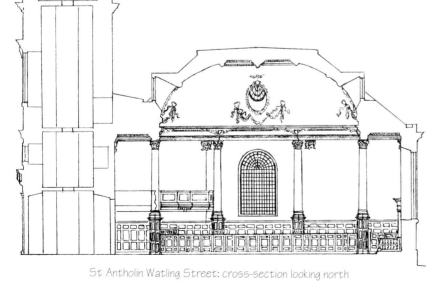

St Antholin Watling Street: cross-section looking north

St Antholin Watling Street: section looking east

ST MARY ALDERMARY with ST THOMAS APOSTLES

St Mary Aldermary Church stands on the east side of Bow Lane, between Watling Street and Queen Victoria Street. It was first mentioned in the late 11th century, and probably in existence by 1020. The name means 'elder Mary', and was probably given to distinguish it from the 'new' St Mary le Bow (built in the late 11th century) at the other end of Bow Lane. The church was rebuilt in Perpendicular style between 1510 and 1518 at the expense of Henry Keeble, Mayor of London in 1511. The tower, completed in 1629, survives, restored by John Clarke under the supervision of the Commissioners (with possible input to the design from Wren or Hawksmoor) in 1701-3. The church was burnt in the Great Fire, and rebuilt by Samuel Fulkes in stone to Wren's design between 1679 and 1682, probably incorporating much of the surviving fabric of the medieval church. Henry Rogers, whose estate provided £5,000 for the rebuilding, is reputed to have stipulated a copy of the old church, and St Mary Aldermary is one of Wren's few essays in 'modern Gothick'. Nevertheless it is characteristic of the usual manner in the plainness of the exterior (except for the panelled octagonal buttresses of the steeple, which are similar to those of the planned but unexecuted tower of King's College Chapel in Cambridge), contrasting with the elaboration of the interior, where the plaster fan vaults nod towards the 'Gothick' past, but the baroque plasterwork of the arcade spandrels is uninhibitedly 'modern'. The Victorian 'restoration' of 1867 set out to make the church as Gothic as possible, in particular the south aisle which, having previously merely faced the churchyard, was then being opened up on a prominent corner site on the new Queen Victoria Street. The restoration involved clearing away almost all of the 17th-century furnishings, pepping up the south doorway, and replacing Wren's restrained pilasters with proper buttresses.

The church of St Thomas Apostles was first mentioned in 1170. It stood on the north side of Great St Thomas Apostle. After the Great Fire Queen Street was laid out across its site. Part of the churchyard remains as the gardens in front of the Georgian houses on the corner of Queen Street and Cannon Street; adjacent to it was a house occupied from 1763 to 1805 by John and Francis, the Baring brothers, wool merchants, who developed their business into one of London's premier merchant banks, exploiting their connection with the great Amsterdam trading house, Hope & Co.

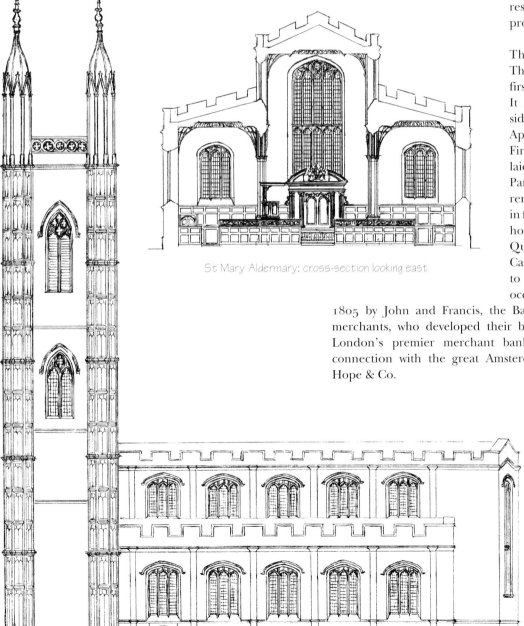

St Mary Aldermary: cross-section looking east

St Mary Aldermary: Aldermary churchyard frontage

NEW COURT

New Court, now Grovelands Court, was surrounded by late 17th-century brick houses, of which the 'front house' was reputedly the residence of several Lord Mayors. In 1739 it was taken over by Robert Williamson as Williamson's Hotel, an establishment which has remained on the same site since. In the early 20th century the premises were rebuilt in their original style, and Williamson's today, with the William and Mary wrought-iron gate which originally barred the entrance to the court from Bow Lane, is still redolent of the 17th-century City.

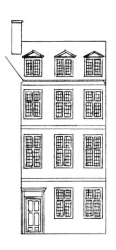

New Court,
Bow Lane: facade of west end

ALL HALLOWS BREAD STREET
WITH ST JOHN THE EVANGELIST FRIDAY STREET

All Hallows' Church stood on the south-east corner of Watling Street and Bread Street, on the site occupied by the north-west corner of Watling House. First mentioned in the late 12th century, it was the church of the Company of Salters, and the scene of John Milton's baptism in 1608. All Hallows' was burnt in the Great Fire and rebuilt with Portland stone facings by Samuel Fulkes to Wren's design from 1677 to 1684; the tower was completed in 1698. The view shows the long, grand Watling Street frontage and the south-west tower, the top storey of which was lightened and enriched by a tripartite open colonnade on each side, an example of how Wren exploited transparency in his steeples. All Hallows' was demolished in 1876 under the Union of Benefices Act, and All Hallows' Church in Poplar was built with the proceeds of sale; some of the fittings are now dispersed among St Mary Abchurch, St Andrew by the Wardrobe, and St Vedast Foster Lane.

St John the Evangelist Watling Street was mentioned in 1349; it was originally dedicated to St Werburga, the daughter of King Penda of Mercia, who was Abbess of Ely. It stood at the south-east corner of Watling Street and Friday Street, on a site now occupied by 25 Cannon Street.

All Hallows Bread Street:
cross-section looking east

All Hallows Bread Street: Watling Street frontage

CORDWAINERS' HALL, Distaff Lane. A company hall, whose site is now the corner of Cannon Street and New Change, which was rebuilt by 1670 (appearance unknown), and again in 1788 and 1910; bombed in 1941. The Company, which acquired ordinances in 1272, controlled the shoe, leather bottle, and horse-harness trade.

WHITE HORSE INN, Friday Street. The White Horse was an important inn which surrounded a courtyard off the west side of Friday Street, just north of Old Fish Street, on a site now covered by Bracken House (formerly the offices of the *Financial Times*, now the Industrial Bank of Japan). The Wednesday Club met there under William Paterson, a Scottish merchant, in the late 17th and early 18th centuries; it was devoted to discussing economic and political issues. Paterson presented there his proposal for introducing stability to Government funding (as opposed to the *ad hoc* raising of loans and stoppages of the Exchequer which did nothing for investor confidence) by means of a permanent National Debt. The proposal gave rise to Paterson's and Michael Godfrey's plan for the Bank of England in 1691; the Bank was established in 1694.

ST MILDRED BREAD STREET
WITH ST MARGARET MOSES

St Mildred Bread Street:
Bread Street frontage

St Mildred's Church stood on the east side of Bread Street on the site now occupied by No. 30 Cannon Street, the old Credit Lyonnais building. It was first mentioned in 1170 and burnt in the Great Fire. Plans to reroof the surviving structure were abandoned when the walls were found to be unstable, and the church was rebuilt completely by Edward Strong to Wren's or Hooke's design between 1681 and 1687, with a narrow, elegant pedimented façade, a domed interior with intricate plasterwork by Henry Doogood and John Grove, and a simple brick south steeple, whose lead-covered square spire on a concave base contrasted with the alternating concavity and convexity of the pedimented parapet of the Portland stone west front. Percy Bysshe Shelley and Mary Godwin were married in the church in 1816. St Mildred's survived the depredations of both Victorian restorers and the Union of Benefices Act, and by the early 20th century it was the best preserved of all the Wren City churches, with its original fittings (by William Cleere) complete. All was destroyed by a direct hit in 1941, except for the tower which survived forlorn until 1960, and a few fragments of the fittings which are now at St Anne and St Agnes. *(See plate 42, p.136.)*

St Margaret Moses was first mentioned in the early 12th century. It was probably named after an early benefactor or incumbent. The site is in the street at the corner of Cannon Street (which here follows the line of the medieval Pissing Alley) and Friday Street.

St Mildred Bread Street: cross-section looking east

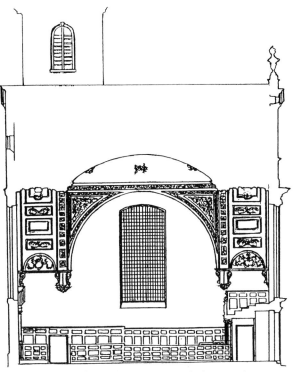

St Mildred Bread Street: section looking south

41 Interior of St Antholin Watling Street, H.
and J. Mathews, 1876. (National Monuments
Record)

42 Interior of St Mildred Bread Street,
Frederick Mackenzie, 1838. (Guildhall Library)

ST NICHOLAS COLE ABBEY WITH ST NICHOLAS OLAVE

St Nicholas Cole Abbey was first mentioned in about 1134. It was probably named after a nearby mansion. Enlarged in the late 14th century, it stood on the south side of Old Fish Street, the principal early medieval fish market, and was formerly closely associated with the London fishmongers. It was burnt in 1666 and rebuilt by Thomas Wise to Wren's design between 1671 and 1677, making it one of the first of the new London churches to be completed (unlike almost all later churches, the steeple, with its lead-covered octagonal concave spire, was completed at this early stage as well, since the enthusiasm with which it was carried forward pre-dated the halt on steeple-building of the late 1670s). The church consists of a simple nave with a quite elaborately ornamented north frontage (previously overlooking the important thoroughfare of Old Fish Street), with Portland stone facings. The aspect of the church was substantially altered by the cutting of Queen Victoria Street in the early 1870s, which exposed the south frontage. The fine furnishings and plasterwork were largely destroyed when the building was gutted by fire-bombs in 1941; the damage was restored in the early 1960s, and St Nicholas is now used by a Presbyterian congregation.

St Nicholas Olave, also called St Nicholas Bernard or St Olave Bread Street, was mentioned from the late 12th century. Its site is now the south side of Queen Victoria Street opposite the entrance to Bread Street.

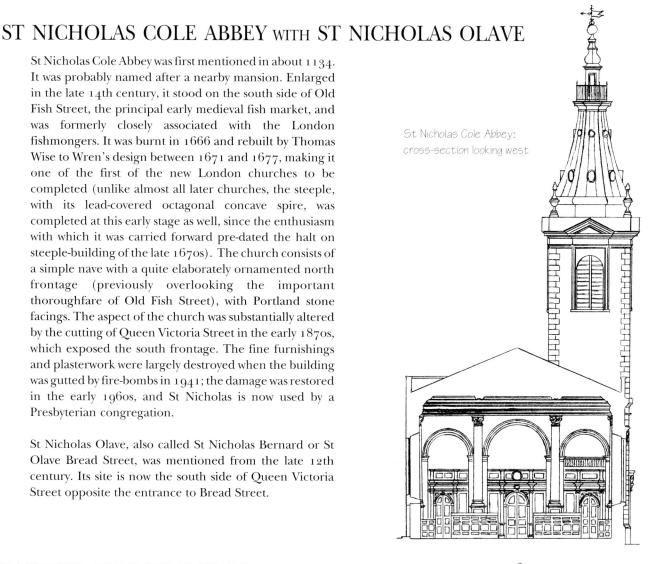

St Nicholas Cole Abbey:
cross-section looking west

St Nicholas Cole Abbey: cross-section looking east

PAINTER STAINERS' HALL

Sir John Browne, Serjeant-Painter to Henry VIII, left his mansion to the Painter Stainers' Company in 1532. The Hall was burnt in 1666 and rebuilt by 1670, with a narrow brick façade with a finely ornamented doorcase; it was also noted for its Painted Chamber, lined with panel paintings executed in 1705 – some of them survive in the modern hall on the site, rebuilt in 1961 after extensive wartime damage to the original hall, which had already been substantially reconstructed in the late 19th

Painter Stainers' Hall:
Little Trinity Lane
frontage

and early 20th centuries. The fraternities of Painters (who originally worked on wood) and Stainers (who worked on cloth) both date from the 13th century; they merged in 1502 to form the Painter Stainers' Company, which had a long-running dispute with the Plaisterers' Company over control of the trade, and with the College of Arms over the right to paint coats of arms. Until the establishment of the Royal Academy the Company was the main fraternity of London artists, and it tried to retain control over the trade until the 19th century. Notable members included Sir Peter Lely, Antonio Verrio, Sir Godfrey Kneller and Sir James Thornhill.

GERMAN CHURCH

German Church: Great Trinity Lane frontage

The German Church was built in brick on the site of the burned church of Holy Trinity the Less (on the south-east corner of Great and Little Trinity Lanes) by the Lutheran congregation of the German Steelyard merchants between 1666 and 1675, perhaps to the design of Caius Gabriel Cibber. Rebuilt in 1773, it was finally demolished in 1867. The finely carved reredos from the 17th-century church survives in the Hamburg Lutheran Church in Hackney.

CUTLERS' HALL

The Cutlers' Company acquired a Hall on the south side of Cloak Lane, between College Hill and Dowgate Hill, in about 1420. Burnt in 1666, it was rebuilt by 1671, its plain street frontage marked only by the doorway with the Company's arms in its pediment. The Cloak Lane Hall was demolished in 1882, when the Cutlers moved to their present Hall in Warwick Lane. The Cutlers' Company was chartered in 1416. It controlled the London cutlery trade, which included the manufacture of swords and surgical instruments as well as knives. Sheffield took over most of London's share of the market in the 17th century, and the Cutlers' Company lost control over what was left during the 18th.

Cutlers' Hall: Cloak Lane entrance

WHITTINGTON'S COLLEGE, College Hill, Vintry. The College of St Spirit and St Mary was established by Richard Whittington, thrice Mayor of London (1397, 1406, 1419) in 1409 in the church of St Michael Paternoster Royal. The College (which was suppressed at the Reformation) and attached almshouses occupied the site of Whittington's mansion on the east side of College Hill. The almshouses were rebuilt after the Great Fire with two spectacularly elaborately carved stone gateways which survive today; they flank what was the main entrance to the almshouses' courtyard. The almshouses moved to Highgate in 1808 and for most of the 19th century the building was part of the Mercers' School (founded 1447, refounded by the Mercers' Company 1541, now defunct). In a nearby courtyard remains, much altered, one of Nicholas Barbon's houses, built in 1688.

43 Whittington's College, photograph. (National Monuments Record)

44 Courtyard of Skinners' Hall, photograph. (National Monuments Record)

ST MICHAEL PATERNOSTER ROYAL
WITH ST MARTIN VINTRY

The church of St Michael Paternoster Royal was first mentioned in about 1100. Its double name derives partly from Tower Royal, a large medieval mansion which stood nearby in College Hill, and partly perhaps from a local community of paternosterers (makers of rosaries). St Michael's was the parish church of Richard Whittington, whose mansion adjoined, who rebuilt it as a collegiate church in 1409. Burnt in the Great Fire, the church was rebuilt by Edward Strong the Elder to Wren's design from 1685 to 1694, with a large rectangular nave and south front faced with Portland stone. The stone steeple was added at the south-west corner from 1713 to 1717 by Edward Strong the Younger, one of the last of the City steeples, with a finely detailed tiered octagonal spire – Hawksmoor may have had a hand in its design. The reredos was substantially altered in early 19th-century restorations – the view shows a conjectural reconstruction of the original based on Hatton's account. The church was damaged by bombing in 1944 and restored in 1967, with the reinstatement of some of its original fittings and part of the space given over to offices.

St Martin Vintry was first mentioned in the late 11th century. Standing in the middle of the Vintry, where now is the east corner of Upper Thames Street and Queen Street, it was the Vintners' church. The churchyard survived until it was removed for street widening in the mid-20th century.

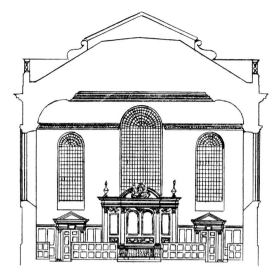

St Michael Paternoster Royal: cross-section looking east

INNHOLDERS' HALL, College Street, Dowgate. One of the better preserved company halls, much of the interior decoration survives, notably in the livery hall and court room, and the replica early 18th-century entrance from College Street. The Hall was rebuilt 1669-71. The guild of Hostellers and Haymongers existed by 1327; by 1473 they had become Innholders (with the term 'ostler' being applied to inn servants); the Company was chartered in 1514. It controlled the innholding trade, and its influence declined with the demise of the City coaching inns after the arrival of the railways in the mid-19th century.

SKINNERS' HALL, Dowgate Hill. The best preserved of all the major companies' halls. Originally a mansion called Copped Hall, the Skinners acquired it in 1409. It was rebuilt by John Oliver from 1668-9, with brick frontages and a loggia around a small courtyard. The interior is much altered, but the superb Court Room survives, with Virginian cedar panelling and exuberant woodcarving. The Company, first chartered in 1327, controlled the fur trade until the 18th century. It had many connections with royalty and nobility because of the high social status of furs, with strict controls in the Middle Ages over who was allowed to wear them. The Skinners were closely involved (along with Prince Rupert) in the formation and operation of the Hudson's Bay Company, chartered in 1670 to manage the fur and skin trade of British North America.

TALLOW CHANDLERS' HALL, Dowgate Hill. This is one of the best preserved of the 17th-century company halls, built by John Caine, perhaps to Jerman's design, from 1670 to 1672, with impressive brick ranges around a small courtyard. The livery hall and parlour have fine original panelling and woodcarving, and the court room is uniquely well preserved. The guild, which existed by the mid-14th century and was chartered in 1462, controlled the trade in tallow and tallow candles (the main source of lighting), as well as vinegar, oils, butter and soap.

45 Courtyard of Tallow Chandlers' Hall, Thomas Shepherd, 1852. (British Museum)

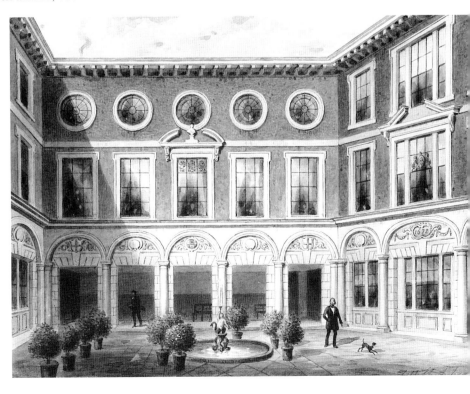

WOOD STREET

ANOTHER CENTRE of the cloth trade clustered around the main street northwards out of Cheapside, leading towards Cripplegate. This was also a district with a great concentration of inns, almshouses, and livery halls.

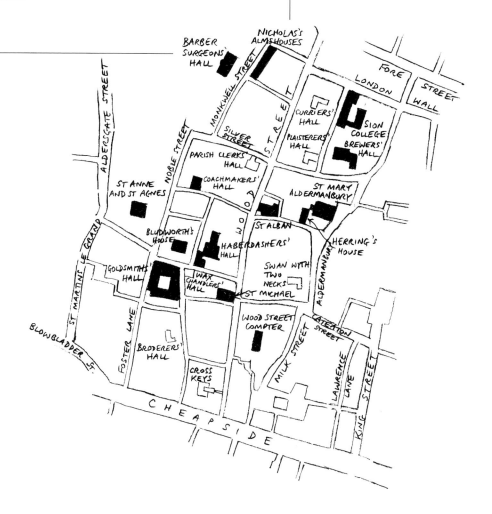

St Michael Wood Street: cross-section looking east

CROSS KEYS INN, Wood Street. Standing in a courtyard opening off the west side of Wood Street, just north of Cheapside, the Cross Keys became one of the chief coaching inns of London in the 18th and early 19th centuries, latterly owned by William Chaplin. Its later appearance was recorded by Shepherd. Dickens first arrived in London there, as memorialised in *Great Expectations*.

WOOD STREET COMPTER

Wood Street Compter was one of the two sheriffs' prisons, and was also used as an overflow for Newgate Gaol. It was opened on the closure of Bread Street Compter in 1555, burnt in 1666, and rebuilt by 1670. Its 70 cells were divided between the Masters' Side (for the wealthy), the Knights' Side (for the comfortably off), and the Hole (for the poor). The Compter was closed in 1791 when its prisoners were transferred to the new and larger Giltspur Street Compter, near Newgate, and demolished in 1816. Its site is now occupied by the south end of Clements House on the east side of Wood Street.

Wood Street Compter: west (courtyard) frontage

ST MICHAEL WOOD STREET WITH ST MARY STAINING

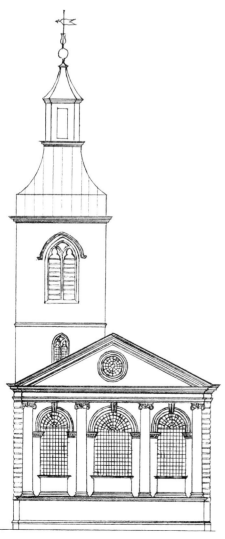

St Michael Wood Street: Wood Street frontage

St Michael's Church stood on the west side of Wood Street, just south of its junction with Gresham Street. It was mentioned in about 1170, and enlarged with a new steeple in 1442. It was burnt in the Great Fire, but substantial parts of the fabric, as well as rubble from Old St Paul's, were incorporated in Thomas Wise's rebuilding to Wren's design which occurred between 1670 and 1673. The steeple was essentially medieval, with the addition in 1687 of a simple baroque lantern; in an early 19th-century restoration the upper stage of the tower was replaced by a spire. As at St Matthew Friday Street, the main decorative display was on the east front, tripartite with pilasters and pediment. The church was demolished in 1894, and the remaining furnishings are now at St George's, Southwark, and St Mark's, Kennington.

St Mary Staining was mentioned from the late 12th century. It was perhaps attached to the town house of the people of Staines. It stood at the north end of Staining Lane, where its churchyard still remains.

SWAN WITH TWO NECKS INN, Lad Lane, Wood Street. One of the main London coaching inns from the 17th to the 19th centuries, extensively rebuilt in Georgian times, so that its more diminutive immediate post-Fire appearance is not recorded; the name was a corruption of 'Swan with Two Nicks', i.e. the beak marks by which the Vintners' Company identified its swans. William Chaplin acquired it in 1825; with its rebuilt galleried ranges around the central courtyard and underground stabling, it became the centre of his extensive coaching business to the North Country. It was demolished piecemeal in the second half of the 19th century.

ST ALBAN WOOD STREET with ST OLAVE SILVER STREET

St Alban's Church stood on the east side of Wood Street, north of the corner of Love Lane. The steeple remains on a traffic island in the middle of the widened Wood Street; most of the site of the church is now occupied by Wood Street Police Station. St Alban's, dedicated to the first British martyr, was first mentioned in the late 11th century, but excavations showed it to have dated from the eighth or ninth century, and Matthew Paris recorded a tradition that it was the chapel of King Offa of Mercia's London palace. The church was restored or rebuilt, reputedly by Inigo Jones, between 1633 and 1634. It was burnt in the Great Fire and rebuilt in Portland stone between 1682 and 1687 by Samuel Fulkes to the design of Wren, reportedly reproducing the old church with its elaborate lierne vaults, one of Wren's few Gothic buildings. The tower was completed in 1697. St Alban's was gutted by bombing in 1940, and the ruins demolished (except for the tower) in 1955. The view shows the west front, most of which in fact survives, although the window of the nave is now at Wrotham church in Kent.

St Olave Silver Street, also referred to as St Mary Olaf, was first mentioned in the late 12th century. It was the church of the silversmiths who lived in Silver Street, which disappeared under the redevelopment of London Wall after the Second World War. St Olave's churchyard survives on the south side of the new London Wall, and marks the old corner of Noble Street and Silver Street.

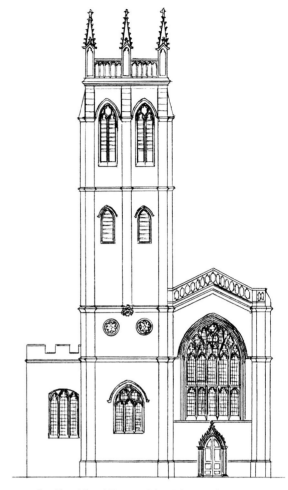

St Alban Wood Street: Wood Street frontage

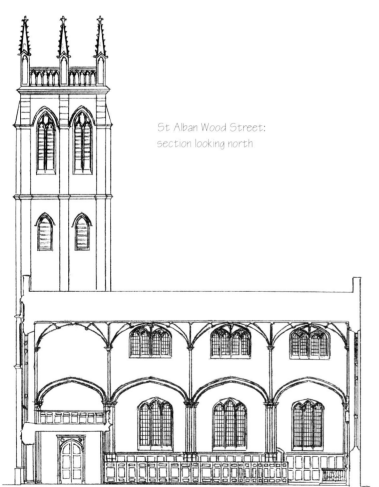

St Alban Wood Street: section looking north

St Alban Wood Street: cross-section looking east

46   Interior of St Alban Wood Street, Robert Billings, 1838. (Guildhall Library)

47   Interior of Brewers' Hall, photograph. (National Monuments Record)

HERRING'S HOUSE

Shortly after the Great Fire Lady Herring rebuilt her house in Love Lane in brick in a plain baroque style with giant pilasters at the angles. One of the most notorious examples of peculation in the aftermath of the Fire was the sale to her by the churchwardens of a slice of the St Mary Aldermanbury churchyard to serve as her garden. The house survived until the early 20th century; its site is now covered by the south-east corner of Wood Street Police Station.

ST MARY ALDERMANBURY

The church of St Mary Aldermanbury stood at the head of the widest part of Aldermanbury, just north of the junction with Love Lane. It was first mentioned in the early 12th century, and was famous in the Middle Ages for the enormous human bone which was displayed in its cloister. Burnt in the Great Fire, it was rebuilt by Joshua Marshall to Wren's designs between 1671 and 1674. The south and east frontages were faced with Portland stone; although the clearest view of the church was from the south down Aldermanbury, the main show front, with exaggerated volutes either side of the main window, and central pediment flanked by voluted aisle parapets setting up a dynamic pattern of convex and concave curves, was at the east end. The steeple, as was often the case with the churches distant from both the river and the main thorough-fares, was not specially elaborate, with a simple turret, and incorporated some of the medieval fabric; it was completed in 1681 by Samuel Fulkes. The plan consisted of nave and aisles, with a central clerestoreyed cross-vault. The Victorian restoration involved the insertion of Italianate window tracery and new furnishings. St Mary's was gutted by bombs in 1940. The ruins were removed in 1964 to Fulton, Missouri, where the church was re-built from 1965 to 1969 in its original form (without the Victorian accretions) as a memorial to Winston Churchill's 'Iron Curtain' speech; St Mary Aldermanbury is thus the only 'lost' Wren church to survive in its entirety, albeit 4,000 miles away from its original site, which is now a garden.

CURRIERS' HALL, London Wall, Cripplegate. A small company hall, on a site which is now beneath St Alphege Highwalk, occupied by the Curriers since 1516. The Hall was rebuilt in 1670 and replaced in 1820 (its plain street entrance was illustrated by Shepherd; the appearance of the Hall itself is unknown). The last Curriers' Hall, built in 1874-6, had a very elaborate Gothic street frontage; it was bombed in 1940. The Curriers were an offshoot of the Cordwainers; they performed the final processing of leather after tanning. The guild existed by 1300 and was chartered in 1605.

PLAISTERERS' HALL, Addle Street, Cripplegate. The Plaisterers' Company took over the Pinners' Hall in 1556, and rebuilt it in 1669 after the Fire; the Hall was burnt again in 1882. The Plaisterers now have a Hall nearby in London Wall. The original site is occupied by Royex House, at the west end of Aldermanbury Square. Chartered in 1501, the Company controlled the plastering trade.

St Mary Aldermanbury: cross-section looking east

St Mary Aldermanbury: Aldermanbury (south) frontage

BREWERS' HALL

Brewers' Hall was in existence by 1403 (when it already incorporated a 'tresaunce' or cloister). Amongst others who used the premises in the 15th century was a company of 'Footballplayers'. The Hall was burnt in the Great Fire and rebuilt between 1670 and 1673 in brick to the design of Thomas Whiting and John Caine, standing on an open arcade (replicating the tresaunce) facing the court, to which access was gained via a highly ornamented gateway in Addle Street. The livery hall itself, above the arcade at first-floor level and approached by a grand staircase which wound around the courtyard, was furnished with finely carved panelling and screens, and remained one of the best and most completely preserved of the City's 17th-century company halls until it was entirely destroyed by bombing in 1940. A new Brewers' Hall was built on almost the same site in 1960. The Worshipful Company of Brewers, which was first mentioned in 1292 and chartered in 1437, controlled the London brewing trade, and remains influential in it. *(See plate 47, p.143.)*

Brewers' Hall: Brewers' Hall Court frontage

Brewers' Hall: section of hall, looking south

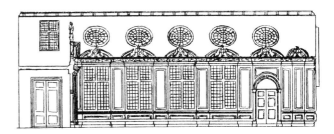

Brewers' Hall: cross-section of hall looking east

Brewers' Hall: Addle Street entrance

St Mary Aldermanbury: Aldermanbury (east) frontage; Herring's house beyond

SION COLLEGE

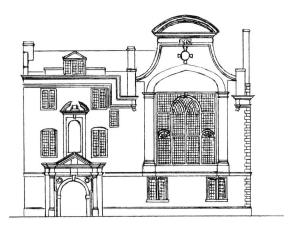

Sion College: London Wall frontage

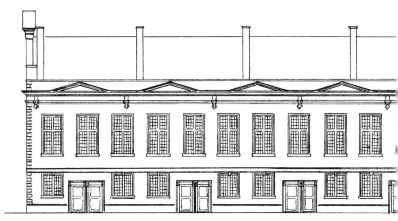

Sion College: Philip Lane frontage

Sion College was a college of clergymen, founded by Thomas White, rector of St Dunstan in the West, in 1624. Its London Wall premises were built in 1631, incorporating a library (on the site of the Hospital of Elsing Spital, now occupied by St Alphege Highwalk, opposite St Alphege's churchyard and its well-preserved fragment of the City wall). About two-thirds of the library was saved from the Great Fire, which destroyed the buildings; the College was rebuilt in brick in 1678 around a courtyard, with the library occupying the first floor of a long range along Philip Lane with an impressive Dutch gable at its north end and 20 almshouses below it (theirs was a better lot than the inhabitants of the almshouse which Richard Whittington's executors built above the Whittington's Longhouse public lavatory in the Vintry in 1428). Between 1710 and 1836 Sion College was a copyright library, entitled to a copy of every book printed in London. The almshouses were vacated in 1845 because of the fire hazard to the library, and the entire premises demolished in 1886 when Sion College moved to a grand new building on Victoria Embankment. The site is now covered by the London Wall dual carriageway, opposite Brewers' Hall. (See plate 48, p.150.)

NICHOLAS'S ALMSHOUSES

Sir Ambrose Nicholas, a salter, founded 12 almshouses in Monkwell Street in his mayoral year, 1575. They were managed by the Salters' Company. Burnt in the Great Fire, the almshouses were rebuilt as a long brick range with a central frontispiece feature in 1668. They were demolished in 1864 to provide a site for warehouses; the almshouses were re-established in Watford, where they remain. The original site is now covered by the north-west corner of the Alban Gate block in London Wall.

Nicholas's (Salters') Almshouses: Monkwell Street frontage

PARISH CLERKS' HALL, Silver Street, Cripplegate.
The Parish Clerks' Company (not a livery company) moved from the Vintry after the Great Fire, and rebuilt in Cripplegate from 1669 to 1672. The small and well-preserved Hall survived until the Blitz. The fraternity, of clerks of London parishes, existed from 1274 and was chartered in 1442. From 1625 to 1858 it published the Bills of Mortality, a weekly summary of the numbers and causes of deaths in London parishes.

BARBER SURGEONS' HALL

The Barber Surgeons' Hall was in existence by 1440. The Guild of Barbers existed by the early 14th century; they were the senior practitioners of surgery in medieval London, and had continuing disputes with a separate fraternity of surgeons until the two companies were formally united by Act of Parliament in 1540. There was substantial rebuilding of Barber Surgeons' Hall, reputedly to Inigo Jones's design, in the early 17th century – this included the court room and anatomical theatre (modelled on Fabricius's lecture theatre at Padua), both of which survived the Great Fire. The southern part of the Hall had to be rebuilt from 1667 to 1671 by Thomas Cartwright after it was destroyed in the Fire, with a brick frontage with pedimented centre which overlooked the courtyard, and an elaborately decorated entrance doorway from the street (its coat of arms survives in the new Hall). The theatre was demolished in 1784 and most of the Hall followed it in 1869. The *coup de grâce* was delivered by German bombing in 1940, when the old court room and entranceway disappeared. The Hall was rebuilt as part of a substantial block in a neo-Georgian style on the same site in the 1960s.

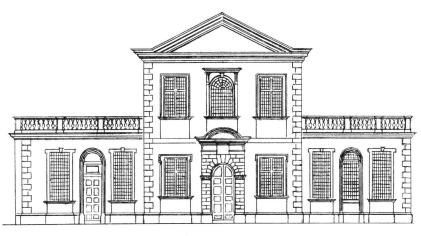

Barber Surgeons' Hall: east (courtyard) frontage

Barber Surgeons' Hall:
Monkwell Street entrance

COACHMAKERS' HALL

The Company of Coachmakers and Coach Harness Makers purchased their Hall in Oat Lane from the poverty-stricken Scriveners' Company (who had had a Hall on this site since 1631, rebuilt after the Fire between 1671 and 1675) in 1703. The Coachmakers were becoming increasingly

Coachmakers' Hall:
hall screen

wealthy because of the expansion of coach traffic, and celebrated their new acquisition by installing the elaborate screen, which survived two 19th-century rebuildings of the Hall itself, only to be finally destroyed in the Blitz in 1940; the site is now approximately covered by Pewterers' Hall. The Coachmakers' monopoly of their trade lasted from the chartering of the Company in 1677 until 1804. The Scriveners, who received their charter in 1617 although the guild dates back to the 14th century, controlled the production of legal documents; the Company is still responsible for regulating public notaries.

ST ANNE AND ST AGNES with ST JOHN ZACHARY

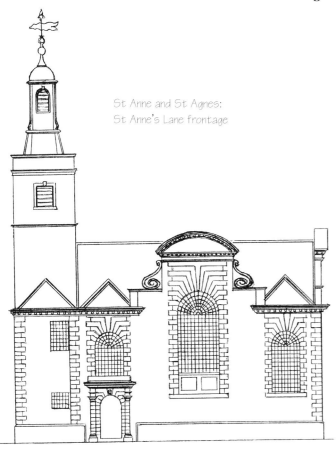

St Anne and St Agnes:
St Anne's Lane frontage

The church was first mentioned in the mid-12th century. Until the mid-15th century it seems to have been called alternatively St Anne (with the suffix Aldersgate, or in-the-Willows) or St Agnes. After its destruction in the Great Fire, St Anne and St Agnes was rebuilt to either Wren's or Hooke's design (the vaguely Dutch character of the exterior and the centralised plan – perhaps derived from the Nieuwe Kerk at Haarlem, Holland – is usually associated with the latter) by William Hammond and Robert Waters from 1676 to 1687. The rubbed-brick east, north and south fronts each have three arched windows and a central pedimented gable, whose flanking scrolls were replaced in the 19th century by much simpler concave scrolls. The tower, which was rebuilt in 1714, contains some medieval fabric. The interior has a central cross-vault supported on four Corinthian columns, and saucer domes in each corner. The church was bombed in 1940 and rebuilt in the mid-1960s. Most of its furnishings were either destroyed or dispersed, but they have been replaced by pieces from other churches, including St Mildred Bread Street, St Michael Wood Street, and St Augustine Watling Street. St Anne and St Agnes is now used by the London Lutheran congregation of the Baltic states.

The church of St John the Baptist was first mentioned in the early 12th century. It was named after one Zachary who held the living in the late 12th century, and was closely associated with the goldsmiths, whose Hall is nearby. The churchyard remains on the corner of Noble Street and Gresham Street.

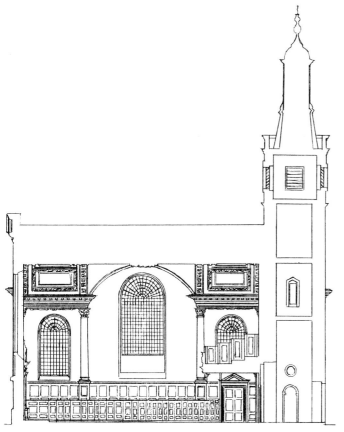

St Anne and St Agnes: section looking south

St Anne and St Agnes: cross-section looking east

BLUDWORTH'S HOUSE

Bludworth's House, Maiden Lane: courtyard frontage

Sir Thomas Bludworth, vintner, wealthy Turkey merchant, and member of the Levant and African Companies, had the misfortune to be Lord Mayor in the Great Fire year. His initial complacency about the Fire, and his poor management of the fire-fighting (he hesitated to pull down houses in the path of the Fire because of the compensation liability which the City would incur), probably contributed substantially to the eventual magnitude of the devastation. Bludworth's own house in Gracechurch Street was consumed, and afterwards he built himself a substantial mansion in a courtyard north of Maiden Lane, on the site now covered by No 29 Gresham Street, just north-east of St John Zachary churchyard. This tentative reconstruction is based on the view in Morgan's 1682 map.

HABERDASHERS' HALL

Haberdashers' Hall was built in 1478, burnt in the Great Fire, and rebuilt by Thomas Cartwright to the design of Edward Jerman from 1667 to 1668. The buildings stood around a courtyard with the grand livery hall on the north side and an embellished entrance from Maiden Lane to the south. The Hall was burnt in 1840 and 1864, and each time rebuilt; the Victorian Hall was destroyed by bombing in 1940, and replaced by a new building of the mid-1950s on the same site, itself recently demolished for replacement by the offices of Schroder Investment Management (with a new Haberdashers' Hall in Smithfield). The Haberdashers' Company, at eighth in the order of precedence one of the great companies, received ordinances in 1371 and was chartered in 1448. The haberdashers were originally an offshoot of the Mercers, and the Haberdashery was next to the Mercery in the Cheapside market. Until 1502 there were two branches of the Company – the hurriers or cappers, who made and sold hats, and the milliners, who dealt in sundry small fashion goods imported from Milan, and in the early 16th century briefly became 'merchant haberdashers', trading to the Levant. The influence of the Company on the trade declined from the 17th century onwards.

Haberdashers' Hall: Maiden Lane frontage

Haberdashers' Hall: north frontage of court (hall)

WAX CHANDLERS' HALL, Maiden Lane, Wood Street. The Company had a Hall on the site by 1525. It was rebuilt after the Great Fire to Jerman's design, 1668-70, and rebuilt again in 1793, 1853, and 1958 (after bombing). The guild received ordinances in 1358 and was chartered in 1484. It controlled the trade in wax candles (more expensive than tallow candles, they were used principally by churches).

BRODERERS' HALL, Gutter Lane, Cheapside. A small company hall, on a site now occupied by Saddlers' Hall, rebuilt from 1670 and again in the 19th century; finally destroyed in 1940. The Company existed by the 14th century and was chartered in 1561. It controlled the London embroidery trade, whose products (*opus anglicanum*) were once famous throughout Europe.

48 Sion College.
(Guildhall Library)

49 Goldsmiths' Hall, Thomas
Shepherd, 1829, with St John
Zachary churchyard to the left.
(Guildhall Library)

GOLDSMITHS' HALL

The Goldsmiths were the first of the City's livery companies to acquire a hall, in 1339. Goldsmiths' Hall was rebuilt several times during the Middle Ages, and again in 1636 to the designs of Nicholas Stone. It was gutted by the Great Fire, and restored by 1669 to Jerman's designs, its brick buildings with stone dressings surrounding a courtyard. The Goldsmiths have always been one of the most powerful and rich of the City companies (they stand fifth in the order of precedence), and their hall was correspondingly grand. It was replaced between 1829 and 1835 by the still more impressive surviving hall, which was designed by Philip Hardwick and which retains some of its predecessor's interior decoration. The guild of goldsmiths was in existence by 1180, and the Company was chartered in 1327. The goldsmiths congregated around the nearby western end of Cheapside, which therefore came to be known as Goldsmiths Row; in the later Middle Ages the goldsmiths' houses were the most lavish and ostentatious in London. Until the 17th century the display of goldsmithry in their shop windows was one of the sights of London, and fulfilled an important role in demonstrating the wealth and power of the City to monarchs and foreign dignitaries during ceremonial processions along Cheapside; the early Stuart kings even tried to legislate to prevent goldsmiths from leaving Cheapside when the trade ebbed away to other locations. The Goldsmiths' Company exercised complete control over the quality of gold and silver wares produced in London, and continues to do so; the system of assay and hallmarking with the leopard's head emblem was first introduced in 1300. Until the development of sophisticated credit techniques in the late 17th and 18th centuries, gold and silver plate constituted the most important store of wealth, and the power of the goldsmiths derived from their skill in storing and handling precious metals belonging not only to merchants but to sovereigns as well. The goldsmiths were indeed the first bankers, and their issuing of promissory

Goldsmiths' Hall: Foster Lane frontage

frontage of east side of courtyard

notes against deposited plate provided an important impetus to the expansion of credit and the development of banking in the late 17th century. The great goldsmith bankers, men such as Vyner, Backwell, and Child, were major financiers of the Crown, but the late Stuarts were notoriously bad servicers of their debt, and the series of shocks to the emergent credit system which were administered by successive royal moratoria on debt repayment led to the establishment of the Bank of England in 1695 specifically in order to administer the National Debt. The goldsmith bankers meanwhile developed into the private banks, which gradually yielded power to the merchant bankers and later the joint stock bankers, who were able in their turn to develop yet more sophisticated means of responding to London's booming credit market.

Cross-section of livery hall looking south

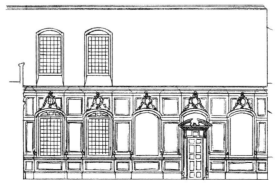

Section of livery hall looking west

NEWGATE AND ALDERSGATE

FROM THE WEST END of Cheapside and through the north-west quadrant of the City ran two of the most important thoroughfares from London to the rest of England: Newgate Street, leading through the City's principal gate towards the West Country and Midlands, and St Martin's le Grand through Aldersgate, the beginning of the Great North Road. Here were important inns serving the carrier trade, the lavish (by City standards) premises of Christ's Hospital school, and the centre of London's administration of criminal justice – the Old Bailey sessions house and the notorious Newgate gaol.

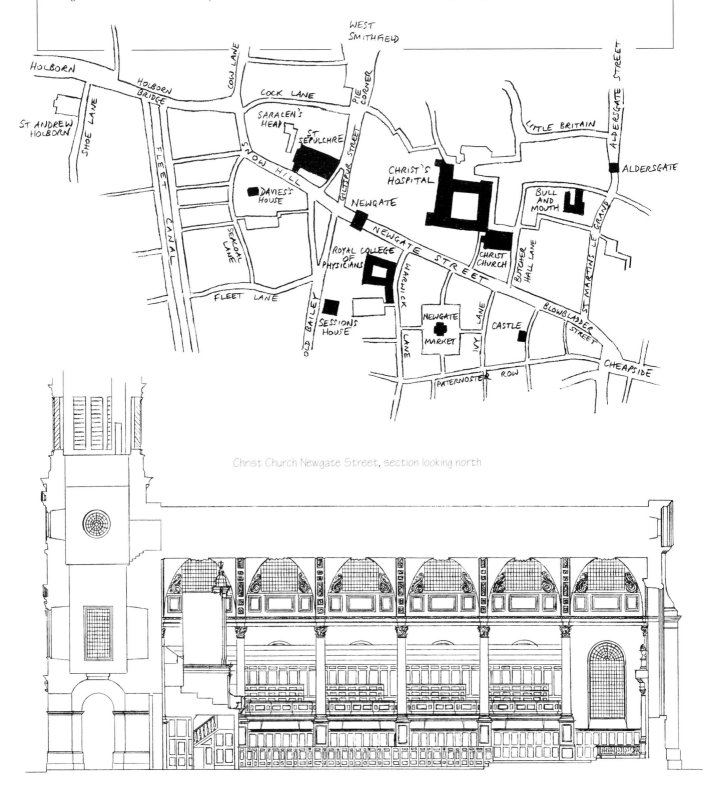

Christ Church Newgate Street, section looking north

CHRIST CHURCH NEWGATE STREET
WITH ST LEONARD FOSTER LANE

Christ Church was established in the choir of the old church of the Franciscan (Greyfriars) friary in 1547. The parish was formed by combining the parishes of St Ewen and St Nicholas in the Shambles, both of whose churches were demolished. The church was burnt in the Great Fire and rebuilt in Portland stone by John Shorthose and Richard Crooke to the designs of Wren between 1677 and 1687. The steeple was completed by Edward Strong the Younger in 1703-4, perhaps with involvement from Hawksmoor. The total cost was £13,750. Christ Church was one of the largest of the City churches, and its interior one of the most impressive, with broad aisles and huge raking galleries which accommodated the boys of the adjoining Christ's Hospital, for whom the church served as a school chapel. Christ Church had a relatively plain exterior, pedimented at each end, while the interior contained fine plasterwork (by Henry Doogood) and furnishings. The steeple is one of Wren's most elaborate, Portland stone, on a square plan throughout, with diminishing colonnaded tiers and urns. The church was gutted by bombs in 1940 and not rebuilt, except for the steeple. Parts of the exterior walls survive and now enclose a rose garden, although the east wall was demolished in the 1980s for the widening of King Edward Street. *(See plate 50, p.156.)*

St Leonard Foster Lane was first mentioned in the mid-13th century. It was a small church which stood on the west side of Foster Lane, almost opposite St Vedast's Church, its site now occupied by Empire House.

Christ Church Newgate Street, Butcher Hall Lane frontage

Christ Church Newgate Street, cross-section looking east

CHRIST'S HOSPITAL

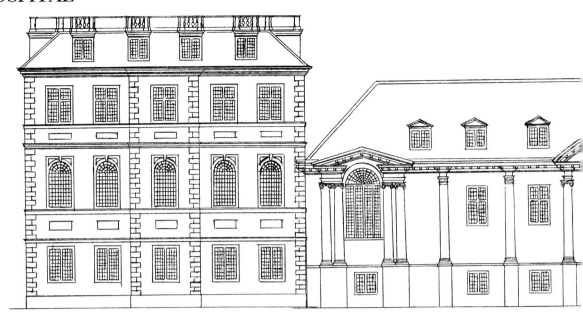

Christ's Hospital
Mathematical School:
west frontage

Christ's Hospital was founded in 1553 by Edward VI as a hospital for orphans. It occupied the conventual buildings of the Greyfriars Franciscan friary, established in 1225 and dissolved in 1538. A school, also known as the Bluecoat School after the Tudor uniform which is still worn by the scholars, was established shortly after the hospital. The accommodation was hugely more generous than that of any other City schools, enabling rebuilding and expansion on an ample scale after the destruction wrought by the 1666 Great Fire. Much of the stone-built medieval fabric was incorporated in the reconstruction, including Whittington's Library on the north side of the central courtyard, called the Garden, and the allegedly haunted Dead Cloister which surrounded it. The brick south front of the school, with its broad segmental

Christ's Hospital: frontage of west side of the
Garden courtyard (great hall)

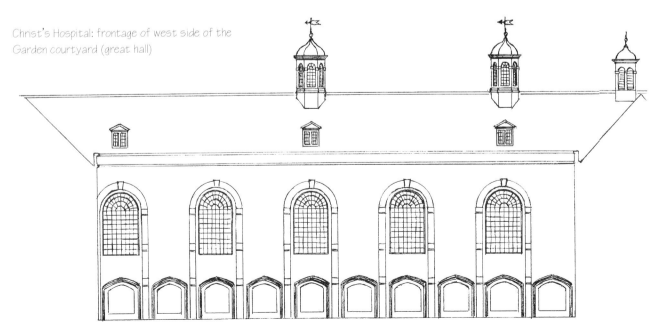

pediment and pedimented entrance incorporating a statue of Edward VI, was built probably to Wren's design in 1675. The dining hall, also of brick, in the west range above the cloister, was built in 1680. Sir Robert Clayton contributed £10,000 to the cost of rebuilding; he also endowed the Mathematical School, established by Samuel Pepys under the patronage of Charles II in 1673 to train boys in navigation, which was added by Wren to the west end of the south range, its main frontage facing west. The Writing School was an addition on the north side, probably to the design of Wren or Hawksmoor, in 1694. The Mathematical School was demolished in 1825 to make way for the huge new Gothic school hall by James Shaw, the hall and Whittington's Library soon followed it, and the whole of the school buildings eventually succumbed in 1902 when Christ's Hospital moved to Horsham in Sussex (where the new buildings incorporate a number of fragments from the old, including Wren's gatehouse), and the new King Edward Building of the General Post Office was put up on the site (recently demolished to make way for new offices for Merrill Lynch, the American investment bank). The boys were involved in an extensive round of annual City customs and processions. They included Edmund Campion, William Camden, Samuel Taylor Coleridge, and Charles Lamb. From 1695 and throughout the 18th century scholars drew the winning tickets in public lotteries. *(See plate 52, p.159.)*

Christ's Hospital: east frontage of Writing School

Christ's Hospital: frontage of the north side of the Garden courtyard (Whittington's Library and Dead Cloister)

50 Interior of Christ Church Newgate Street, photograph, 1929. (National Monuments Record)

Newgate: west frontage (Newgate Street)

Newgate: east frontage (Newgate Street)

Newgate was commonly regarded as the principal gate of London. It led to the Oxford Road and was in fact one of the oldest of the City's gates, having probably been opened by the Romans in about A.D. 200. It was first called Newgate in about 1188, probably because of a recent rebuilding; in the early Middle Ages it was also called Chamberlaingate. A prison was established in Newgate by 1236, and later expanded into adjoining buildings. The gate was rebuilt by Richard Whittington's executors in the 1420s, and again after a fire in the 1550s. Repaired in the 1620s, when some classical decoration was introduced with statues of virtues in niches above the gateway, it was damaged in the Great Fire and subsequently repaired (work was completed in 1672), although much of its medieval fabric was retained, especially on the outer face. This was the Newgate Prison from which the notorious condemned thief and gaolbreaker Jack Sheppard escaped (twice) in 1724, and in which John Gay's Macheath was incarcerated in *The Beggar's Opera* (as shown in Hogarth's painting). It was finally demolished in 1767 for street widening (the last of the old City gates to go), after which a new and much larger Newgate Prison was built on the corner of Old Bailey and Newgate Street to the design of George Dance the Younger; this was itself demolished in 1902 to make way for the Central Criminal Court, opposite the north end of which is the site of the original gate.

ST SEPULCHRE NEWGATE STREET

The church of St Sepulchre without Newgate was first mentioned in 1137. It was originally dedicated to St Edmund, but was later rededicated to the Holy Sepulchre presumably by association with the Crusades and the Jerusalem pilgrimage. It was rebuilt with funds provided by Sir John Popham, the Lord Treasurer, in 1450. The result is the largest parish church in the City, with eight-bay nave and aisles, commensurate with its importance as the centre of a large parish, standing just outside one of the principal gates. The three-storeyed south porch with its fine lierne vault, the west tower, and much of the walling (all repeatedly and heavily restored) survive from Popham's building. The church was gutted in the Great Fire, but being situated towards its edge was not so badly damaged that much of the fabric could not be incorporated into the rebuilding – this was done by Joshua Marshall, and the work was complete by 1670. St Sepulchre's was thus one of the first City churches to be reinstated. Outwardly it was almost identical in appearance to its pre-Fire state. Internally the church was rebuilt with the extant Tuscan arcades, galleries in the aisles, and baroque furnishings, some of which survive. In 1790 the windows of the church were themselves replaced in Tuscan style, but the Perpendicular gothic design was reinstated in the aisle windows in the 1880 restoration.

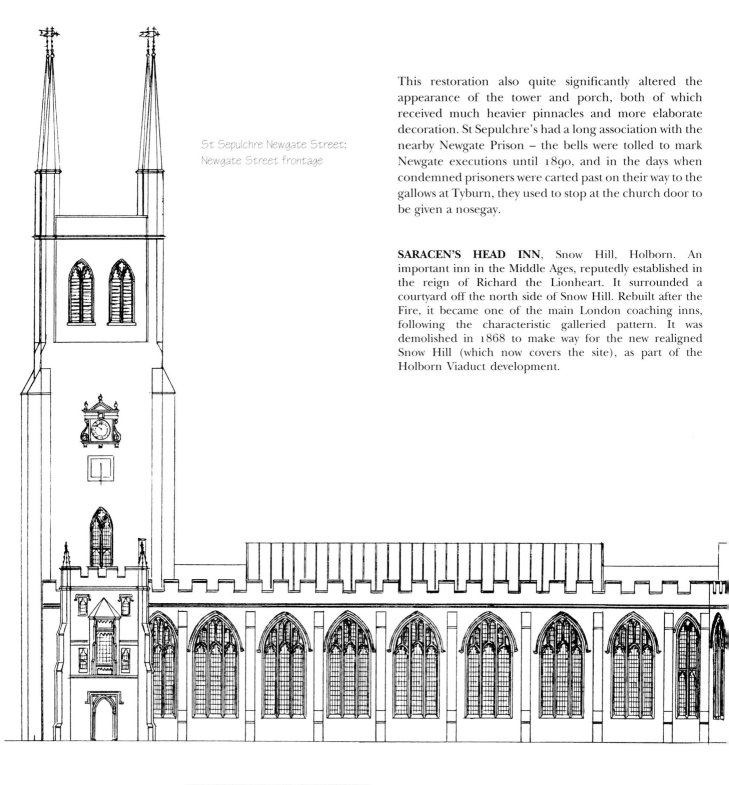

St Sepulchre Newgate Street:
Newgate Street frontage

This restoration also quite significantly altered the appearance of the tower and porch, both of which received much heavier pinnacles and more elaborate decoration. St Sepulchre's had a long association with the nearby Newgate Prison – the bells were tolled to mark Newgate executions until 1890, and in the days when condemned prisoners were carted past on their way to the gallows at Tyburn, they used to stop at the church door to be given a nosegay.

SARACEN'S HEAD INN, Snow Hill, Holborn. An important inn in the Middle Ages, reputedly established in the reign of Richard the Lionheart. It surrounded a courtyard off the north side of Snow Hill. Rebuilt after the Fire, it became one of the main London coaching inns, following the characteristic galleried pattern. It was demolished in 1868 to make way for the new realigned Snow Hill (which now covers the site), as part of the Holborn Viaduct development.

ST ANDREW HOLBORN. St Andrew's Church was first mentioned in 959, and rebuilt in the 1440s. It was not touched by the Great Fire, but was rebuilt in Portland stone from 1684 to 1686 by Edward Pierce and William Stanton to Wren's design, perhaps because of dilapidation, but more probably because of the huge expansion of the large parish's population as the suburbs spilled into it during the 17th century. It is a large church with galleried aisles. The old tower was retained, but its upper stages were rebuilt at a later stage, perhaps to Hawksmoor's design (the baroque tension of the round and segmental arches in the belfry windows hints at his style). The church was gutted by bombs in 1941 and the interior rebuilt in replica by 1966.

51 St Andrew Holborn, photograph. (National Monuments Record)

52 Christ's Hospital and Christ Church Newgate Street,
W. Toms, 1740. (Guildhall Library)

53 Courtyard of the College of Physicians, David Loggan,
1677. (Guildhall Library)

DAVIES'S HOUSE

Sir Thomas Davies was a stationer and bookseller of St Paul's Churchyard who, with his brother Alexander (a scrivener who died in the 1665 Great Plague), in 1662 inherited from Hugh Audley a fortune which included the Manor of Ebury in Westminster. His wealth enabled him to enter City politics, and he became Lord Mayor in 1676. The Westminster estates went as dowry to Alexander's daughter Mary on her marriage to Sir Thomas Grosvenor in 1677; the enormously valuable Grosvenor estate, including much of Mayfair and Belgravia, was built on them in the 18th and 19th centuries. Sir Thomas's own house was in a curiously unfashionable location, at the end of the long and tangled Angel Court, between Snow Hill and the Fleet River, on a site later covered by Holborn Viaduct Station and now by the Fleet Place development. The view is a suggested reconstruction based on the schematic view in Morgan's 1682 map.

Sir Thomas Davies's House: south frontage

OLD BAILEY SESSIONS HOUSE

Old Bailey Sessions House: Sessions House Yard frontage

The sessions house of the Lord Mayor and Justices of the City of London and county of Middlesex was built on the east side of Old Bailey, adjacent to the City wall, in 1539. Destroyed in the Great Fire, it was rebuilt by 1671 with a courtroom open on its north side to the courtyard (in order to reduce the risk of prisoners infecting the court officials with gaol fever) and a finely decorated dining room above. The building was demolished in 1774 to make room for George Dance the Younger's new Newgate Prison, and a new sessions house was rebuilt further south;

this became the Central Criminal Court in 1834, and its successor, the 'Old Bailey', expanded northwards back over the site of Newgate Prison in Mountford's neo-baroque rebuilding in the first decade of the 20th century. Perhaps the most significant trial in the old sessions house was that of Penn and Mead in 1670 – the appeal of the jury members in 'Bushell's Case' against being fined for refusing to bring a guilty verdict established the principle of the independence of jurors.

ROYAL COLLEGE OF PHYSICIANS

Royal College of Physicians: east frontage of courtyard

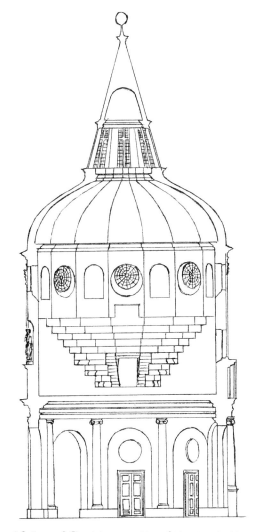

Royal College of Physicians: section of theatre, looking north

The Royal College of Physicians was built on the site of Warwick Inn, the town house of the Earls of Warwick (one of whom was Warwick the Kingmaker), after it had been burnt out of its old premises in Amen Corner in the Great Fire (the College was established in 1518 in Thomas Linacre's house in Knightrider Street). The buildings surrounded a courtyard off the west side of Warwick Lane, and the west range, which contained the state rooms, had an elaborate pilastered and pedimented frontage with a statue of Sir John Cutler (merchant, grocer, and benefactor of the college) in a niche and a lantern on its roof. The courtyard was entered through a highly original domed octagonal range which contained a lecture theatre on its upper floor. The conical glazed lantern (designed to give maximum natural light to the theatre below) and the 'gilded pill' which surmounted it gave it a distinctive profile when viewed along Warwick Lane or across the rooftops. The buildings were traditionally attributed to Wren, but were more likely to have been designed by Hooke. Building lasted from 1674 to 1683. The College moved to a new building in Trafalgar Square in 1827 (it now forms part of Canada House), and on to Regents Park at a later date, where what remains of the fittings of the Warwick Lane building (notably the panelling of the Censors' Room) is now located. The College's old home

Royal College of Physicians: west frontage of court

was converted into a meat market and eventually demolished in the late 19th century; Cutlers' Hall was built on the site in 1887. A diploma from the Board of Censors of the College was necessary in order to practise as a physician within seven miles of London; the physicians tended to attend to the medical needs of the wealthy, while the poorer classes patronised the apothecaries. *(See plate 53, p.159.)*

Warwick Lane: frontage of west side from Warwick Court northwards, including Royal College of Physicians

WARWICK LANE

Warwick Lane, linking Ludgate Hill with Newgate Street, was named after the town house of the Beauchamps, Earls of Warwick, which stood on its west side on the site later occupied by the Royal College of Physicians; before the mid-14th century it was called Old Dean Lane. The view shows a typical row of the second category of City house, for 'streets and lanes of note', which formed the foreground to views northwards towards the dome of the Royal College of Physicians. There remained at the corner of Warwick Lane and Newgate Street (the site is now being redeveloped) one of the very few stone house signs surviving from the Great Rebuilding; it shows Guy, Earl of Warwick, and is dated 1668.

NEWGATE MARKET

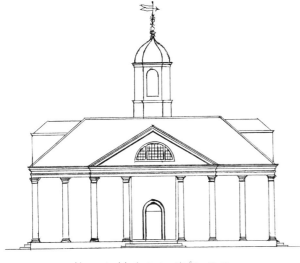

Newgate Market: south frontage

As part of the street improvements following the Great Fire, the provisions markets which had encumbered the passage of traffic through the City were cleared away from the main thoroughfares. Newgate Street had for centuries been the main London meat market, as reflected in its previous name, the Shambles. It retained a large number of butchers' shops until the 19th century, but the main market was removed to a newly cleared square between Newgate Street and Paternoster Row. In the centre stood the market house, its columniated ground floor on a cross plan with pedimented arms. The detail of its appearance is (like Honey Lane Market's) poorly documented, and this reconstruction is based on Leybourn's plan, the schematic view in Morgan's 1682 map, and contemporary descriptions. It was rebuilt in the early 19th century, but the market was removed to Smithfield in 1869; the site is now covered by Paternoster Square.

CASTLE TAVERN

In the late 16th century the Castle Tavern was kept by Richard Tarlton, Shakespeare's fellow-actor, and frequented by the Blackfriars players. It was burnt in 1666 and rebuilt in a plain style in brick; in the early 18th century the building became Dolly's Chop House, a famous City eating house named after one of its early cooks. Dolly's was closed, and the building demolished, in 1883. The site is now covered by the Paternoster development.

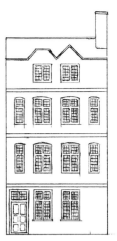

Castle Tavern: Queen's Head Passage frontage

BULL AND MOUTH INN

The Bull and Mouth, whose name was a corruption of 'Boulogne Mouth' (commemorating a siege by Henry VIII) was established in 1630. Rebuilt after the Great Fire with galleried ranges around a courtyard which opened into Bull and Mouth Street, it became one of the most important of the London inns which serviced the coach and carrier trade to the North Country and Scotland, especially after its acquisition by Edward Sherman in 1823; he pioneered long-distance day coaches to the cities of the north. The Bull and Mouth was rebuilt on a larger and grander scale in 1830 to accommodate this expansion of business. Even long after the coaching trade had been killed off by the railways, the Bull and Mouth, renamed the Queen's Hotel, continued to be much patronised by Manchester textile merchants visiting London. It was finally demolished in 1890 to make way for the extension of the General Post Office on the north side of Angel Street (now the London office of Nomura, the Japanese securities house).

Bull and Mouth Inn: frontage of west side of courtyard

ALDERSGATE

Aldersgate: north frontage (Aldersgate Street)

A gate in the wall of Londinium was opened to the west of the Cripplegate fort probably in the late Roman period to provide an additional route out of the city to the north; in the medieval period it became the principal north gate of the City, the start of the Great North Road. It was named after one Ealdred, and is first mentioned in about 1000. It was rebuilt in 1617, perhaps by Gerard Christmas, with a large equestrian relief of James I above the arch, commemorating that monarch's ceremonial entry into the City at the end of his journey from Scotland after his accession in 1603. The flanking towers had statues of Jeremiah and Samuel, and over the inside of the gate was another statue of King James, seated in his chair of state. The gate was damaged by the Great Fire, which came to a halt a short distance outside it, restored in 1670 (though probably retaining much of its early 17th-century appearance), and cleared away in 1760 along with the other City gates to ease the flow of traffic; it stood across Aldersgate Street just north of the Lord Raglan public house.

LUDGATE HILL AND BLACKFRIARS

LUDGATE HILL, part of the main route towards Westminster and the south-west and an important shopping street with a number of inns, ran steeply down the east flank of the Fleet valley from St Paul's Churchyard. To the south the semi-autonomous district of Blackfriars was a tangle of alleyways running down towards the Fleet Canal and the Thames.

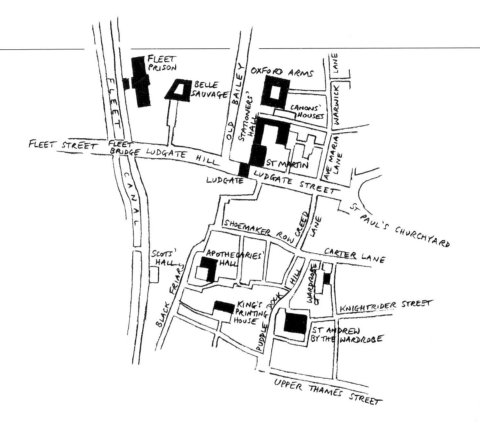

Ludgate: west frontage (Ludgate Hill)

ST MARTIN LUDGATE

St Martin's is one of the handful of the new City churches which are almost unchanged from their original state, having escaped the worst depredations of both Victorian improvers and the Luftwaffe. It was first mentioned in the mid-12th century, although Geoffrey of Monmouth recorded a tradition that it was founded in the seventh. Burnt in the Great Fire, it was rebuilt by Nicholas Young to the design of Wren or Hooke from 1677 to 1686. The compact Portland stone south front has large stone volutes flanking the central tower, whose light lead-covered spire, ringed at its base by a railed balustrade, standing on a small bell-shaped dome (echoed by the ogee caps on the western towers of the Cathedral), provides a highly effective foil to the dome of St Paul's in views up Ludgate Hill. The foreground of this view was until 1760 provided by the broad front of Ludgate, and the view shows the church's relation to (a conjectural reconstruction of) the inside face of the gate. St Martin's has an interior whose plan consists of a groin-vaulted cross within a square, in the Dutch tradition which is usually associated with Hooke, separated from the street by a vestibule and gallery. The furnishings are mostly of the late 17th century, the work of William Draper, William Newman and William Emmet, lacking only the box pews, and are of the highest quality.

St Martin Ludgate: diagonal view of Ludgate Street frontage, with conjectural view of inner face of Ludgate

LUDGATE

Ludgate was traditionally supposed to have been named after the legendary British king Lud, who was said to have built it in 66 B.C.; Eilert Ekwall interpreted it more prosaically as meaning 'back gate'. It was probably built by the Romans, and first mentioned by name in 857. Spanning the main highway towards Westminster, it was one of the main gates through the City wall. It was rebuilt in the early 13th century, in 1463 (when it was enlarged to incorporate a gaol), and again in 1586, and had to be extensively repaired after damage sustained during the Great Fire; reconstruction was complete by 1672. Above the archway on the west side was a statue of Queen Elizabeth I; on the inside (eastern) face of the gate were corresponding statues of King Lud and his sons. These statues, carved by William Kerwin in 1586, were saved when Ludgate was demolished for road-widening in 1760, and they are now at St Dunstan in the West. The view of St Martin Ludgate shows how Ludgate straddled Ludgate Hill just west of that church.

STATIONERS' HALL

OXFORD ARMS INN

The Stationers' Company acquired Abergavenny House, previously the residence of Lord Abergavenny, in 1611. It rebuilt it as its Hall from 1670 to 1674 following its destruction by the Great Fire; the bricklayer was Robert Wapshott. The interior of the Hall is one of the few in the City which remains substantially as it was in the late 17th century, notably the livery hall with its fine panelling and carved screen by Stephen Colledge and Henry Foord. The appearance of the brick-faced exterior, shown in the view, was substantially changed by the addition of a neo-classical stone frontage to Stationers Hall Court in 1800. The Stationers' Company was chartered in 1557 at the instance of Queen Mary's government, which wished to control heretical publications, although a fraternity had existed since the early 15th century. It was responsible for the regulation of the publishing industry, which was controlled via the Stationers' Register, established in the early 16th century (registration was compulsory from 1662 to 1911, although by then the company had already lost its power); in the early days proscribed books were burnt in the courtyard behind Stationers' Hall. Incineration was a fate which befell many of the London stationers' books, first in the Great Fire, when the books stored in the crypt of St Paul's for safety caught fire (the fuel they provided contributed substantially to the irreparable damage that the cathedral sustained), and later in 1940, when Paternoster Row, the centre of the London book trade, was reduced by an inferno of fire bombs to a smouldering wasteland.

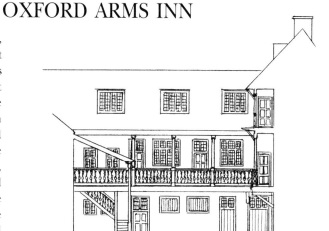

Oxford Arms Inn: frontage of north side of courtyard

Frontage of entrance from Oxford Arms Passage

Stationers' Hall: Stationers' Hall court frontage

The last survivor of the City's many galleried coaching inns stood against the City wall west of Warwick Lane. It originated before the Great Fire, and was rebuilt by 1673 with galleries around three sides of its courtyard. Coaches ran from it to Oxford. It was later occupied by Edward Sherman, the famous innkeeper and coach operator of the Bull and Mouth. It closed as an inn in 1868, after which it was converted into tenements. Before its demolition in 1878 its appearance was extensively recorded, especially by the recently formed Society for Photographing Relics of Old London, and more is therefore known of what it looked like than any other old City inn. The site is now occupied by canons' houses in Amen Court.

CANONS' HOUSES, Amen Court, St Paul's. The three brick houses in Amen Court (perhaps named, like Paternoster Row, Ave Maria Lane, and Creed Lane, after medieval text-writers) were built by Edward Woodroffe between 1671 and 1673 for the Canons Residentiary of St Paul's. Sydney Smith and Richard Harris Barham lived there in the 1830s and 1840s.

54   Canons' Houses, nos. 1, 2 and 3 Amen Court, photograph. (National Monuments Record)

Oxford Arms Inn: frontage of east side of courtyard

55 Oxford Arms Inn, looking over the rooftops towards St Paul's, photograph, c.1875. (National Monuments Record)

BELLE SAUVAGE INN

Originally called Topfield's Inn after the family which occupied it in the 14th century, the house was called Savage's Inn, or the Bell, by the mid-16th century, so the myth that it was named after Pocahontas, who stayed there in 1616 and 1617, must be discounted. In the 16th century its yard was used for performances of plays, and was supposedly the scene of the alleged appearance of the Devil himself in Marlowe's *Dr Faustus*, an event which, according to John Aubrey, prompted Edward Alleyn to found Dulwich College. Rebuilt with a galleried inner courtyard after the Great Fire, it became one of the principal London coaching inns in the 18th century. Grinling Gibbons lived in one of the houses in the outer yard in the 1660s – it was there that he was 'discovered' by John Evelyn as a result of the exquisitely carved pot of flowers which he kept in his window as an advertisement. The Belle Sauvage was eventually demolished in 1873; the premises of Cassells the publisher replaced it until they were destroyed in the 1941 Blitz. The site now lies under the offices on the east side of Seacoal Lane.

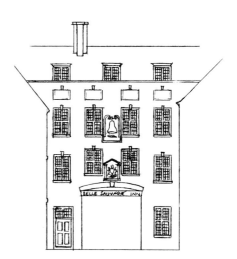

Belle Sauvage Inn: frontage of north side of outer courtyard

Belle Sauvage Inn: frontage of south side of inner courtyard

FLEET PRISON

Fleet Prison: Fleet Canal frontage

SCOTS' HALL, Blackfriars. Scots' Hall stood on the east side of the Fleet Canal, just south of Bridewell Bridge. The Scottish Corporation, a charitable foundation for the support of Scotsmen in London, was founded in the early 17th century and chartered in 1665. It built Scots' Hall, consisting of a hall and almshouses, from 1672 to 1676. The building was removed in the 1760s for the New Bridge Street development.

APOTHECARIES' HALL

Named after the river, the Fleet was a royal prison, in existence by 1130; it was a debtors' prison by 1290. It stood on the east bank of the Fleet River (now covered by Farringdon Street), just north of Ludgate Circus. Burnt in the Great Fire, it was rebuilt shortly thereafter, and burnt again in the 1780 Gordon Riots. The appearance of the late 17th-century prison is poorly documented, and this hypothetical reconstruction of its entrance is derived from the 18th-century print 'Begging at the Gate'; the main range of buildings lay behind, in a walled courtyard. Rebuilt in 1782 by George Dance the Younger, the prison closed in 1842 and was demolished in 1846. Poor conditions in it attracted the attention of John Howard in the late 18th century and Charles Dickens in the 1830s. Latterly it was mainly a debtors' prison, with the quality of accommodation varying according to the means of the prisoner. The Fleet was a liberty exempt from the City's jurisdiction, and 'Fleet marriages', performed without licence by imprisoned clergymen, were popular until voided by the 1753 Marriage Act. The site is now covered by the Fleet Place development.

Apothecaries' Hall is one of the best preserved of the late 17th-century company halls. The Society of Apothecaries (chartered in 1617 as an offshoot of the Grocers' Company) acquired Cobham House, a mansion in Blackfriars which had formerly been the guesthouse of the Dominican friary, in 1632. Burnt in 1666, it was rebuilt by Thomas Locke between 1669 and 1673 around a quadrangle, and especially in its interiors remains largely unchanged, with finely carved woodwork. The courtyard frontages were altered in the late 18th and 19th centuries by the addition of a shallow pediment above the livery hall frontage, the infilling of the colonnade on the north side, and the rendering over of the brick walls. The Apothecaries acquired wide influence as poor men's doctors; the Society still administers the Licenciate in Medicine and Surgery. The Apothecaries Act of 1815 granted the Society powers which meant that it dominated early 19th-century medicine; this influence was eroded by the development of industrial pharmacy and the Medical Act of 1886. The Society founded the Chelsea Physic Garden in 1673. Members have included Cromwell, Goldsmith, Keats, Jenner, and Davy.

Apothecaries' Hall:
frontage of east side of courtyard (livery hall)

WARDROBE COURT

Nos.8 and 9 Wardrobe Court

Wardrobe Court opens off the south side of Carter Lane just east of St Andrew's Hill. It occupies the site of the courtyard of the King's Wardrobe, a large house which originally belonged to the Beauchamp family, and was acquired by Edward III in 1366 to house the royal wardrobe, which included the garments of the royal household and the Order of the Garter, as well as the royal account books. The King's Wardrobe was burned in the Great Fire. Wardrobe Court was built up in the late 17th and early 18th centuries. The view shows two of the late 17th-century brick houses which stood on the east side until the early 20th century. Nos.3, 4 and 5, which date from about 1710, survive today.

ST ANDREW BY THE WARDROBE WITH ST ANNE BLACKFRIARS

St Andrew's Church was first mentioned in the late 12th century, and acquired its name as a result of its proximity to the King's Wardrobe. The church was burnt in the Great Fire, and rebuilt by Nicholas Young to the designs of Wren from 1685 to 1697, the last of the new City churches to be completed. The parishes were poor ones, and unusually the furnishings as well as the fabric were provided out of public funds. St Andrew's is brick-built with stone dressings, on a basilican plan with tunnel-vaulted nave and plain south-west tower. Originally closely hemmed by buildings, the south side was opened up to the newly constructed Queen Victoria Street in the 1870s; at the same time this frontage was embellished and the entrance moved one bay westwards. The church was gutted by bombing in the Second World War and most of its furnishings destroyed. As part of the

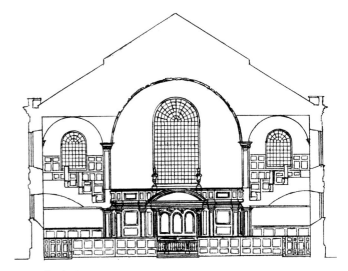

St Andrew by the Wardrobe: cross-section looking east

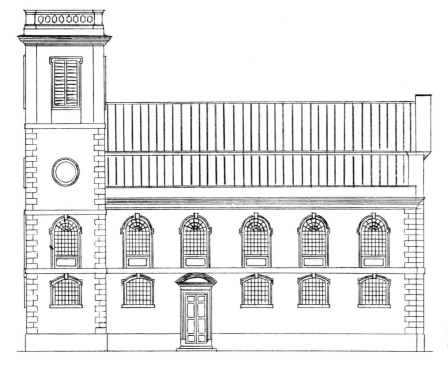

St Andrew by the Wardrobe: south (churchyard) frontage

King's Printing House: Printing House Square frontage

KING'S PRINTING HOUSE

restoration by Marshall Sisson between 1959 and 1961 the Victorian external decorations were removed (their scars remain) to return the church to more or less its original appearance, and the interior was considerably altered.

St Anne Blackfriars was originally a chapel in the large church of the Dominican friars which stood in the western angle of the City wall, above the Fleet River to the south of Ludgate Hill. After the suppression of the friary in 1538 the parishioners were left without a place of worship until Queen Mary ordered a new church to be built in the mid-16th century. Its site lies in the churchyard on the corner of Ireland Yard and Church Entry.

Bonham Norton and John Bill, King's Printers, took over Hunsdon House, previously the mansion of Baron Hunsdon, Lord Chamberlain and Queen Elizabeth's cousin, in 1627. The *London Gazette* was published there from 1665, and also the 'Wicked Bible', which commanded 'Thou shalt commit adultery'. The Printing House was rebuilt in the early 1670s after its destruction in the Fire; this reconstruction is based on the view in Morgan's 1682 map. It was rebuilt again in a similar style after a further fire in 1738. The King's Printers remained there until 1769. In 1784 John Walter established the *Daily Universal Register* (from 1788 *The Times*) there; it remained in Printing House Square (and was rebuilt on the same site, on the north side of Queen Victoria Street, just east of the Blackfriars railway, in the 1870s and 1960s) until 1974. The new Times Square building is now being built on the site.

FLEET STREET

WEST of the Fleet Canal, Fleet Street led up the hill towards the Strand and Westminster, flanked by the legal Inns, inns for refreshment and transport, printing houses, the narrow alleys of Whitefriars, the telescopic steeple of St Bride's, and the maze of new housing developments which stretched northwards towards Holborn. A few doors short of Temple Bar, the grand new gateway which marked the western boundary of the City, an abrupt transition from neat new brick houses to irregular gabled timber-framed structures marked, as it did in a great arc all the way round to Tower Hill, the limit of the flames of 1666.

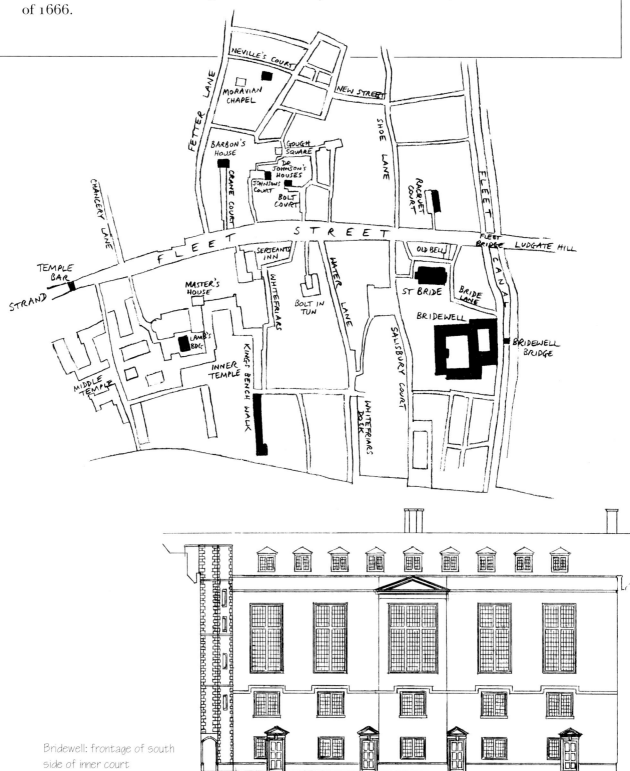

Bridewell: frontage of south side of inner court

BRIDEWELL

King Henry VIII built Bridewell Palace, which was named after the nearby well in St Bride's churchyard, from 1515 to 1523. It was the last royal palace to be built in the City, and was the scene of several conferences relating to the king's divorce from Katherine of Aragon. Edward VI granted it to the City in 1553 to house orphans, vagrants, petty offenders, and 'disorderly women'. From 1557 it was managed jointly with the Bethlehem Hospital for lunatics (Bedlam) in Bishopsgate, later in Moorfields. It incorporated a prison (for short-term prisoners only, who were put to hard labour and flogged twice weekly in public), a hospital, and workrooms, and became the model for hundreds of 'Bridewells' or 'Houses of Correction' throughout the kingdom. Religious offenders were imprisoned in Bridewell in the late 16th and early 17th centuries. The three courtyards of the Tudor building were burnt in the Great Fire, and Bridewell was rebuilt around the two northern courtyards, incorporating much of the original fabric, between 1666 and 1676. The eastern, outer, courtyard, with its gatehouse opening from Bride Lane, was demolished as part of the

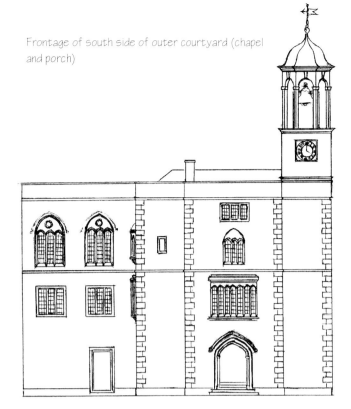

Frontage of south side of outer courtyard (chapel and porch)

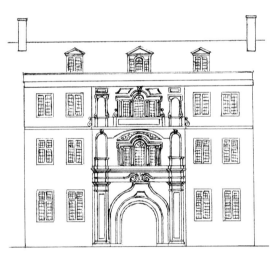

Bridewell: Bride Lane frontage

reconstruction of the eastern part of Bridewell which accompanied the covering over of the Fleet Ditch to form New Bridge Street at the end of the 18th century. Bridewell was closed in 1855, and the prisoners moved to Holloway; the entire complex, except for the surviving early 19th-century gatehouse in New Bridge Street, was demolished in 1863. Its site is now covered by the buildings around Bridewell Place.

Bridewell: frontage of west side of inner court

BRIDEWELL BRIDGE

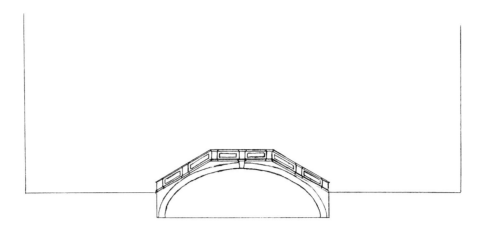

Bridewell Bridge, Fleet River, looking north

The Fleet River was a tributary of the Thames which flanked the west side of the City wall. In the early Middle Ages it was used by boats for both passenger and goods traffic, but later became clogged with rubbish, in spite of repeated municipal efforts to clean it out. Between 1671 and 1674 the Fleet was deepened, widened, and improved to the design of Wren and Hooke as the 'New Canal', 40 feet broad and flanked by 30-foot-broad quays, lined by brick houses and warehouses, with a view to encouraging the revival of a shipping trade; the scheme cost £51,000. Its appearance was very much what Wren and others intended for the unrealised Thames quay. The waterway was crossed by street bridges at Holborn Bridge and Fleet Bridge, and the footbridge opposite Bridewell, built in 1672; the appearance of the last, with its elegant high arch to provide clearance for boats, is known from Samuel Scott's painting of the mouth of the Fleet and Hayman's illustration for Pope's *Dunciad* (the Fleet was the scene of the diving and filth-flinging contest in that poem). (Bridewell Bridge must have stood close to the site of the gallery which was built for the Emperor Charles V's state visit to England in 1522, linking Henry VIII's Bridewell Palace with the Blackfriars Friary, where the Emperor stayed.) The hoped for revival of river traffic did not materialise, and neither the scour of the river nor the energy of the City was sufficient to prevent the Fleet's reversion to an open sewer and rubbish dump – as Pope described it: 'The King of dykes! than whom no sluice of mud/ With deeper sable blots the silver flood'. The part of the river above Fleet Bridge was paved over for the Fleet Market in the 1730s, and the rest was paved and straightened in 1766 to form New Bridge Street, the approach to the new Blackfriars Bridge; it was at this stage that Bridewell Bridge was removed – its site is on the east side of New Bridge Street opposite Bridewell Place. (*See plate 57, p.176.*)

RACQUET COURT

Racquet Court was probably developed in the 1680s, part of the infilling on the north side of Fleet Street, between Shoe Lane and the Fleet River. It survived relatively intact until the later part of the 20th century, with this fine row of brick houses occupying its east side. The site was until recently occupied by the Express Newspapers printing works.

OLD CHESHIRE CHEESE TAVERN, Wine Office Court, Fleet Street. A late 17th-century tavern with a Georgian frontage; in the 18th and 19th centuries it was a noted chop house, famous for producing giant meat puddings (which could allegedly be smelt in the Stock Exchange). Now a public house, its patrons have included Johnson and Boswell, Reynolds, Garrick, Gibbon, Dickens, Carlyle, Macaulay, Tennyson, Collins, Roosevelt, Conan Doyle and Beerbohm.

Racquet Court: frontage of east side (nos.1 to 3)

JOHNSON'S HOUSE

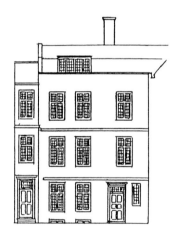

Dr. Johnson's House (no. 8 Bolt Court)

No.8 Bolt Court was a plain late 17th-century brick house which was Dr. Samuel Johnson's home from 1776 until his death in 1784. He wrote the *Lives of the Poets* there. The house burned down in 1819.

JOHNSON'S HOUSE

Dr. Johnson's House (no.7 Johnsons Court)

Dr. Johnson lived at No.7 Johnsons Court from 1765 to 1776; he wrote *Journey to the Western Isles* and edited Shakespeare there. Johnsons Court was named after a 17th-century tailor on whose land it was developed, as part of the infill of vacant plots on the north side of Fleet Street, the warren of alleyways which so excited Samuel Johnson's imagination. *(See plate 58, p.176.)*

JOHNSON'S HOUSE, Gough Square, Fleet Street. The houses in Gough Court were developed in the late 17th century as a speculation by Richard Gough, a wool merchant and China and East India merchant. Nos.1 and 17 survive, rare examples of the sorts of brick houses which abounded in the new courts which infilled behind Fleet Street in the aftermath of the Fire. No.17 was Dr. Johnson's house from 1748 to 1759; he wrote the *Dictionary*, the *Rambler*, and the *Idler* there. It is now the Dr. Johnson's House museum.

BARBON'S HOUSE

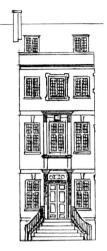

Nicholas Barbon's House (no.7 Crane Court)

Nicholas Barbon, a Fleet Street property speculator, who was a pioneer of fire insurance as well as the author of several treatises on money, developed Crane Court on the land behind his Fleet Street house in the early 1660s. The houses were burnt in the Great Fire, and Barbon rebuilt them in brick between 1670 and 1672 (nos.5 and 6 survive, rebuilt in replica after fire damage in the 1970s, with the fine plaster ceilings reinstated). No.7, the 'front house' at the north end of the court, with a narrow but more elaborately decorated frontage than the others, was Barbon's own house. It was purchased by the Royal Society during Sir Isaac Newton's presidency in 1710 and remained its headquarters until it moved to Somerset House in 1780. Later the house was occupied by the Philosophical Society, and Coleridge delivered his Lectures on Shakespeare there in 1819. It burnt down in 1877. The site is now occupied by Winchmore House.

56 Dr. Johnson's House, Gough Square, photograph. (National Monuments Record)

57   Entrance to the Fleet Canal, showing the steeple of St Bride Fleet Street, Bridewell Bridge, and Fitch's House, after Samuel Scott, mid-18th century. (Guildhall Library)

58   Johnson's Court: Dr. Johnson's house is at the far end, John Crowther, 1881. (Guildhall Library)

59   Neville's Court, photograph, *c.*1880. (National Monuments Record)

NEVILLE'S COURT

No.10 Neville's Court

No.10 Neville's Court, also referred to as Neville's Castle (after the Neville family who had a house on the site) was rebuilt in brick in the late 17th century. It became the 'Great House' of the Moravian community who settled in Neville's Court from the mid-17th century and built their own chapel there. No.10 and other houses in Neville's Court were the last houses in the City to retain their front gardens, but all was either swept away in the early 20th century or destroyed by bombing in the Second World War, and the site is now occupied by the new office blocks on the east side of Fetter Lane.

MORAVIAN CHAPEL, Neville's Court, Fetter Lane. One of the earliest nonconformist conventicles in London, first built by the Moravian community before the Great Fire and rebuilt after it and again in the 18th century. Many of the most famous nonconformists preached there, including Baxter, Wesley and Whitefield.

TEMPLE BAR

Temple Bar was a gate which stood across Fleet Street, marking the western boundary of the liberties of the City of London. A barrier was established probably in the 12th century, and rebuilt as a timber gate by the mid-14th century; by the early 16th century this had reached quite elaborate proportions. Temple Bar was not touched by the Great Fire, but was rebuilt in Portland stone by Joshua Marshall to Wren's design in 1672. It and Moorgate were the only late 17th-century rebuildings of London gates which were carried out in full-blooded baroque style, in spite of the fact that neither was necessitated by damage caused by the Fire itself. Temple Bar was constructed with a broad archway across the street and narrow entrances for pedestrians on either side, and a segmentally-pedimented upper storey which was flanked by large carved volutes. The gate was adorned with fine stone carvings, including John Bushnell's statues in niches of James I and Queen Anne of Denmark, Charles I, and Charles II. From 1684 to 1772 the heads of executed criminals were exposed on spikes on the roof. On state visits by the sovereign to the City, Temple Bar was the scene of a symbolic demonstration of the rights of the City when the gates were closed in the sovereign's face, and a herald had to knock for admission. Nowadays a rather less confrontational ceremony of admission, involving the offering up of the sword of state, still takes place at the memorial on the site of the Bar. Temple Bar was removed for the widening of Fleet Street in 1878, and was re-erected in 1888 in Theobalds Park, Hertfordshire; it remains there in spite of repeated proposals to incorporate it in various schemes for redesigning the surroundings of St Paul's Cathedral. *(See plate 62, p.180.)*

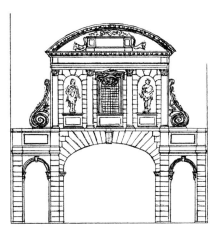

Temple Bar: west frontage (Strand)

INNER TEMPLE: KINGS BENCH WALK

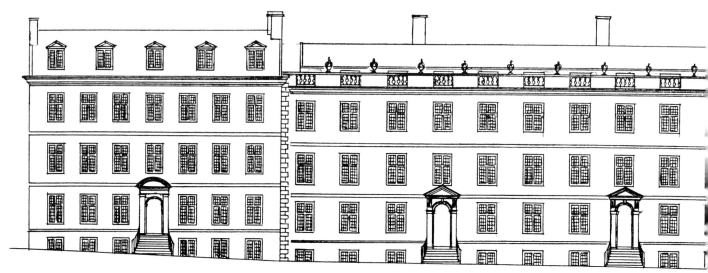

Inner Temple: Kings Bench Walk: facade of east side of the Lower Walks

Inner Temple, one of the four Inns of Court to which barristers practising in England and Wales must belong, marked the furthest point westwards which the Great Fire reached on the river bank – the Temple Gardens were sufficient barrier to prevent its further spread. Many of the buildings of the Temple were affected by a further conflagration in 1677. Kings Bench Walk, a row of barristers' chambers along the eastern boundary of the Temple which was named after the Kings Bench Office which stood at its south end, was completely destroyed in the Great Fire and rebuilt in brick by 1670. It was rebuilt again after the 1677 fire, and the surviving original houses at its northern end, which constitute the finest 17th-century domestic ensemble remaining in the City, date from that time. The view shows the earlier rebuilding of the southern part of the terrace, and derives from a 1671 view of the Temple; the 1677 rebuilding (of which one house survives at the north end, on the corner of the entrance from Tudor Street) was not so grand, and did not have an equivalent river frontage; it was progressively rebuilt from the late 18th to the mid-19th centuries.

60   17th-century houses in King's Bench Walk, Inner Temple, photograph. (National Monuments Record)

Inner Temple: Kings Bench Walk: river frontage

MIDDLE TEMPLE: LAMB BUILDING

Caesar's Building (named after its builder in 1596, Sir Julius Caesar, Master of the Rolls), which stood to the south of the Temple Church, marked the westernmost extent of the area of continuous destruction wrought by the Great Fire (although precautionary demolitions were scattered further westwards along Fleet Street and the Strand). On its site in 1667 the Benchers of the Middle Temple built Lamb Building, a large brick block of barristers' chambers dividing Cloister Court and Tanfield Court. Lamb Building was destroyed by German bombing in the Second World War and not rebuilt; the site is now covered by Church Court. Lamb Building marked the easternmost extent of the Middle Temple, one of the Inns of Court whose members practise as barristers in England and Wales.

61 Master's House, Temple, photograph. (National Monuments Record)

TEMPLE: MASTER'S HOUSE. The residence of the Master of the Temple (who has jurisdiction over both the Inner and Middle Temples) stands just north-east of the Temple Church, its front garden opening onto what used to be Tanfield Court and is now part of Church Court. It was rebuilt in 1667, reputedly but not probably to Wren's design, in brick with stone dressings and a pediment. Destroyed in the Second World War, it has been rebuilt in near replica and is a good example of how the grander City mansions appeared.

SERJEANTS' INN, Fleet Street. The Society of Serjeants-at-Law, the highest order of barristers, which originated as servitors to the Knights Templar and was dissolved in 1877, occupied premises near the Temple at the time of the Great Fire. The Inn was rebuilt by 1670, and again in the 18th century. The site is now occupied by post-war barristers' chambers in traditional style. The Serjeants moved to new premises on the east side of Chancery Lane in 1737.

BOLT IN TUN INN, Fleet Street. A famous inn and coaching house, which stood in a deep courtyard opening southwards off Fleet Street just west of Water Lane (now Whitefriars Street), on the site now occupied by the offices of the solicitors Freshfields. Coaches ran from it to Bath and the West Country, and the last stage coach from London was said to have departed from it. The inn was demolished in the late 19th century.

OLD BELL TAVERN, Fleet Street. The Bell was supposedly the site of the Sun, where Wynkyn de Worde, the first City printer, established his press about 1500. The front house is a modern rebuilding, but the rear, facing onto St Bride's Churchyard, is a survival from 1678.

Middle Temple: Lamb Building: Tanfield Court (west) frontage

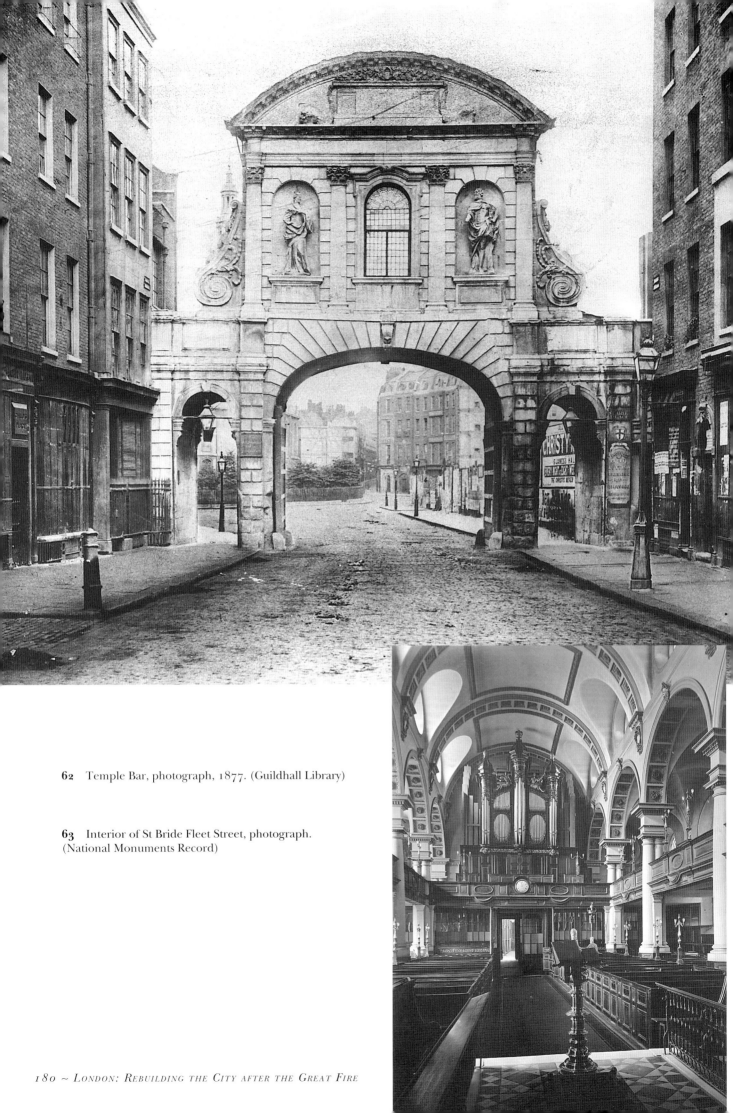

62 Temple Bar, photograph, 1877. (Guildhall Library)

63 Interior of St Bride Fleet Street, photograph.
(National Monuments Record)

ST BRIDE FLEET STREET

St Bride Fleet Street: west (churchyard) frontage

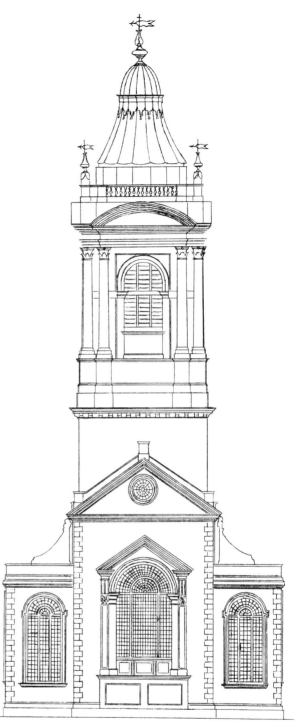

St Bride Fleet Street: Bride Lane frontage, showing original design for steeple

St Bride's Church was founded in the sixth century on the west bank of the Fleet River, at the eastern end of Lundenwic, the early Saxon trading settlement which extended westwards along Fleet Street and the Strand. It was probably dedicated to St Bridget of Kildare, perhaps in connection with Irish traders resident in Lundenwic. St Bride's Well was previously in the churchyard. Rebuilt in the late 12th century, it was large and important enough for a parliament to be held there in 1210. Rebuilt on a yet larger scale in the late 15th century, it was burnt in the Great Fire, and rebuilt in Portland stone by Joshua

Marshall and later Samuel Fulkes to Wren's designs on new, regular foundations, from 1671 to 1678, with a nave and aisles separated by double Tuscan columns (a Dutch motif). The cross-section shows a suggested reconstruction of the elaborate reredos, based on Hatton's description. The vigorous steeple, built in Portland stone from 1701 to 1703 by Fulkes, was at 234 feet the tallest of all Wren's City steeples. Hawksmoor may have had an input to its design, although the concept was originally conceived by Wren in an early project for St Paul's (a similar steeple was already shown in Morgan's panorama in 1682, 20 years before it was built). Its five diminishing octagonal stages, whose open arcades provide transparency in distant views, remains one of the dominant landmarks of the City's skyline (it effectively anchored the skyline at the west end, its great height providing a foil to the bulkier mass of St Paul's Cathedral on the other side of the Fleet valley), and served as the model for the early 19th-century Ludgate Hill pastrycook Rich's wedding cakes. The stages of the steeple and their openings diminish in height at each stage, but the relative height of the openings within each stage increases, thereby heightening the effect of thrusting telescopic expansion. The total cost of the church was some £15,000. The spire was struck by lightning in 1764 and rebuilt eight feet shorter; this disturbed the proportions somewhat, and the view shows the original height (as well as the urns, which were removed in 1803). St Bride's bells were so famous for their musicality that 18th-century high society came specially to listen to them. Bells, and the richly furnished galleried interior were completely burnt out in a fire raid in 1940; the church was restored in 1957 but remains bell-less.

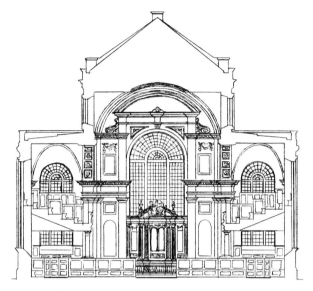

St Bride Fleet Street: cross-section looking east

St Bride Fleet Street: section looking south

ACKNOWLEDGEMENTS

I WOULD LIKE to express my thanks to the following for permission to use original material held by them as sources for my drawings, or to reproduce original material held by them. In all cases any interpretation of that source material is entirely my own responsibility, and the permission of the owners of the material to use it as a source does not necessarily imply their agreement with my interpretation. The use of each source is detailed in the list of sources overleaf.

All Souls' College, Oxford, for permission to use original drawings as source material for several of the drawings of churches.

The British Library, for permission to use original drawings as sources for several of the drawings.

The British Museum, Department of Prints and Drawings, for permission to use original drawings, watercolours, and prints as sources for a large number of the drawings, and also for permission to reproduce original material as illustrations.

The Worshipful Company of Clothworkers, for permission to use original material as source material for the drawings of Clothworkers' Hall.

The College of Arms, for permission to use original drawings as source material for the drawings of the College of Arms.

The Worshipful Company of Drapers, for permission to base the drawing of Drapers' Hall on the original drawing by John Gorham.

English Heritage (National Monuments Record), for permission to base a large number of drawings on original drawings by the National Monuments Record, and on photographs and drawings held by the National Monuments Record, and also for permission to reproduce original material as illustrations.

The French Protestant Church of London, for permission to use original drawings as source material for the drawings of the Threadneedle Street French Church.

The Worshipful Company of Goldsmiths, for permission to use original drawings as source material for drawings of Goldsmiths' Hall.

The Guildhall Library Print Room, for permission to use original drawings, watercolours, and prints as sources for a large number of the drawings, and also for permission to reproduce original material as illustrations.

Lobkowicz Collections, Nelahozeves Castle, Czech Republic/Bridgeman Art Library, for permission to reproduce Canaletto's painting of the River Thames on Lord Mayor's Day.

The Museum of London, for permission to reproduce original material as illustrations.

The Royal Institute of British Architects, for permission to use original drawings as source material for several of the drawings of churches.

The Dean and Chapter of St Paul's Cathedral, for permission to use original drawings as source material for the drawings of St Paul's Cathedral and St Paul's Churchyard.

SOURCES FOR DRAWINGS

Abbreviations

All Souls'	All Souls' College, Oxford
BM	British Museum, Department of Prints and Drawings
GL	Guildhall Library Print Room
NMR	National Monuments Record (measured drawings: after original drawings by the National Monuments Record; photographs and other drawings: based on photographs and drawings held by the National Monuments Record)
RIBA	Royal Institute of British Architects
SPROL	Society for Photographing Relics of Old London
St Paul's	Dean and Chapter of St Paul's Cathedral

Aldermen's Court Room
Photographs (NMR); 19th-century prints and drawings: W. Thornbury, 1872; H. Hodge, 1884 (GL)

Aldersgate
17th- and 18th-century prints: S. Nicholls, 1670; T. Bowles, 1754; B. Cole 1754

All Hallows Bread Street with St John the Evangelist Friday Street
Clayton's measured drawings, 1848; 18th- and 19th-century prints and drawings: T. Bowles, 1730; photographs (NMR); Hatton's description, 1708

All Hallows the Great with All Hallows the Less
Clayton's measured drawings, 1848; 18th- and 19th-century prints and drawings: J. Coney, 1812; J. Crowther, 1884 (GL); photographs; Hatton's description, 1708

All Hallows Lombard Street
Surviving building; Clayton's measured drawings, 1848; photographs (NMR); Hatton's description, 1708

Apothecaries' Hall
Surviving building; 19th-century prints and drawings: T. Shepherd, 1831; T. Shepherd watercolour, 1855 (BM)

Barber Surgeons' Hall
18th- and 19th-century prints and drawings: J. Manson, 1800; G. Shepherd, 1815, 1837 (BM)

Barbon's House
19th-century prints and drawings: C Smith, 1830; T. Dibdin watercolour, 1850

Beckford's House
Measured drawings (NMR); photographs (NMR)

Belle Sauvage Inn
19th-century prints and drawings: G. Shepherd, 1809; Anon, 1820 (GL)

Bethlehem Royal Hospital
17th-century prints: J. Nutting, 1689; R. White, 1676

Beyer's House
18th-century print: Colnaghi, 1800

Billingsgate
18th-century print: A. Vanhaecken, 1736

Blackwell Hall
18th- and 19th-century prints and drawings: Cole, 1754; G Shepherd, 1810; Schnebbelie, 1819; J. Buckler, 1820 (GL)

Bludworth's House
Imaginative reconstruction based on view in Morgan's map, 1682

Boar's Head Tavern
18th-century drawing: Anon, 1800 (GL)

Brewers' Hall
Measured drawings (NMR); H. Waring, 1916 (Builder); 19th-century prints: T. Shepherd, 1830; J. Emslie, 1890; photographs (NMR)

Bridewell
18th- and 19th-century prints and drawings: Kip, 1720; Nicholls, 1725; Strype, 1755; Anon, 1790 (GL); G. Shepherd, 1810 (GL), 1812, 1822; C. Whichelo, 1815

Bridewell Bridge
Samuel Scott's painting of the Fleet Canal, 18th-century (Guildhall Art Gallery); 18th-century print: F. Hayman, 1728

Bull and Mouth Inn
19th-century prints and drawings: G. Shepherd, 1817 (GL)

Butchers' Hall
19th-century watercolour: T. Shepherd, 1855 (BM)

Castle Tavern
19th-century watercolour: T. Shepherd, 1855 (BM)

Chained Swan
Photographs, 1883 (SPROL)

Cheapside
17th- and 18th-century prints: Thacker, 1680; Bowles, 1751; Nichols, 1754

Christ Church Newgate Street with St Leonard Foster Lane
Surviving building; Clayton's measured drawings, 1848; photographs (NMR); Hatton's description, 1708

Christ's Hospital
18th- and 19th-century prints and drawings: W. Toms, 1740; S. Wale, 1761; Measured drawing of south frontage (NMR); Hawksmoor's design drawings for Writing School

Clayton's House
19th-century prints and drawings: G. Shepherd, 1810 (BM); A Beugo, 1812; T Shepherd, 1856 (BM)

Clothworkers' Hall
19th-century prints and drawings: Anon, 1820 (GL); T.

Shepherd, 1830; P. Justyne watercolour, 1856
(Clothworkers' Company)

Coachmakers' Hall
Photographs, 1929 (NMR)

College of Arms
Surviving building; measured drawings (NMR); 17th-,
18th- and 19th-century prints and drawings: Anon,
1673 (College of Arms); B. Cole, 1750; T. White, 1768

Coopers' Hall
19th-century prints and drawings: T. Shepherd, 1831

Cornhill
19th-century print: Tallis, 1838

Custom House
18th-century print: J. Harris, 1715 (details applied to
dimensions of Ripley's building: T. Ripley, 1722)

Cutlers' Hall
19th-century prints and drawings: T. Shepherd, 1850

Davies's House
Imaginative reconstruction based on view in Morgan's
map, 1682

Dean's Corner
19th-century prints and drawings: C. Richardson
watercolour, 1819 (GL); Tallis, 1838

Doctors Commons
19th-century prints and drawings: A. Pugin
(Ackermann), 1808; Shepherd watercolours, 1854
(BM)

Drapers' Hall
17th-century measured drawing: John Gorham
(Drapers' Company)

Duke's Theatre
17th-century prints: R. Sawyer, 1673; W. Sherwin, 1673

Fishmongers' Hall
17th-, 18th- and 19th-century prints and drawings: S
Nicholls, J. Bowles, 1694, 1700; T. Shepherd, 1835

Fish Street Hill
17th- and 18th-century prints: Lodge and Tempest,
1671; W. Toms, 1740; S. Nicholls, 1750; A. Canaletto,
1794

Fitch's House
S. Scott's painting of Fleet Canal, 18th-century (Guildhall
Art Gallery); 18th-century print: Anon, nd (BM)

Fleet Prison
Extrapolation from 17th-century print: 'The Cry of the
Oppressed', Moses Pitt, 1691

Frederick's House
18th-century print: W. Maitland, 1739

French Church
Grellier's measured drawing, 1840 (French Church,
Soho Square); 19th-century prints: W. Thornbury, 1872

French Church (St Martin Orgar)
19th-century prints and drawings: Anon, 1795 (GL); T.
Shepherd, 1830 (GL)

George and Vulture Inn
19th-century drawing: T. Shepherd, 1855 (GL)

German Church
17th-century print: Anon, 1720 (GL)

Girdlers' Hall
Photographs (NMR); 19th-century print: T. Shepherd,
1827

Godliman Street
20th-century drawings: Anon, 1938 (GL); photographs
(NMR)

Goldsmiths' Hall
17th-, 18th- and 19th-century prints and drawings:
J. Ward watercolours (Goldsmiths' Company);
G. Shepherd, 1810 (BM); T. Shepherd, 1827

Grocers' Hall
17th-century print: Wright, 1696

Guildhall
Surviving building; T. Ball's measured drawings in 'The
Mediaeval Guildhall of London', Barron, 1974; 18th-
and 19th-century prints and drawings: H. Jones's and
G. Dance's (1785) drawings (GL); Anon, 1707 (GL); J.
Bowles, 1723; T. Bowles, 1734; J. Carter, 1786; G.
Hawkins, 1816

Guildhall Chapel
19th-century prints and drawings: G. Shepherd, 1810;
J. Neale, 1813; R. Schnebbelie, 1815; J. Buckler, 1820
(GL)

Guildhall Offices
18th-century prints: J. Bowles, 1724 and 1741; T.
Malton, 1783

Haberdashers' Hall
19th-century prints and drawings: T. Shepherd
watercolours, 1830, 1852 (BM)

Herring's House
19th-century prints and drawings: G. Shepherd, 1814 (GL)

Honey Lane Market
Imaginative reconstruction based on Morgan's map,
1682; Cole's map, 1756 and Leybourn's plan, 1677

Houblon's House
18th-century drawings: T. Shepherd (copy of 1733
drawing), (BM)

Inner Temple: King's Bench Walk
17th-century print: Anon, 1671 (GL)

Johnson's House (Bolt Court)
19th-century print: J. Smith, 1835

Johnson's House (Johnson's Court)
19th-century watercolour: J. Crowther, 1881 (GL)

Joiners' and Ceilers' Hall
Photographs (NMR); 19th-century drawings: T.
Shepherd watercolour, 1854 (BM)

King Street
18th-century print: T. Bowles, 1734

Kings' Printing House
Imaginative reconstruction based on Morgan's map, 1682

King's Weighhouse Chapel
19th-century prints: T. Shepherd, 1830

Lombard Street
19th-century drawing: G. Shepherd, 1810 (GL)

Lord Mayor's Court Room
Measured drawings, 1830 (GL); H. Hodge drawings,
1882

Ludgate
17th- and 18th-century prints: S. Nicholls, 1670;
T. Bowles, 1754, B. Cole 1754. East side: imaginative
reconstruction, showing surviving statues

Mark Lane
19th-century drawing: T. Shepherd, 1852 (BM);
photographs (NMR)

Masons' Hall
19th-century watercolour: T. Shepherd, 1854 (BM)

Mercers' Hall
Surviving building; Photographs (NMR); 17th- and 19th-
century prints: R. Morden, 1672 (GL); G. Shepherd (BM)

Merchant Taylors' Hall
Measured drawing of hall screen, 1904 (NMR); 18th-
and 19th-century prints and drawings: Anon, 1780; G.
Shepherd, 1810 (GL), 1820 (BM)

Merchant Taylors' School
18th- and 19th-century prints: J. Mynde, 1756; G.
Shepherd watercolours 1811-15 (BM); J. Buckler, 1827;
photographs (NMR)

Middle Temple: Lamb's Building
Photographs (NMR)

Monument
Surviving building; 17th-century design drawings and
prints: H. Hulsbergh, 1670; Lodge, 1671

Moorgate
17th- and 18th-century prints: S Nicholls, 1670;
T. Bowles, 1754, B. Cole 1754

Navy Office
18th-century print: Taylor, 1714

Neville's Court
Measured drawing (NMR); photographs (NMR)

New Court
Photographs (NMR)

Newgate
17th- and 18th-century prints: S. Nicholls, 1670;
T Bowles, 1754; B Cole, 1754

Newgate Market
Imaginative reconstruction based on Morgan's map,
1682; Cole's map, 1756 and Leybourn's plan, 1677

Nicholas's Almshouses
19th-century watercolours: T. Shepherd, 1851 (BM);
R. Schnebbelie, 1818 (GL)

Old Bailey Sessions House
17th- and 18th-century prints: Anon, 1675 (GL);
J. Bowles, 1740

Old Mansion House
19th-century prints; photographs: H. Dixon, 1883
(SPROL); measured drawing, 1840 (GL)

Oxford Arms Inn
Photographs: H. Dixon, 1875, (SPROL); 19th-century
drawings: T. Dibdin, 1851 (GL)

Painter Stainers' Hall
Searles-Wood's measured drawing (NMR);19th-century
prints: G. Shepherd, 1810 (BM), 1811 (GL)

Paternoster Row
20th-century drawing: H. Fletcher, 1908

Pewterers' Hall
19th-century watercolour: T. Shepherd, 1851 (BM)

Pollexfen's House
18th-century print: T. Prattent, 1795

Pope's House
19th-century watercolour: G. Stewart, 1870 (GL)

Poultry
19th-century drawings and watercolours: G. Shepherd,
1810 (GL)

Poultry Compter
Extrapolation from J. T. Smith's print, 1813

Queenhithe Granary
19th-century prints and drawings: C. Tomkins, 1801;
T. Dibdin, 1854 (GL); T. Shepherd, 1855 (BM)

Racquet Court
20th-century drawings; photographs (NMR)

Royal College of Physicians
17th-, 18th- and 19th-century prints and drawings:
Loggan, 1677; W. Stukeley, 1723; S. Ware's measured
drawings, 1825, 1826; T. Shepherd, 1841

Royal Exchange
17th- and 18th-century prints and drawings: R. White,
1671; C. Campbell, 1716; P. de Loutherbourg, 1788; T.
Malton, 1792

Saddlers' Hall
19th-century drawings: T. Shepherd, 1830, 1855 (BM);
photograph, 1860 (GL)

St Alban Wood Street with St Olave Silver Street
Surviving building; 19th-century prints: R. Billings,
1838; photographs (NMR); Hatton's description, 1708

St Andrew by the Wardrobe with St Ann Blackfriars
Surviving building; Clayton's measured drawings, 1848;
18th-century prints: B. Cole, 1750; Hatton's
description, 1708

St Anne and St Agnes with St John Zachary
Surviving building; Clayton's measured drawings, 1848;
18th-century prints: B. Cole, 1750; Hatton's
description, 1708

St Antholin Watling Street with St John Walbrook
Clayton's measured drawings, 1848; 19th-century prints
and drawings: Anon, 1830 (GL) H. and J. Mathews,
1876 (NMR); Hatton's description, 1708; design
drawings (All Souls')

St Augustine Watling Street with St Faith under St Paul's
Surviving building; Clayton's measured drawings, 1848;
photographs (NMR); Hatton's description, 1708;
Hawksmoor's design drawing (All Souls)

St Bartholomew by the Exchange
19th-century prints and drawings: N. Whitlock, 1835
(GL); R. Billings, 1838; Hatton's description, 1708

St Benet Fink
Clayton's measured drawings, 1848; 18th- and 19th-
century prints: B. Cole, 1750; T. Shepherd, 1827;
Hatton's description,1708

St Benet Gracechurch with St Leonard Eastcheap
Clayton's measured drawings, 1848; 19th-century prints

and drawings: G. Shepherd, 1811; Hatton's description, 1708

St Benet Paul's Wharf with St Peter Paul's Wharf
Surviving building; Clayton's measured drawings, 1848; design drawings (All Souls')

St Bride Fleet Street
Surviving building; Clayton's measured drawings, 1848; 19th-century prints: T. Bowles, 1761; G. Shepherd, 1814; Hatton's description, 1708; design drawings (All Souls')

St Christopher le Stocks
18th-century prints: T. Malton, 1781

St Clement Eastcheap with St Martin Orgar
Surviving building; Clayton's measured drawings, 1848; Hatton's description, 1708

St Dionis Backchurch
Clayton's measured drawings, 1848; 19th-century prints and drawings: G Shepherd, 1818; photographs (NMR); Hatton's description, 1708

St Dunstan in the East
Surviving building; Clayton's measured drawings, 1848; 18th- and 19th-century prints: H. Overton, 1708; G. Shepherd, 1810; J. Neale, 1815; Hatton's description, 1708

St Edmund King and Martyr with St Nicholas Acons
Surviving building; Clayton's (1848) and Crace's (RIBA) measured drawings; 19th-century prints: G. Shepherd, 1813; Hatton's description, 1708; design drawings (All Souls')

St George Botolph Lane with St Botolph Billingsgate
Clayton's measured drawings, 1848; 19th-century prints and drawings: J. Coney, 1814 (GL); Godwin and Britton, 1838; Hatton's description, 1708

St James Garlickhythe
Surviving building; Clayton's measured drawings, 1848; Hatton's description, 1708

St Lawrence Jewry with St Mary Magdalen Milk Street
Surviving building; Clayton's measured drawings, 1848; measured drawings (NMR); photographs (NMR); Hatton's description, 1708

St Magnus the Martyr with St Margaret Fish Street Hill
Surviving building; Clayton's measured drawings, 1848; design drawings (RIBA); 18th-century prints: Anon, 1750 (GL); Hatton's description, 1708

St Margaret Lothbury
Surviving building; Clayton's measured drawings, 1848; 18th-century prints: B. Cole, 1750; Hatton's description, 1708

St Margaret Pattens with St Gabriel Fenchurch
Surviving building; Clayton's measured drawings, 1848; 18th- and 19th-century prints: B Cole, 1750; J. Coney, 1814; Hatton's description, 1708

St Martin Ludgate
Surviving building; Clayton's measured drawings, 1848; 19th-century prints; Hatton's description, 1708

St Mary Abchurch with St Laurence Pountney
Surviving building; Clayton's measured drawings, 1848; design drawings (All Souls')

St Mary Aldermanbury
Clayton's measured drawings, 1848; 19th-century prints and drawings: G. Shepherd, 1814 (GL); T. Shepherd, 1830; photographs (NMR); Hatton's description, 1708

St Mary Aldermary with St Thomas Apostles
Surviving building; 18th- and 19th-century prints: Anon, 1750; F. Mackenzie, 1839; Hatton's description, 1708

St Mary at Hill with St Andrew Hubbard
Surviving building; measured drawings of Clayton (1848), Crace (RIBA) and NMR; 18th- and 19th-century prints and drawings: 'Prospect of London', 1710; Bucks' panorama, 1749; Anon, 1750 (GL); Anon, 1825 (GL); T. Shepherd, 1829; Hatton's description, 1708

St Mary le Bow with All Hallows Honey Lane and St Pancras Soper Lane
Surviving building; Clayton's (1848) and A Pugin's (1826) measured drawings; Hawksmoor's design drawing for steeple (All Souls') and loggia; 17th- and 18th-century prints: Thacker, 1680; Bowles, 1751; Nichols, 1754; photographs (NMR); Hatton's description, 1708

St Mary Somerset with St Mary Mounthaw
Surviving building; Clayton's measured drawings, 1848; 19th-century prints: J. Coney, 1812; Hatton's description, 1708

St Mary Woolnoth with St Mary Woolchurch Haw
Surviving building; 19th-century measured drawings: A Pugin, 1826; Hatton's description, 1708; old steeple – Morgan's panorama, 1682

St Mary Magdalen Old Fish Street with St Gregory by St Paul's
Clayton's measured drawings, 1848; 19th-century prints: G. Shepherd, 1812; Hatton's description, 1708

St Matthew Friday Street with St Peter Cheap
Clayton's measured drawings, 1848; 19th-century prints and drawings: J. Coney, 1814; J. Crowther, 1881 (GL); Hatton's description, 1708

St Michael Bassishaw
Clayton's measured drawings, 1848; 19th-century prints: G. Shepherd, 1810; J. Coney, 1812; photographs (NMR); Hatton's description, 1708

St Michael Cornhill
Surviving building; 19th-century prints: T. Shepherd, 1830; R. Billings, 1838; Hatton's description, 1708; Dickinson's design drawings (British Library)

St Michael Crooked Lane
19th-century watercolour: G. Scharf, 1830 (GL); measured drawings of steeple (British Library)

St Michael Paternoster Royal with St Martin Vintry
Surviving building; Clayton's measured drawings, 1848; Hatton's description, 1708

St Michael Queenhithe with Holy Trinity the Less
Clayton's measured drawings, 1848; 18th- and 19th-century prints and drawings; B. Cole, 1756, J. Coney, 1811 (GL); photographs (NMR); Hatton's description, 1708

St Michael Wood Street with St Mary Staining
Clayton's measured drawings, 1848; 18th- and 19th-

century prints: 'Prospect of London', 1710; B. Cole, 1750; photographs (NMR); Hatton's description, 1708

St Mildred Bread Street with St Margaret Moses
Clayton's measured drawings, 1848; 19th-century prints: J. Coney, 1812; F. Mackenzie, 1838; photographs (NMR); Hatton's description, 1708

St Mildred Poultry with St Mary Colechurch
Clayton's measured drawings, 1848; measured drawings (NMR); 19th-century prints: T. Shepherd, 1829; Hatton's description, 1708

St Nicholas Cole Abbey with St Nicholas Olave
Surviving building; Clayton's measured drawings, 1848; photographs (NMR); Hatton's description, 1708

St Olave Jewry with St Martin Pomary
Surviving building; Clayton's measured drawings, 1848; 19th-century prints and drawings: J. Coney, 1818; J. Emslie, 1883 (GL); J. Crowther's watercolour, 1887 (GL); photographs (NMR); Hatton's description, 1708

St Paul's Cathedral
18th-century prints and drawings: S. Wale and J. Gwynn, 1755; J. Kip, 1720; Hawksmoor's design drawings for 'baptistry' (St Paul's)

St Paul's Churchyard
Hawksmoor's design drawings (St Paul's)

St Paul's School
17th-, 18th- and 19th-century prints and drawings: Hollar, 1670; B. Cole, 1750; S. Rawle, 1807; Pugin, 1826

St Peter Cornhill
Surviving building; Clayton's measured drawings, 1848; Hatton's description, 1708

St Sepulchre Newgate Street
Surviving building; 18th-century prints: W. Toms, 1737; R. West, 1739

St Stephen Coleman Street
Clayton's measured drawings, 1848; 19th-century prints and drawings: J. Coney, 1814; Anon, 1815 (GL); photographs (NMR); Hatton's description, 1708

St Stephen Walbrook with St Benet Sherehog
Surviving building; Clayton's measured drawings, 1848; 18th- and 19th-century prints: T. Malton, 1798; Hatton's description, 1708

St Swithin Cannon Street with St Mary Bothaw
Clayton's measured drawings, 1848; 19th-century prints: J. Coney, 1812; photographs (NMR); Hatton's description, 1708

St Vedast Foster Lane with St Michael le Querne
Surviving building; Clayton's measured drawings, 1848; photographs (NMR); Hatton's description, 1708

Salters' Hall
18th- and 19th-century prints: T. Shepherd, 1822; W. Angus, 1800

Shades Tavern
Bucks' panorama, 1749

Ship Tavern
19th-century watercolour: T. Shepherd, 1857 (BM)

Sion College
18th- and 19th-century prints and drawings: W. Wise, 1800

Smith's Almshouses
19th-century watercolour: T. Shepherd, 1855 (BM)

Spread Eagle Inn
19th-century watercolour: R. Schnebbelie, 1814 (GL)

Stationers' Hall
18th-century print: B. Cole, 1750

Steelyard
18th- and 19th-century prints and drawings: Bucks' panorama, 1749; C. Tomkins watercolour (GL); T. Shepherd watercolour, 1856

Stocks Market
18th-century prints: S. Nicholls, 1728; T. Bowles, 1751; J. Nichols, 1752

Temple Bar
Surviving building; photographs (including NMR); 17th-century prints: S. Nicholls, 1670

Trinity House
19th-century prints and drawings: Anon, 1856 (BM); Anon, 1840 (GL)

Vintners' Hall
18th- and 19th-century prints and drawings: Wilson watercolour, 1750; G. Shepherd drawing, 1810

Vyner's House
18th- and 19th-century prints: S. Nicholls, 1710; Anon, 1829 (GL)

Waldo's House
18th-century prints: Bowles, 1751; J. June, 1761

Wardrobe Court
Photographs (NMR)

Warwick Lane
19th-century prints: C. Whichelo, 1804

Watermen's Hall
18th-century print: 'Prospect of London', 1710

Wood Street Compter
18th-century print: N. Smith, 1793

Wren's House
Measured drawing (NMR); 19th- and 20th-century drawings: C. Richardson watercolour, 1871 (GL); P. Norman, c.1900 (Museum of London)

BIBLIOGRAPHY

Amery, Colin, *Wren's London*, 1988

Archer, Ian, *The History of the Haberdashers' Company*, 1991

Ash, Bernard, *The Golden City*, 1964

Barker and Jackson, *History of London in Maps*, 1990

Barron, Caroline, *The Mediaeval Guildhall of London*, 1974

Beard, Geoffrey, *The Work of Sir Christopher Wren*, 1982

Beier and Finlay (ed.), *London 1500-1700. The Making of the Metropolis*, 1986

Bell, Walter, *The Great Fire of London*, 1920

Besant, Walter, *London in the Eighteenth Century*, 1902

Besant, Walter, *London in the time of the Stuarts*, 1903

Besant, Walter, *London City*, 1910

Borer, Mary, *The City of London*, 1977

Bradley, Simon, *The City of London*, 1987

Britton and Pugin, *Illustrations of the Public Buildings of London*, 1825

Buck, Samuel and Nathaniel, 'Panorama of London' (reproduced in *A Prospect of Britain*, Ralph Hyde, 1994), 1749

Builder, The, The City Companies and Their Halls, 1916-20

Bush, Graham, *Old London* (Society for Photographing Relics of Old London photographs), 1975

Carswell, John, *The South Sea Bubble*, 1960

Clark, Sir George, *A History of the Royal College of Physicians of London*, 1964

Clarke, Charles, *Architectura Ecclesiastica Londini*, 1819

Clayton, John, *The Works of Sir Christopher Wren*, 1848-9

Cobb, Gerald, *The Old Churches of London*, 1941, 1948

Cobb, Gerald, *London City Churches*, 1977, 1989

Corporation of London, *The Corporation of London*, 1950

Cunningham, Peter, *Handbook of London*, 1849

Downes, Kerry, *The Architecture of Wren*, 1982

Downes, Kerry, *Hawksmoor*, 1970

Downes, Kerry, *Sir Christopher Wren: The Design of St Paul's Cathedral*, 1988

Ekwall, Eilert, *Street Names of the City of London*, 1954

Evelyn, John, *Diary* (edited by de Beer), 1955

Fletcher, Hanslip, *London Passed and Passing*, 1909

Godwin and Britton, *The Churches of London*, 1839

Harben, Henry, *Dictionary of London*, 1918

Hatton, Edward, *A New View of London*, 1708

Hearsey, John, *London and the Great Fire*, 1965

Hobhouse and Saunders, *Good and Proper Materials: The Fabric of London since the Great Fire*, 1989

Horwood, Richard, 'A Plan of the Cities of London and Westminster with the Borough of Southwark' (reproduced in *A to Z of Regency London*, Ralph Hyde, 1985), 1799, 1813

Huelin, Gordon, *Vanished Churches of the City of London*, 1996

Hunting, Penelope, *A History of the Drapers' Company*, 1989

Imray, Jean, *The Mercers' Hall*, 1991

Inwood, Stephen, *A History of London*, 1998

Jeffery, Paul, *The City Churches of Sir Christopher Wren*, 1996

Jeffery, Paul, 'The Lost Crace' in *London Topographical Record*, 1995

Kent, William, *Dictionary of London*, 1937

Kent, William, *The Lost Treasures of London*, 1947

Kynaston, David, *The City of London*, 1994-9

Lang, Jane, *Rebuilding of St Paul's after the Great Fire of London*, 1956

Leake and Hollar, *Exact Surveigh of the Streets, Lanes and Churches contained within the Ruines of the City of London*, 1667

Lillywhite, Bryant, *London Coffee Houses*, 1963

Lobel, Mary, *The British Atlas of Historic Towns: City of London*, 1989

London Survey, *College of Arms*, 1963

London Survey, *Survey of London*, Vol.XV, 1934

Maitland, William, *History of London*, 1739, 1756

Malton, Thomas, *Picturesque Tour through the Cities of London and Westminster*, 1790

Masters, Betty, *The Public Markets of the City of London Surveyed by William Leybourn in 1677*, 1974

Matthews and Atkins (ed.), *A History of St Paul's Cathedral*, 1957

McKellar, Elizabeth, *The Birth of Modern London*, 1999

Metcalf, P., *The Halls of the Fishmongers' Company*, 1977

Milne, Gustav, *The Great Fire of London*, 1986

Morgan, William, *London Actually Surveyed* (map and panorama), 1682

Norman, Philip, *London Vanished and Vanishing*, 1905

Ogilby and Morgan, 'A Large and Accurate Map of the City of London' (reproduced in *A to Z of Restoration London*, Ralph Hyde, 1992), 1676

Ogilvy, James, *Relics and Memorials of London City*, 1910

Ordnance Survey, *Map of London* (5 feet to the mile), 1873

Pepys, Samuel, *Diary* (edited by Latham and Matthews), 1970-83

Pevsner, Niklaus, *The Cities of London and Westminster*, 1973

Phillips, Hugh, *The Thames about 1750*, 1951

Porter, Stephen, *The Great Fire of London*, 1996

Pugin and Rowlandson, *The Microcosm of London*, 1808-9

Raydon, Arthur, *Mercers' Hall*, 1947

Reddaway, T.F., *The Rebuilding of London after the Great Fire*, 1940

Roque, John, 'A Plan of the Cities of London, Westminster, and the Borough of Southwark' (reproduced in *A to Z of Georgian London*, Ralph Hyde, 1981), 1746

Royal Commission on Historical Monuments, *The City of London*, 1929

Rudé, George, *Hanoverian London*, 1971

Saunders, Ann (ed.), *The Royal Exchange*, 1997

Shepherd, Thomas, *London and its Environs in the Nineteenth Century*, 1829

Stamp, Gavin, *The Changing Metropolis*, 1984

Stow, John, *Survey of London*, 1603

Strype, John, *Survey of London*, 1720

Summerson, John, *Georgian London*, 1945, 1988

Summerson, John, *Architecture in Britain, 1530-1830*, 1953

Summerson, John, *Drawings for the London City Churches*, 1952

Tallis, John, *London Street Views*, 1838-40

Thornbury, Walter, *Old and New London*, 1872-8

Vincent, Thomas, *God's Terrible Voice in the City*, 1667

Weinreb and Hibbert, *London Encyclopaedia*, 1983, 1993

Welch, Charles, *History of the Monument*, 1893

Wheatley, Henry, *London Past and Present*, 1891

Wren, Christopher, *Parentalia: Memoirs of the Family of the Wrens*, 1750

Wren Society, *Volumes I, II, III, XIII, XIV, XV, XVI: St Paul's Cathedral*, 1924-39

Wren Society, *Volumes IX and X: The Parochial Churches of Sir Christopher Wren*, 1932-3

Wren Society, *Volume XIX: The City Churches, Vestry Minutes, and Churchwarden's Accounts*, 1942

Young, E. and W., *Old London Churches*, 1956

ARCHIVES AND MUSEUMS

All Souls' College, Oxford

British Library

British Museum, Department of Prints and Drawings

Geffrye Museum, Shoreditch

Guildhall Library, Print Room (some material accessible on http://collage.nhil.com)

Museum of London

National Monuments Record (English Heritage)

Royal Institute of British Architects

Victoria and Albert Museum

INDEX

References given in **bold** indicate the main entry for each building (with drawings).

HOLBORN

WEST
SMITHFIELD

ALDERSGATE STREET

PIE CORNER

SNOW
HILL

CHRIST'S
HOSPITAL

NEWGATE

STREET

WOOD ST.

FLEET CANAL

FLEET LANE

FETTER LANE

ST MARTINS LE GRAND

ST MARTINS

OLD BAILEY

CHEAPSIDE

FLEET STREET

LUDGATE HILL

LUDGATE ST.

ST PAUL'S

WATLING

STREET

BRIDEWELL

ST PAUL'S CHURCHYARD

BREAD STR

TEMPLE

DOCTORS
COMMONS

↑

LIMIT OF
DESTRUCTION
BY THE
GREAT FIRE

UPPER THAMES STREET

QUEENHITHE

R I V E R

T H A M E S